Creativity and the Management of Change

creativity

and the management of change

Tudor Rickards
Manchester Business School

Foreword by Authur B. VanGundy, Ph.D.
University of Oklahoma, and Principal of VanGundy & Associates

First published 1999

2 4 6 8 10 9 7 5 3 1
Blackwell Publishers Ltd
108 Cowley Road
Oxford OX4 1JF
UK

Blackwell Publishers Inc.
350 Main Street
Malden, Massachusetts 02148
USA

British Library Cataloguing in Publication Data

A CIP catalogue record for this book is available from the British Library.

A Library of Congress Cataloging-in-Publication record is available for this book.

ISBN 0-631-21067-9 (hbk)
ISBN 0-631-21068-7 (pbk)

Typeset in Galliard 10/12 pt
by Best-set Typesetter Ltd., Hong Kong
Printed in Great Britain by MPG Books, Bodmin, Cornwall

This book is printed on acid-free paper

Contents

Figures

Foreword

I vividly can recall an exercise I found in a book about 20 years ago, which challenged me to cut a pie into eight pieces using three cuts. I then was referred to the back of the book for the 'correct' solution. 'The' solution was a picture of a circle divided into quarters by two lines at right angles and a small, concentric circle drawn through these lines. The caption read 'Pie Exercise Solution'. The text noted that the problem did not specify that the cuts must be straight lines.

I was somewhat puzzled by this response because I thought of many other solutions. The author had intended that I assume his (or her) 'platform of understanding'. In this case, I should assume that there is a 'correct' solution to such problems and that this solution can be achieved by testing 'a' major assumption.

Fortunately, I refused to accept such a platform (a trait which used to cause me trouble on standardized tests which also assumed one 'correct' solution). Instead, I began looking for other options. I took it upon myself to expand my initial problem. In effect, I gave myself permission to be creative and to challenge the expected or traditional platform of understanding.

I began asking a lot of questions (for instance, What is a cut? How long can a cut be? What shape must the pieces be? What cutting instrument may I use?). Answering these and other questions enabled me to leap-frog from one platform of understanding to another. As this occurred, I gained additional insight into what was and was not 'permitted' by my problem. Moreover, the more questions I asked, the more solutions I generated, and the more I learned about the relationship between problems and solutions (sometimes there is a very fine line between the two).

Professor Rickards has written a book which discusses how life's discoveries are attained by searching for knowledge. However, we should not always accept that knowledge as given as soon as we discover it (for instance, not accepting only one solution). Throughout *Creativity and the Management of Change* he exhorts the reader to challenge the wisdom and assumptions of business orthodoxy, to reject doing things because 'That's the way we've always done things here!'

This is a book on how to link abstract learning and practical acts during the discovery process. As such, it spans boundaries between academe and business, between theory and practice. Moreover, Professor Rickards sounds the alarm to alert business educators to break free from the chains of orthodoxy while encouraging organizational managers to test their conventional wisdom as well.

The author accomplishes his objectives using a well-crafted jigsaw puzzle metaphor. By fitting together the pieces for the reader, he makes it easier to grasp concepts across a variety of topics and disciplines. These topics range from creativity and innovation to leadership and the management of change, and then finish with cogent observations on postmodern 'puzzling' and the role of economic paradigms.

In each chapter he 'puzzles' out bits of a jigsaw with the objective of creating new platforms of understanding. Sometimes philosophic, sometimes theoretical, and sometimes simply practical, Professor Rickards moves the reader to examine existing paradigms in any field of endeavour, instead of blindly accepting a culture of tradition.

The author doesn't just deconstruct platforms of understanding; he also moves towards reconstructing existing platforms with novel alternatives. This is a common thread throughout the book. And it helps the reader understand current orthodox platforms and devise new platforms for increased understanding and improved performance.

The more you read this book, the more the pieces of the business puzzle begin to fall into place. The result is a desire to embrace old platforms of understanding afresh. During the discovery journey, a lot of territory is covered. Importantly, this material is treated in ways that facilitate understanding and learning.

Creativity and the Management of Change is a soundly written, tightly wrapped compendium of management knowledge presented in a novel way. As you read it, think about your own platforms of understanding and whether you should reconstruct them in novel ways. I think you'll enjoy the discovery process ahead.

Arthur B. VanGundy, Ph.D.
Professor of Communication, University of Oklahoma,
and Principal of VanGundy & Associates, Norman, Oklahoma, USA

Preface

Contemporary management involves both acquiring knowledge and putting that knowledge to use in specific circumstances. Although business school courses have much to offer through delivering codified encapsulated information, they are less successful in helping business students to develop skills in penetrating beyond the received wisdom. There is undoubtedly criticism that business graduates fresh from their MBAs seem unable to apply much of their knowledge to the practical demands of their new jobs.

The basic premise of this book is that 'what they teach at business school' is a base from which each student of management has subsequently to develop creative insights to deal with specific tasks – be these tasks in marketing, strategy formation, product development, leadership, or decision-making.

There is nothing particularly new in this as a general principle of experiential learning. The received wisdom helps us understand the nature of the organizational box. In practice, we need to break out of the box and explore what lies beyond its boundaries.

The entire book is intended to be read as a guide, or a description of a series of journeys of exploration and discovery into important 'territories' of interest in business studies, such as marketing, strategy, decision-making, and even economic orthodoxy. The most accessible materials can be found in the main body of the text, towards the start of each chapter. These materials will provide concise summaries of current received wisdom or business orthodoxy.

If the reader is content to accept the received wisdom, then he or she can concentrate on the early part of each chapter, dipping into the book for the topics of interest. However, such an approach misses the point of the book – to demonstrate how to develop skills in pinpointing where conventional wisdom can be challenged effectively. These skills require the reader to share the journey of exploration with the author chapter by chapter. This illustrates the techniques and processes used in various journeys of discovery. The reader will then be better able to encounter real business situations in an appropriately challenging manner. The more advanced researcher or educationalist is provided with information about the primary source materials that contributed to the ideas in the text.

The journeys of exploration begin with a study of creativity, one of the most silenced voices in MBA courses. After that, the chapter sequence reflects my personal journey towards topics more central to business school orthodoxy.

Creativity, Science, and the Nature of Discovery Processes

In the 1960s, I worked as a technical manager in a research laboratory. My experiences there stimulated an interest in the nature of discovery processes that has remained an important part of my working life ever since. As a scientist, I took for granted that the methods of studying natural phenomena in test tubes could be simply reapplied in studying the workings of individuals and teams. At the time, I did not realize that my approach might unkindly have been termed naive positivism. It was naive because I had unthinkingly applied methods that were appropriate in one field of knowledge-seeking to a very different field. It was positivist in the sense we will encounter it in subsequent chapters. I believed that the safest way to establish truth was through conducting controlled experiments designed to test hypothetical outcomes.

I was unaware that my assumptions were the subject of considerable contention within the field of social science. Nor was I aware that more sophisticated methods of the positivist approach had made major contributions to a range of organizational and economic subjects.

I grew increasingly disappointed with the results obtained from my studies of creativity within the processes of scientific discovery. Over time, I rejected the possibility that the methods that worked within the empirical sciences could be simply transferred to work into the nature of social systems. More specifically, the methods that my fellow scientists and I used to discover scientific knowledge did not seem to work so well when turned in on them to examine processes of discovery.

Beyond Managerial Orthodoxy

These early experiences help explain my interest in writing a book about exploring the orthodox views held of business studies. After my time as a technical researcher, I became associated with a well-known business school. There I learned that the orthodox approach to understanding business studies was essentially similar to the one I was in the process of rejecting. I also discovered alternative approaches, particularly from researchers and writers in the social sciences.

This book shows a way of studying the material found in business courses to reveal its generally accepted wisdom. It also indicates the ways in which that wisdom can be challenged so that the reader is better equipped to discover 'what they don't teach you (yet) at business school'. The process is simple to state, if difficult to achieve consistently. Meaningful discovery always involves a search of existing knowledge for evidence of core beliefs and assumptions that shape its messages. The search has to explore knowledge of a personal kind for the searcher, and of a kind that has become accepted as conventional wisdom of the topic of interest. To benefit from business orthodoxy we have to be skilled at challenging its wisdom.

Is this book heretical? In one sense it is. To challenge received wisdom is to be on the side of the heretics. Yet it is not a call for a rejection of most of the accumulated knowledge found in established business disciplines. Rather, it is a handbook illustrating how each of us might approach academic knowledge to discover possibilities that are typically concealed. If we become more skilled in these discovery processes, we also increase our chances of becoming more effective in the practical application of our business knowledge.

TR
Woodford, November 1998

Acknowledgements

I would like to thank, in particular, Professor Teresa Amabile, Dr Christian de Cock, Professor Peter Frost, Dr Julie Hass, Dr Frederick Hsu, Richard Hudson-Davies, Susan Moger, Dr Naresh Pandit, Professor Alan Pearson, Professor Peter Swann, Professor Paul Torrance and Professor Hari Tsoukas.

I would also like to thank other colleagues, and graduate and doctoral students at Manchester Business School who made numerous suggestions that helped shape my thinking.

chapter 1
The Basic MBA and Beyond

In general management, the ability to conceptualize how parts and functions fit together is critical . . . This synthesizing ability is related to creativity, most of which consists not of conjuring up totally new ideas but in putting common elements together in novel ways, often by borrowing from a separate context.

Ross Webber[1]

In retrospect, I felt I had been working on a giant jigsaw puzzle, with many missing pieces. Some of the pieces I had seemed to fit in obvious places, and once enough of them were in place, an image began to appear in my mind. Thereafter, each new piece in place clarified that image. By the time I had finished [the book], I felt I had found a logical place for all the pieces available to me. In fact, the image had become so sharp that I felt confident in describing some of the missing pieces.

Henry Mintzberg[2]

As I began my study of creativity, over 20 years ago, I envisioned myself as carefully and methodically adding planks to the grand framework of psychological science. In retrospect, my work over these two decades seems rather more like a surprising journey in search of the pieces to an important puzzle; although much of it was unpredictable, it does nonetheless fit together.

Teresa Amabile[3]

The idea that one voice could drown out the rest is an attractive one to the pulmonarily gifted but it is a dream that can never be realized fully. There will, thank goodness, always be the voices of dissent and the clamour of alternatives vying for aural space.

Gibson Burrell[4]

Introduction

'If you think education is expensive . . . ' A few years ago, Sir John Harvey-Jones, then the CEO of ICI plc, addressed an audience in a lecture theatre packed with business executives, many engaged in courses of business education. They had listened enthralled to his proposals for business transformation. He was at great pains to emphasize the importance of continuous learning and development. At question time he was quizzed about the well-known reluctance of his company to hire MBAs. 'We do hire MBAs,' he corrected the questioner. 'But we hire them for their personal potential and technical and professional capabilities. We don't pay any extra for the MBA. We are more concerned with management performance in our plants than on formal degrees.'

Harvey-Jones lucidly expressed a problem facing those who embark on a course of business education and those who design and teach such courses. Are MBAs getting the right sort of education, one that permits them to perform better in practice?

Some critics of business education make their views quite clear. Mark McCormack saw the potential in sports sponsorship and is widely regarded as someone who helped create a new and significant industry. He also found time to write a book entitled *What they don't teach you at Harvard Business School.*[5] The core of the criticism is straightforward. Few people deny the potential benefits of studying how business operates in theory and through case examples. The big question is how to convert such learning into enhanced practice.[6]

The skills that connect abstract learning with practical actions involve some form of discovery process. 'Book learning' is only part of it. This book provides an illustration of one such approach, which encourages each individual to approach business situations with a creative orientation that combines knowledge with a willingness to 'think outside the box' of prevailing theory and best practice. The approach illustrates the general principles of developing a learning discipline, as advocated by Peter Senge in his influential text *The Fifth Discipline.*[7] If received wisdom helps us understand the nature of the organizational box, we need different kinds of skills to break out of the box and explore what lies beyond its boundaries.

Before outlining the various components within the approach, we should perhaps take a quick look at an additional complication – the widely held view that we are moving into a rapidly changing world in which many old ideas of management and control are no longer appropriate.

The contemporary business and cultural scene

It has become popular to introduce business texts with the affirmation 'we are living in a fast-changing world'. Microsoft, the dominant organization at the end of the decade, had grown from nowhere in a few tumultuous years. The Millennium threatened to end 'not with a bang but a virus' (or at least a very unpleasant bug). Scientists are well on the way to mapping the fine detail of the human genetic structure. In 1997, Dolly, the most famous sheep outside nursery rhymes, moved cloning from the realms of the theoretical to the realms of the feasible and frightening. The Asian economic miracle seems to have run its course.

The traditional business disciplines are being subjected to serious re-examination. The new era has been marked by assertions that many old ideas are dead or dying. As we will see later in this book, serious commentators have asked whether the classical organizational pyramid is heading for extinction, to be replaced by firms with indistinct boundaries, operating in virtual networks. Some have challenged the continued viability of economics as it is taught, asking 'Is economics dead?', pointing to the continued failure of economic modelling to predict business cycles. Others have asked a similar question of marketing in its traditional format. Even science is no longer the absolute arbiter of the real and the feasible. Scientists seek explanations of human consciousness with models that seek to connect mathematical theories and cosmic notions of universality of being. A range of voices of varying degrees of sophistication can be heard asking: 'Is science dead?' 'Is history dead?' 'Is religion dead?' 'Is Elvis dead?' Alongside these voices are others making claims for the existence of aliens, alien abductions, and mystical means of predicting the future. From time to time charismatically led cults still organize their extinction through mass suicide.

These are but a few selected themes and instances of relevance to our Millennium-spanning generation. Almost everything to be found in current business education predates these themes. At the very least, the challenge is on to take the old knowledge and find ways in which it makes sense in this new and complex world.

The business orthodoxy and its hidden voices

This first chapter puts in context the general approach for discovering and then escaping from the received wisdom of business school theories. It outlines the nature of contemporary business orthodoxy, which is termed a managerialist perspective, and indicates how that orthodoxy may suppress other possibilities. A range of devices is introduced for examining the orthodoxy in new ways, including an approach for dealing with confusions arising through lack of generally accepted definitions. These devices make use of various metaphors of discovery, among which the metaphor of the personal quest or journey, the jigsaw-puzzling metaphor, and the handful of books metaphor are particularly important. These metaphors permit access to the contemporary business orthodoxy expressed as another metaphor, its platform of understanding. We will also see how such studies contain a powerful method of understanding the nature of definitions and for dealing with what are often represented as intractable difficulties in arriving at satisfactory definitions.

Studying the platform of understanding reveals the hidden voices silenced by the orthodoxy, and regarded as heresies. The strengths and weaknesses of such an approach are briefly considered, which leads to the conclusion that the approach deserves to be tested particularly as a means of exposing more appropriate ways of evaluating the heresies than from the perspective of the dominant orthodoxy or paradigm. The chapter ends with an outline of the overall journey of discovery that will be covered in the subsequent chapters in the book.

The Bits of Jigsaw of Contemporary Business Courses

Throughout this book we will be referring to the process of puzzling out business. This jigsaw analogy or metaphor reminds us that the overall picture may be incomplete, and that we may have to work hard to find some of the missing pieces. Regardless of the business school you care to visit, you will find that the courses share a common set of disciplines that closely match the academic groupings or departments. In many parts of the world, business schools have followed the North American model, and the disciplines and courses show many commonalities. These disciplines make it easy to identify 'what they do teach you on an MBA programme'.

However, the courses are not totally uniform in content. For any specific course we would expect to find some common bits of the jigsaw, which are augmented with a few bits that reflect special interests of the specific school. Figure 1.1 shows the bits of the jigsaw with labels that would be recognized within well-certificated business studies courses. The pieces of its (still incomplete) jigsaw give a clear indication of the origins of business education – which were from the earlier disciplines of economics and its offshoot of financial studies. Operations Management came in with the arrival of 'scientific management', while marketing and then strategy were added after the Second World War. More recent additions reflected developing interests in human behaviours, although that economic dimension can again be seen in the categorization of human beings as a resource to be managed. Most recently the importance of technology and of information management have been acknowledged.

However, there are other topics, many of them of considerable practical significance, that are covered in business courses to greater or lesser degree. These additional topics – the gaps in the jigsaw in figure 1.1 – may command a place in the core curriculum, or may be included as optional extras, or electives. For example, some business schools offer excellent electives on leadership, although other schools do not deal with the leadership topic. Other schools have introduced creativity, entrepreneurship and extended options on change management.

Figure 1.2 shows these topics and indicates the chapters in this book where these topics are considered.

The Platform of Understanding of Business Orthodoxy

Introduction to the concept of building a platform of understanding

Throughout this book the notion of building a platform of understanding is used as a metaphor. It indicates a process for seeking those ideas shared by a social group on some topic of concern to the group. It is repeatedly used to indicate the shared knowledge base of an academic discipline such as economics, or a sub-discipline such as organizational decision-making. The assumption made is that a group operates within a shared set of assumptions, meanings and values that contribute to the way it deals with its internal 'world' and with its external 'environment'.

The purpose of studying a platform of understanding is to establish some firm ground on which to stand in order to find fresh ground and alternative

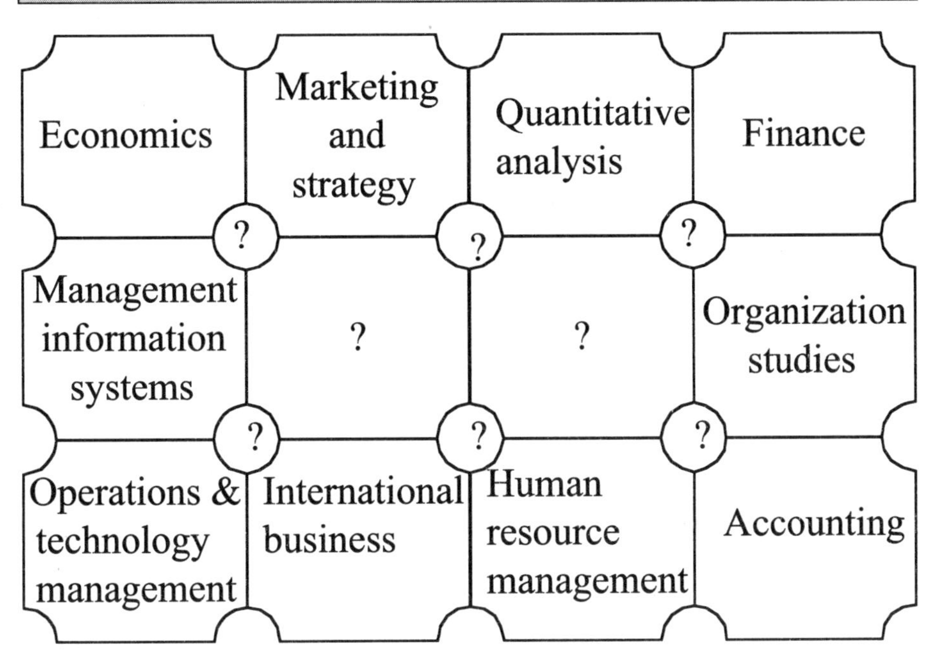

Figure 1.1: The business disciplines jigsaw (common pieces and its variable core)

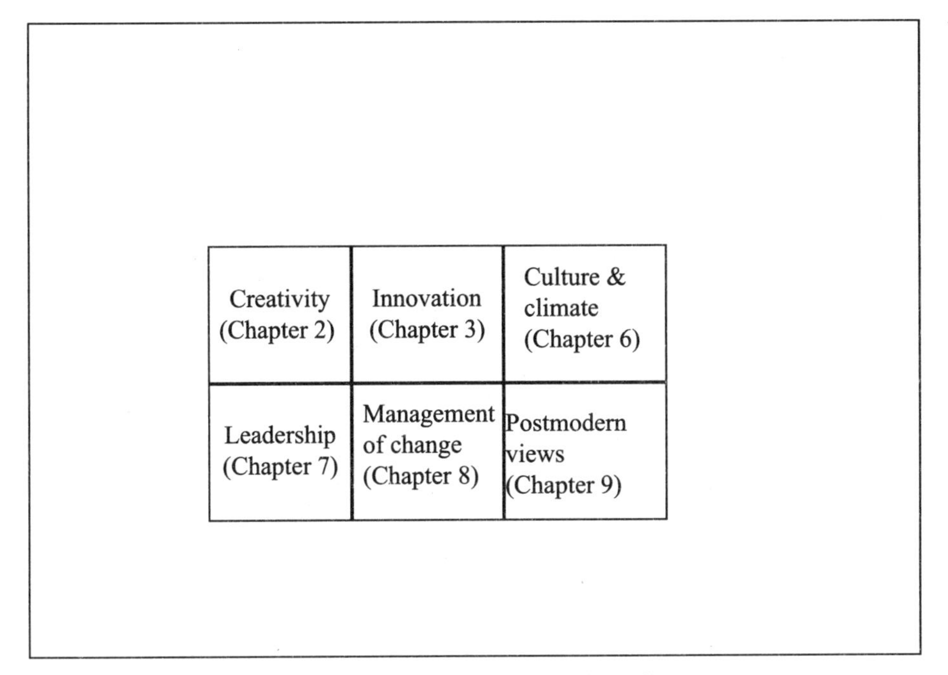

Figure 1.2: The optional core to the business disciplines jigsaw

possibilities. We are not concerned with the 'rightness' of the platform. That is a much longer process, and is of prime concern for those committed to the social group and to its platform of understanding. We are concerned with the existing orthodoxy in order to find new possibilities that it has largely denied.

How studying the platform of understanding leads to new possibilities

Each chapter after this one takes a topic of importance to business education and practice. The first part of the chapter describes an exercise that builds a platform of understanding of that topic. The reader is repeatedly introduced to platform-building, so that he or she can become increasingly aware of approaches and techniques for capturing the essential features of rather complex business areas. The platform of understanding is referred to as the orthodox view, or received wisdom of that topic as far as it could be established. This is knowledge that can be checked against the indicated sources, or used to support any business studies that the reader may have undertaken.

Then various alternative approaches are introduced as contrary to the orthodox view. This is where we try to go beyond conventional wisdom. The approach is a version of the very general one found in everyday life. All conversation attempts to establish a platform of understanding, perhaps in a mutually supportive way, perhaps in a more combative way. When a researcher reads a technical paper he or she is trying to build a platform of understanding with what is in the text. The process metaphorically provides an appreciation of 'where we stand'.

Platforms and paradigms

From an understanding of 'where we stand' it becomes easier to investigate the grounds for our stance. These contain a great deal of knowledge and experience. They also are shaped by unconsciously held assumptions and beliefs. These are sometimes referred to as paradigmatic beliefs. We will have a lot more to say about paradigms throughout the book. If the reader is content to accept the orthodox view covered in the early sections of each chapter, he or she has arrived at the platform of understanding of that orthodoxy. The platform of understanding serves as a foundation of received knowledge. Those readers still facing examinations to test their know-how as business graduates will find this of some value of itself. It permits communication with other graduates, business academics and professionals.

Why MBAs should learn how to challenge established wisdom

It is believed by some employers that MBAs fresh from business school are unable to apply what they have learned to the practical challenges of their new jobs. There is an element of truth in such assertions. Some students find the competitive pressures so intense that the main learning objective is to retain enough of what they have been told to gain good grades in the examinations and continuous assessment assignments. Learning to pass examinations in management is clearly different from learning how to manage effectively. The pressure extends to the teachers, who concentrate on presenting information in a form best suited for the students to reproduce the knowledge in essays and exams. This approach is likely to minimize the uncertainties and conceals unresolved issues present. At the end of such a programme, students have a good grasp of what is currently believed to be 'sound' theory, and 'best practice' applications of that theory. Passing the exams is partly a rite of passage to show that the initiate has assimilated a code of conduct. Indeed, for this kind of discipline acceptance there is little need to know why the information is true. What is important is that the students are able to communicate with other MBA-trained managers, using their shared platform of understanding to signal their affinity, and shared education and sets of values.

Beyond the platform of understanding

Sharing a platform of understanding is a means of joining an exclusive club. However, it does not provide the means of differentiating between which rules make sense and which are outmoded or inconsistent. Clearly it is in the interests of MBAs, their educators and employers to seek more from a business education than a guarantee that the recipient can say the right words in the right order. This is the challenge that educators set their best students. It is one that leads to the second, and more ambitious type of learning. It is sometimes known as reflective or experiential learning.

In the vocabulary of the knights of the economic order, the first approach leaves the knights to rely on blind faith in what they have been taught. The second approach adds thoughtfulness about beliefs and values that will lead to accumulating wisdom from each new challenge taken up.

Those readers opting for an overview of conventional wisdom can concentrate on the technical content in the first part of each chapter. Those willing to go more deeply will be interested in the approach taken to identify the information, and to get at less conventional possibilities. The notes at the end of each chapter are supplied for those wishing to carry out a deeper study of the original source materials.

Dealing with definitions

An important aspect of understanding a topic is reaching conclusions on definitions of key concepts. Managers and professionals have as a first fallback the definitions found in the platform of understanding. Some concepts are reasonably well defined (current cost accounting; FTSE index; bounded rationality). Others lead to many definitions and little resolution of the definitions (creativity; inflation; unemployment rate; corporate culture).

The platform of understanding is used as a starting point to establish what concepts are taken to mean within a given context. A term such as creativity is not taken to have a universally correct definition. Rather, we approach the term as if to ask: 'what work is the term creativity doing in the context in which it is being used?' If we find there are many definitions and much debate about them we conclude that the word is put to use in various contexts. We will even then be able to make further progress if we have some notion of the ways in which words are needed within the dominant orthodoxy and within less orthodox 'heresies'.

This is an approach to defining terms that is well understood and accepted in the social sciences. Readers who have not come across it before might wonder why it would not have been possible to follow the simpler expedient of looking up the term in a dictionary. Those within the particular paradigm have already spent time checking dictionary definitions (and indeed contributing to them). Furthermore, the dictionary offers only a set of all possible definitions. A student in a field is better advised to build a platform of understanding (or, in this book, to take advantage of the ones custom-built) to find which definitions have been favoured by those who have already spent a lot of time on just such activities.

Challenging the Platform of Understanding: Images of Discovery

So how will we be challenging the platforms of understanding once we have established them? I have resorted to methods that are not commonly found in traditional business textbooks. The techniques are generally ways of becoming engaged in processes of discovery. With new ways of seeing may come new discoveries. Each can be described as an image of discovery.[8] The images of discovery are tactics in a multi-pronged attack to challenge the platform of understanding.

The images of discovery crop up time and again in subsequent chapters. Here I will mention the most frequent images and some of the new possibilities to which they sensitize us.

The platform of understanding metaphor

We have already come across this metaphor. Its use to go beyond the platform of understanding is a constant reminder that social beliefs are constructions and that other constructions are also possible. In this sense, the metaphor is a simple way of approaching the concerns of postmodern thinkers (we will meet them in chapter 9). For example, the traditional belief (found or implied in the platform of understanding of all the orthodox topics of management studies) is the potential for the establishment of scientific truths (give or take estimates of statistical confidence). The postmodern belief (shared in some aspects by other theorists in the social sciences) is that such 'truths' have to be inspected to reveal the deep hidden assumptions. The postmodernists have their own ways of deconstructing the platform of understanding. Our metaphor is more concerned with reconstructing alternative platforms. It also provides a more traditional approach for 'getting at' a set of beliefs from the outside – which is a challenge to all who want to study social systems.[9] For example, as indicated above, we have a way, through studying a platform of understanding, of approaching the often tricky problems of vocabulary and definitions.

The metaphor of the personal quest or journey

The book is written as a story of a personal quest by the author. This may seem dangerously 'subjective' and even self-indulgent from the perspective of the dominant business orthodoxy. Yet the processes of discovery and change have resisted orthodox analysis. Increasingly the telling of stories has become recognized as a way through which new sense can be made out of old difficulties. Furthermore, the story can serve as a means of taking readers through an experience, in the first instance, vicariously (as I describe it) and then as an encouragement to try out their own personal journies of exploration.[10]

The metaphor of jigsaw puzzling

Within the quest metaphor can be found the second metaphor of jigsaw puzzling. Suppose we think of searching for knowledge as trying to fit together a monstrously complicated jigsaw puzzle. Large numbers of people have devoted their lives to this task, and many still do. To date, much has been achieved, but the jigsaw remains incomplete. Unlike simple mass-produced jigsaws, this one has no systematic replication of pieces. Each piece may fit into one or more other pieces.[11] One of the many difficulties is that no one knows exactly how many pieces there are; no one knows what the final picture will be.

In our jigsaw-building we may have reasonable information about the state of existing knowledge, how much of the picture has already been filled in, even where there are gaps remaining. We obtain further bits of jigsaw through dipping into the world of experience and sometimes pulling out a few pieces to examine. Each such effort allows us to look for fits with our beliefs ('theories'). A convincing fit gives us a good feeling, as we have linked up a new discovery with a theoretical position. That also gives us confidence that the theory helps explain new knowledge. That is how theory and practice reinforce each other.

The story so far is one of engaging in a widespread and pleasant pastime. Now let us introduce a little more tension into it. Suppose that making sense of part of the jigsaw is very important to us. Suppose also that progress is slow. We find that pieces are hard to come by, and the ones we find do not fit. It is likely that we become unsure and discouraged. Each piece is tested more and more thoroughly. We turn them over to make sure we are examining the right side. There is still no satisfactory fit.

We may not have the right pieces, or it may be that the order in which we fit them together is important. That is a particularly shocking and disorienting thought. In more familiar jigsaws it does not matter too much the sequence in which we study the bits, or even the sequence in which we fit them together. It does not matter where we start: we always finish with the same picture.[12]

I now want to connect this metaphoric tale of jigsaw-making to the business of discovery or 'thinking outside the box'.[13] In our studies we will be treating knowledge as bits of a jigsaw, looking for fits and misfits. The misfits 'do not make sense'. Our task then has to be to look for new sense, new explanations, and, as a result, the assembly of better-fitting new pictures. For each chapter we puzzle out the orthodox picture, then look for misfits and possible new pictures.

There is a second level of puzzling out to deal with: the difficulty of getting a good sequence to our overall journey. Each of the chapters represents a group of ideas, or a picture to be puzzled out. To increase the chances of challenging the orthodox platform of understanding we will begin with some of the themes that do not fit easily into that orthodoxy.

The handful of books metaphor

If discovery is a journey, it involves a search for short cuts. To put this more literally, no one has sufficient time to analyse and evaluate all available information. The short cuts involve various calculated risks and assumptions. The handful of books metaphor is one such short cut, framed in terms of someone approaching a very large library. He or she knows that in the time available it is advisable to scan widely and then return to the reading desks with no more documents than can be carried in one trip! The process is not automatic, and selecting the handful of books requires creative thought for each new topic studied.

The approach worked in the creation of this text to the extent that it quickly got me to a platform of understanding of each topic to which it was applied. Selecting the handful of books technique might be seen as another form of jigsaw puzzling. It was never quite the same in use. Each puzzle set its own new challenges. Descriptions of how it worked will be found in various chapters. Not surprisingly, the technique has to be used with some appreciation of its scope and limitations. The accounts illustrate the processes of discovery, and make up one of the ways in which readers may choose to study discovery processes and develop understanding of their own jigsaw puzzling (or discovery processes).

The hidden voices metaphor

The hidden voices metaphor is used to indicate how a dominant point of view effectively silences the other viewpoints, which are ignored, or dismissed as in error, false, or irrelevant.[14] It is a favourite metaphor among writers interested in 'deconstructing' orthodox views to arrive at fresh perspectives. This is covered in more detail in chapter 9, on postmodernism.

Thinking Outside the Box: Developing 'Thinking About Thinking Skills'

As we experiment with the various metaphors we find ourselves hitting up against new possibilities of a deep kind. The most immediate possibilities simply add a texture to existing ideas. The deeper possibilities are those that force us to think about our thinking. Here is where we may part company with the readers who are happy to take 'on trust' the view of the 'experts'.

Once we have arrived at different 'ways of seeing' we are faced with a tough question. How are we to reach a view on the value of any particular way over others? (One of the advantages of identifying with the views constituting a platform of understanding is that it makes plain what is the 'correct' way of seeing things.) This is the key challenge of those independent souls who seek to find things out for themselves.

One of the shortcuts is to look for evidence of 'voices' and to seek understanding of their platforms of understanding. The voices have to be studied in terms of the beliefs about knowledge and reality. The theory of theory deals among other things with the 'what, how and why' of 'what how and why'. Not surprisingly, this moves us away from the content and process of everyday thinking.

The simplest way of thinking about some of these abstractions is in terms of methods, knowledge and reality. Methods of studying are themselves influenced by beliefs about the reasoning processes for establishing knowledge. These beliefs for establishing knowledge are themselves directed toward understanding the nature of reality.

Borrowing the language of paradigms to assist our 'thinking about thinking'

For several hundred years the methods of investigation through empirical examination were synonymous with 'real' science and 'real' knowledge. Only within the last three decades of the twentieth century were these issues to be revisited. The initial impetus came from a young American philosopher and theorist, Thomas Kuhn, who proposed a theory of theories based on his studies of major scientific controversies. Kuhn showed how any belief system could be regarded as a framework with all sorts of built-in mechanisms to protect it from attacks by other belief systems. His work was to popularize the term paradigm as a belief system. He also suggested that successful paradigms persisted, even if some of the beliefs about knowledge and realities ('theories') were found to be in error. The resistance to fundamental change, according to Kuhn, can be overcome. When that happens there is a radical, perhaps catastrophic, disruption of the paradigm, followed by the emergence of its successor.

The great paradigmatic systems of human thought have been described in various ways. Historically we might consider the pre-industrial, and industrial eras as paradigms that emerged as the dominant world-view of their times. At the turn of the twentieth century many commentators had begun to anticipate the end of the industrial paradigm, and the emergence of the post-industrial one – perhaps also to be labelled the informational paradigm.

Today the term 'paradigm' has found its way into the vocabulary of organizational management, in such terms as 'paradigm shift', 'paradigm switch' and 'paradigm breakthrough'. The expressions are broadly taken to imply that a traditional belief system – the old paradigm – has been replaced by a new way of understanding, the new paradigm. The implication is that the process has been one within which a fundamental assumption has been successfully challenged.

Kuhn suggested that his own studies – of discovery in the pure sciences – did not match with the picture of science (i.e. scientists) making progress by such rational and formal methods. He proposed that at a particular period of time knowledge was bounded within a set of beliefs that were so broadly accepted that they resisted empirical refutation. That is to say, evidence that could disconfirm the basic beliefs was ignored, or treated as in error in some way. The concept of paradigm shifting represented the world of knowledge as essentially one that carried within it hidden assumptions and beliefs. It threatened the idea that science was engaged in correcting errors, and substituted the notion that science was a process whereby one set of beliefs was replaced by another set of beliefs.[15]

Managerialism and three 'suppressed voices'

Approximately a decade after Kuhn's ideas had attracted the attention of social scientists, another influential theoretical text on paradigms appeared. The book, *Sociological Paradigms and Organisational Analysis*, by the British sociological theorists Gibson Burrell and Gareth Morgan, was concerned with paradigmatic beliefs within the social sciences. 'Our proposition,' they wrote, 'is that social theory can usefully be conceived in terms of four key paradigms based upon different sets of metatheoretical assumptions about the nature of social science and the nature of society. The four paradigms are based upon four mutually exclusive views of the social world. Each stands in its own right and generates its own distinctive analyses of social life. With regard to the study of organizations, for example, each paradigm generates theories and perspectives, which are in fundamental opposition to those generated in other paradigms.'[16]

This set of procedures resulted in a 'theory of theories' matrix within which theories could be classified according to their assumptions. We have borrowed from the original classification that had one dominant paradigm, and three competing paradigmatic positions as shown in figure 1.3. We have used the term 'managerialism' to replace the earlier term of 'functionalism' (and the related term structural-functionalism).

The diagram can be taken as a window, which we can look into, and see a distinctive paradigmatic grouping in each of the window sections.[17] In the original text the four paradigms received labels that were based on the earlier leading theories placed in each category.

The dominant paradigm was originally labelled as the *functionalist paradigm*.[18] Once the reader becomes sensitized to the possibility, it becomes easy to identify the influence of the dominant paradigm in every major component of the business studies curriculum. We sometimes refer to the paradigm by its original label if we are examining material that uses that vocabulary. Otherwise we will refer to a managerialist paradigm to indicate that we are examining the paradigm in a way that will unfold itself in subsequent chapters.[19]

The beliefs within the managerialist paradigm – its platform of understanding – are hinted at in the willingness of managers and management theorists alike to

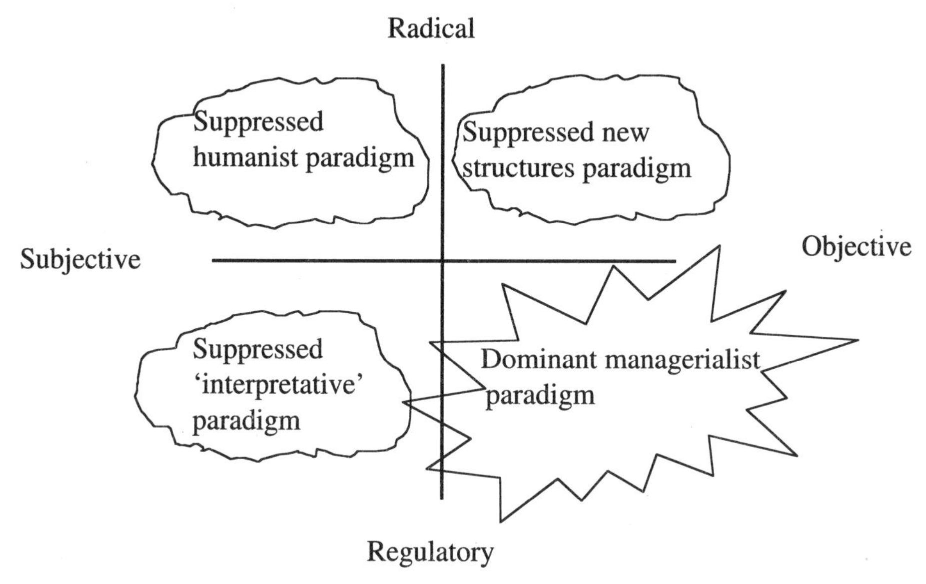

Figure 1.3: Managerialism, and the three suppressed 'heresies'

treat management studies as a form of scientific endeavour. Management science and scientific management have direct links into beliefs of how science 'works' in understanding the physical world of objects and the abstract world of mathematical relationships. The methods are the methods of benchmarking, measuring, and accounting (for) things. The beliefs are summed up in the old expression 'what gets measured gets managed'. The sense of what is real comes from these beliefs.

We must emphasize that the managerialist paradigm can rightly claim great advances in the practice of management, as this has been studied from the orthodox platform of understanding. Many of the principles are indeed 'what they teach at business school'.[20] The application of measurement-based methods happens to have served managers well in a whole range of different fields such as operations management and financial analysis, where it contributes to greater efficiencies in ways of 'doing things better'. We will argue that it begins to lose its impact when the need is for greater effectiveness or 'doing better things'. Then the confidence in 'the numbers' turns into a misplaced opposition to those hidden paradigms or voices that rely on different methods for achieving knowledge and change.[21]

So what are the suppressed voices? The voices heard directly above the managerialist space in our window-frame have been described as expressions of radical structuralist views. This concerns itself with revolutionary alternative structures that can substitute for existing social structures. We might expect new and innovative structures for stimulating organizational change to be radical structural challenges to orthodox approaches. In some ways Tom Peters has been encouraging a revolution against the structural orthodoxies of big business organizations. The most famous radical structuralist theory was built up by Karl Marx and his followers as an alternative to capitalism.

Alongside, and spatially to the left of the objective managerialist paradigm, can be found its subjective mirror image. This set of beliefs has been labelled the *interpretative paradigm*. Organizational systems within this paradigm have existence ultimately only in terms of the sets of meanings developed by people within the organization. Their actions provide clues as to the meanings and give sense to their mutual interactions. Researchers in this tradition seek to understand and explain the 'real' significance of everyday transactions, rejecting studies of large samples in favour of deeper investigations of specific contexts.[22] While this sounds highly theoretical, I recently came across a sign pinned to a dividing wall of one open-plan department of marketing in a large consumer goods organization. The sign captured much of the platform of understanding of interpretivistic thought. It read 'reality is what is perceived as reality . . . We are in the perceptions business'.

Finally, and differing on two dimensions from the dominant functionalist one, we come to the radical humanist paradigm. Here the radicalism of the radical structuralists and the subjectivity of the interpretivists combine to give an approach to social systems that seeks to find radical ways of understanding and liberating human needs.[23] Radical and humanistic ways of engaging in organizational life might include communitarian approaches based on ethical rather than economic beliefs. We will look later at the possibilities for new radical humanist insights within the postmodern movement.

One important outcome is that researchers exploring the suppressed voices find themselves following the rules and requirements of truth-seeking from the position of the dominant paradigm. This has been called the process of *abstracted empiricism*, whereby the alternative paradigms are distorted and submitted to inappropriate methods of investigation. The rules are rigged so that the dominant paradigm tends to win out. For example, the marketing department may feel compelled to back up its belief in perceptions to convince 'hard-headed accountants' how they have measured the perceptions of their customers, and how this translates into percentage points on their market-share. The language of debate is the language of the most powerful voice.

In figure 1.4 we see the four groupings we have been discussing. Each of the three 'heresies' is shown as being pulled towards the dominant orthodoxy. This gives us a clue to what we have to do, while also indicating why the task will not be straightforward. Specific versions of this figure will appear in other chapters, as we look for evidence of this happening. This kind of examination helps us to consider what contributions to our thinking might be possible if the voices were given 'more of a say'.

The Start of a Journey of Exploration

After all these preliminary remarks it is now time to outline the journey that is more fully described in subsequent chapters of the book. I have simplified the journey a little while retaining some accounts of culs-de-sac and false trails. The

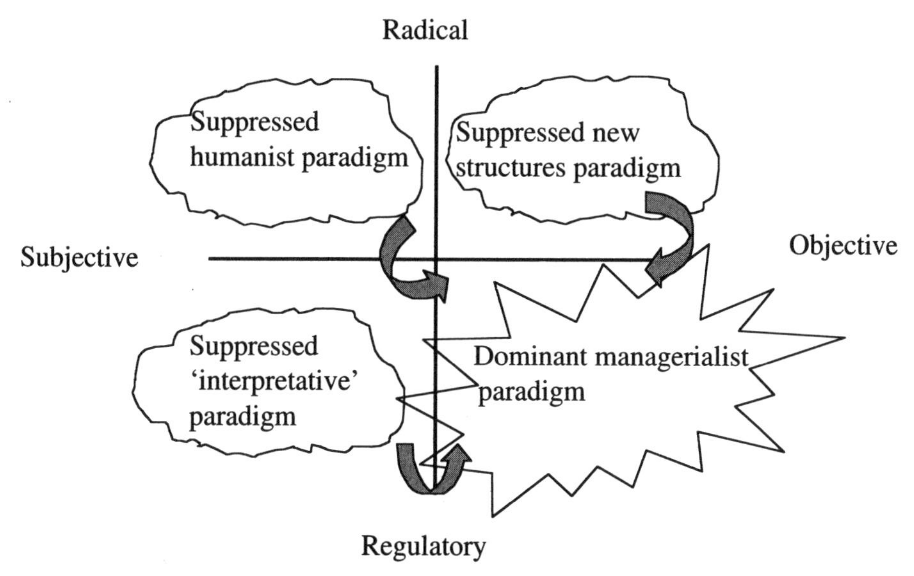

Figure 1.4: The powerful pull of the dominant paradigm

route has been split up into stages or chapters. Each chapter describes the jigsaw puzzling challenge encountered in some business territory. Its platform of understanding is described as I assembled it from the bits of the jigsaw.

Discovery by wandering about

The sequence of explorations which is shown in figure 1.5 deserves an explanation. Whatever insights I derived in my journey arose because I started close to my own personal knowledge base of creativity. As it happens, that particular starting point is a promising one for contrasting the orthodox business view with that of the less conventional ones. Then I worked outwards, away from my starting point, and towards other territories. The important learning occurred in terms of what was found – but also in terms of how the findings were obtained. There is a case for readers to walk along in my footsteps for a first reading. It is also possible to go straight to regions of special interest, and then strike out toward other regions in a 'random-walk' kind of way. In either case, it is advisable to study the map before setting out on the journey.[24]

In chapter 2 we encounter clear and substantial evidence that creativity is difficult to fit into the dominant business paradigm. Yet, if creativity is treated from various less orthodox positions it offers ways of humanizing the ways we think about organizations and organizing. Here, as elsewhere, creativity has tended to be intellectually 'defined away'. This serves to preserve an assumption that business can be managed so as to arrive at the right answers through logical thought processes. The assumption denies the legitimacy of approaches and ideas dismissed as 'illogical', 'irrational' or even 'insane'.

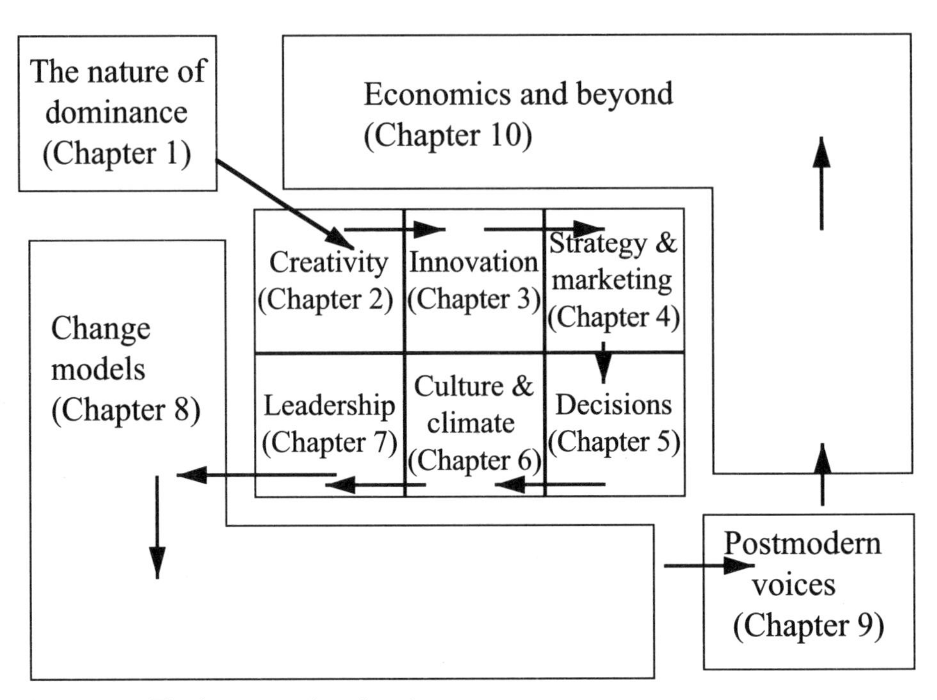

Figure 1.5: The journeys of exploration

In chapter 3 the journey shows that innovation has had a little more success as a credible topic in business studies without quite making it to the status of a core topic. Efforts to make innovation credible have produced linear models that are still widespread although they have been criticized as unreliable. Innovation seeks to retain its respectability by isolating creativity in a stage at 'the front end' of the process. Once this process is recognized it becomes easier to consider creativity and innovation as highly interdependent processes within change management. These ideas bring innovation closer to recent ideas about knowledge management.

Chapter 4 takes us closer to the core business topics in studies of marketing and strategy. These formal disciplines deal with interface between the firm and its economic market environment. Their high status is supported by their methods, which have become highly quantitative and analytical. This has led to the relative suppression of creativity in the dominant theories, although creativity is often proposed in more practical treatments. Efforts to introduce creativity as an 'emergent' strategy mode are treated as controversial. Intangibles such as brand image and relationship excellence are managed through application of quantification methods.

Chapter 5 continues the journey into the heart of business orthodoxy. The regions of applied decision-making have high status. Claims have been made that decision-making is the fundamental managerial activity. In its most orthodox form, decision-making is regarded as rational and analytical, only bounded by the inadequacies of human information processing. Creativity is thoroughly tamed, with claims that anything a human can create an electronic computer can create in principle and, increasingly, in practice. We show how such a claim might arise and be taken seriously from within the orthodoxy of decision-science. We also show that other beliefs about creativity have to be suppressed, if such a claim is to be taken seriously outside the dominant paradigm.

In chapter 6 we describe how our journey returns from the heights of business orthodoxy to the domains of culture and climate. Both constructs (sometimes referred to as metaphors in the literature) are increasingly being studied for insights into organizational factors that support innovation and creativity. By now we are able to anticipate the ways in which the topics have been tamed to increase their acceptability within the dominant paradigm. Climate has tended to be regarded as some quantifiable entity possessed by organizations. Culture, in contrast, has its origins in the social-anthropological tradition, and again tends to be weakened by efforts to measure and codify it. There are welcome signs of recognition of the need for more radical approaches of studying change-orientated cultures, including those of a visionary kind.

Visionary cultures lead us into the subject of leadership, covered in chapter 7. The managerialist approach has been active in one great branch of the literature, in what has become known as transactional leadership. This approach tames leadership and limits the impact of individual differences on organizational outcomes. Interestingly a more radical approach to leadership has gradually become more visible, namely transformational leadership. This approach suggests that a greater connection between creativity studies and leadership studies might be one that benefits both topics.

After chapter 7, our journeying takes another turn towards a mostly unmapped region, concerning the management of change (chapter 8). All our previous experiences suggest that the orthodoxy will seek to deal with change as a process susceptible to logical analysis and deliberate control processes. One approach that gained international recognition was connected with control of the quality of production and service (Total Quality). Under the conditions of uncertainty we have already discussed, such approaches proved insufficient, permitting more radical alternatives to appear, such as the business process re-engineering variant. Both these approaches, however, paid their dues to the orthodox need for rational and logically delineated structures. In each system the scope for human creative contribution seems to have been restricted. The more humanistic approaches to change, such as action research and (soft) systems dynamics, struggle to gain acceptance. Our treatment of this confused field leaves us with the impression that the search is on for ways of admitting participative and humanistic contributions into organizational theory and practice.

In search of such alternatives, we head in chapter 9 to the controversial realms of postmodernism. The approach has a spirit of radicalism and excitement about it, and more than a dash of mystery and self-contradiction. It sets out to rupture old assumptions and beliefs. We might expect ways of breaking free of conventional ideas. Here in particular we have to postpone a potted explanation, as we do not quite have the vocabulary for it, and so we risk 'taming' it in the vocabulary of the old orthodoxy (something that postmodernists object to as, we suggest, do all suppressed and non-dominant voices). It turns out that postmodernism may have common cause with some of the more radical creative voices outlined in this book. It certainly shared a few common enemies! Among these we find opposition to the idea of a dominant voice of authority; and the idea that efforts to break from such orthodoxy are worthwhile. Postmodernism also offers thoughts on the benefits of creativity freed from the restrictions of a managerialist culture.

After the somewhat exhausting mental gymnastics of postmodernism, we make one final excursion in chapter 10 to the high ground of orthodoxy. Here we take a non-economic look at economic orthodoxy. Our platform of understanding reveals a subject that historically embraced rather liberal views and philosophical values. However, economic orthodoxy was the influence that shaped management studies. It was from economic values that managerialism sprang. Economics and its associated managerial disciplines seem to have developed into a more qualitative and restricted format over time. Its dominance has been earned by its adherence to a formalistic and quantitative set of methods known as the neoclassical orthodoxy.

Now we can see the consequences of such a position. Many rich and elegant advances have been made. These strengths have justified the recognition earned by economics in such fields as macroeconomic modelling. However, the costs of a claim of a 'pure and positive' scientific base for economics include some uncomfortable trade-offs. There has emerged a tricky gulf between macroeconomics and microeconomics that is hard to bridge. Matters of ethical concern have to be wrapped up in the so-called normative or non-positive mode. Neoclassical theory has trouble with concepts such as human altruism. Innovation and mechanisms for growth are mainly treated as outside the scope of the mathematical models. A few revolutionaries dare to suggest the death of conventional economics.

Hundreds of books and articles have chewed these subjects over. One more perspective as suggested in this book can act only like another straw on the back of a complaining camel, or one more drop of water on the stony surface of orthodoxy. Nevertheless, the straw has been put in place, the idea-droplet directed on to the stone. Readers have to decide if these straws in the wind or droplets on to the surface of orthodoxy are likely to make a difference. If so, he or she may choose to approach business studies in a more creative and self-directed manner.

Notes

[1] Ross A. Webber, Director of Wharton's Executive Development programme 'The transition from functional to general management', in Dickson & Bickerstaffe (1997: 10).

[2] Mintzberg (1979: xii).

[3] Amabile (1996: xi), preface to the updated version of her (Amabile 1983) book.

[4] Burrell (1996: 645).

[5] McCormack (1984) pioneered today's industry of sport sponsorship. For an even bleaker view of the MBA process see *Snapshots from Hell: The Making of an MBA*, by Peter Robinson (1994).

[6] For a rich discussion on this point see the *Harvard Business Review*, Nov–Dec issue, 1992. The general point was accepted that MBA courses can at best complement practical experience.

[7] Senge, P. (1990).

[8] The term has echoes of *Images of Organization* (Morgan, 1985, 1998), one of the seminal influences of this current work.

[9] See Rickards & Moger (1999) for an example of a practical application of the concept in a study of organizational teams.

[10] For a beautiful account of the power of story telling in sense-making see Weick (1995), especially chapter 5.

[11] We can make this metaphor as complex as we choose. So we could decide that a piece may have no fit at all. This leads us to considerations of what is *real*, what is *true*, and what is *false*. My second choice of guide to these matters is Sayer (1992).

[12] If we consider not real jigsaws, but the processes of discovery, we may note that the various strategies of search will converge on the same discovery. This is known in systems theory as the principle of equifinality.

[13] As we indicated at the start of the chapter, Mintzberg (1979: xii) and Amabile (1996: xi) are among the distinguished researchers attracted to the jigsaw metaphor. The image is helpful inasmuch as it indicates the creative, sense-making processes of discovery, and the issue of aggregation of components into a unified pattern. It is worth remembering, however, that jigsaws tend to be two-dimensional, and that search involves uncertainties in a multitude of dimensions.

[14] Putnam et al. (1996) include the voice metaphor in their detailed review of a range of 'metaphor clusters' found in organizational analyses. See also Burrell (1996) in the same edited work.

[15] The vehemence of the rejection of the Kuhnian view by Popper and his supporters can be interpreted as a reaction to a perceived threat to the contemporary orthodoxy of science. The Popperians were anticipating a difficulty we will address below – that of resolving the claims of one 'paradigm' over another.

[16] Burrell & Morgan (1979: x).

[17] The four fundamental paradigms, often referred to as if they are the only ones of significance, are composed of larger numbers of more coherent paradigmatic groupings. Burrell and Morgan found approximately a dozen 'families' of paradigms from the sociological literature. They located these on the basis of 'best fit' within each of the four of their major divisions (Burrell & Morgan, 1979: 29).

[18] Or, alternatively, the structural functionalist paradigm. The term implies an approach to sociology that draws heavily on the natural science orthodoxy. We have tended to use the term 'managerial' paradigm, which refers to these assumptions when applied to issues relevant to managers.

[19] Burrell and Morgan's theory has come under attack for its internal inadequacies and for helping popularize 'the latest and most pernicious variant of the doctrine that the basis of organizational studies must be general characterizations of organizations' (Ackroyd, 1992). In all the attacks, however, the primacy of the functionalist paradigm in organizational studies is tacitly or explicitly recognized.

[20] Although the hold of managerialism is far from absolute. Not atypically, a Harvard Business School professor explained to me once that 'we don't do plumbing'.

[21] See Art Kleiner's highly readable account of the 'magic of the numbers' in Kleiner (1996).

[22] 'The various interpretative views have in common their focus on an actor's perspective on life in organizations . . .' (Aldrich, 1992: 23).

[23] French existentialism combines trust in subjective beliefs and reaction against conventional authority. Burrell and Morgan located the philosophy of Sartre and associated existentialists in the radical humanist category.

[24] I am painfully aware that some people always consult the appropriate map before starting a journey, whereas others only consult the map after they get lost. As a lifetime member of the second category I would not want to debar such a strategy from any like-minded readers.

chapter 2
Creativity: The Slumbering Giant of Organizational Studies

In the last 100 years we have developed our steel and paper and pulp industries. And just think of Swedish product innovations like the separator, the safety match, the automatic lighthouse, the three-phase electrical generator and motor, the refrigerator and the ball bearing . . . All these very important innovations were the result of inventors and entrepreneurs joining forces with financiers. Often these people were thought to be mad, fooling around with crazy ideas. But history has now taught us that these 'madmen' made it.

Lars Ramqvist, President and CEO Ericsson[1]

The concept of creativity may trail clouds of glory, but it brings along also a host of controversial questions. The first of these is: **What is it?**

Margaret Boden[2]

There is a good deal of agreement on what we mean by 'creativity'.

Hans Eysenck[3]

The jury is in on the current state of creativity research and the verdict is – case dismissed for lack of evidence.

Cameron Ford[4]

The real reason we have done so very little about creativity is very simple. We have not understood it at all.

Edward De Bono[5]

Introduction

The start of a journey

Here we are at the real start of my journey of exploration. Chapter 1 was simply a clearing of the throat. A getting ready for the journey itself. The start of any journey is a time of rare excitement and anticipation. What will happen?

Will it turn out as expected? Or will I be pleasantly surprised, or maybe sadly disappointed?

The trip has been planned and replanned in my mind. It is my intention to visit a number of territories in the realms of organized human behaviours. I am starting with a trip through very familiar territory of creativity and related subjects, subjects I believe to be neglected yet potentially valuable in advancing understanding of the practice of management. What follows is the account of my journey and the various approaches that I used in making progress. These include the approaches for puzzling out jigsaws; ways of building a platform of understanding (including the handful of books approach); and methods for detecting almost silenced voices that contradict the prevailing ways of thinking about management.

The Traveller's Platform of Understanding of Creativity

When I began my journey I already had a set of beliefs and assumptions about creativity. These had developed and been influenced by what I had read and discussed with others interested in the subject all over the world. The platform received a few jolts along the way and these will be indicated in the text. However, the platform retained much of its shape.

I will first of all briefly indicate what I regarded (and still regard) as the essential features of a platform of understanding shared among those who have studied the subject or thought about it in some detail. Then I will outline what my own platform of understanding looked (and still looks) like.

Among theorists and practitioners alike, there is a view that creativity is 'something to do with' processes that produce new and valued ideas. The novelty and value may be primarily an assessment by the person doing the thinking and creating. Or it may be an assessment by wider social groupings. There is something of a split between those who would regard creativity as something extraordinary, and those who consider the process to be as natural as breathing, and a universal human characteristic. There is also mostly agreement that the process is complex and multifaceted. Most authorities agree that there is no universally agreed creativity test, nor universally agreed definition.[6] The processes are regarded as partly unconscious, and may leap into consciousness as a moment of inspiration or insight. Additionally, many practitioners explicitly or implicitly believe that creative processes can be partially influenced by deliberate efforts on the part of the explorer/creator. These interventions may be directed towards securing favourable environmental conditions, including the application of structures or techniques. These views are among the most widely accepted views among practitioners of the so-called creative problem-solving techniques.[7]

My own platform of understanding has some points of departure from the more widely shared views. I tend to support the view that creativity is a universal human characteristic not unlike a form of intelligence.[8] Whatever creativity is, we all have some of it, although we are unlikely to have received the same endowment or the opportunity to develop it. I agree there is no wide agreement about definitions or measures. I do not find this particularly surprising, nor believe it to be a justification for rejecting the concept for a fundamental lack of definitional precision.[9]

Overview of the journey

The motivation for this journey might be summed up as a need to explain a puzzle. Creativity is a concept that finds favour with many managerial professionals, and yet is widely ignored within business research and courses. This is an important issue to clarify, if creativity is to be taken more seriously in business studies.

In this journey I begin by obtaining enough handfuls of books to build a platform of understanding from the point of view of practitioners. I was looking for important bits that did not quite fit. The chapter then moves on to identify the stories that became most influential in the field. The stories were built around individuals who were in some cases concerned with theory development, in other cases with proposing practical steps for assisting the creative process.

In the study of the practitioner literature, creative thinking and creative problem-solving are repeatedly placed in opposition to rational thinking and problem-solving. Various non-orthodox themes are detected dealing with personal transformation, mystery/magic, and the unexplained 'something special' of creativity. In the study of influential stories there is further evidence that creativity deals with issues that are difficult to manage from the dominant rational paradigm. There is also evidence that many researchers have tried to work 'with the grain' of the dominant orthodoxy. This has helped the orthodox view to preserve its integrity. It is as if creativity is a slumbering giant whose strength, once awakened, could be harnessed to bring about much-needed changes in many fields of management theory and practice. This chapter has illustrated how creative methods might be applied to creativity itself. We conclude that the methods have to be applied to those specific fields to support new ideas within them.

Building a Platform of Understanding of Practitioner Perspectives of Creativity

The handful of books shortcut

I was able to take advantage of one very effective shortcut in studying what managers and professionals think about creativity. Because the subject was close to my area of greatest personal expertise, I had almost instant access to a comprehensive collection of books. I wandered around my personal bookshelves and took out as many as I could carry of the popular books dealing with creativity and creative thinking. I noted also another set of books dealing with creative problem-solving. These would be two bits of the jigsaw to be assembled. As a kind of control I took down what might be termed a contrasting set of books that dealt with problem-solving that was not classed by the authors as creative.[10] Figure 2.1 indicates the bits of the practitioners' jigsaw to be puzzled out.

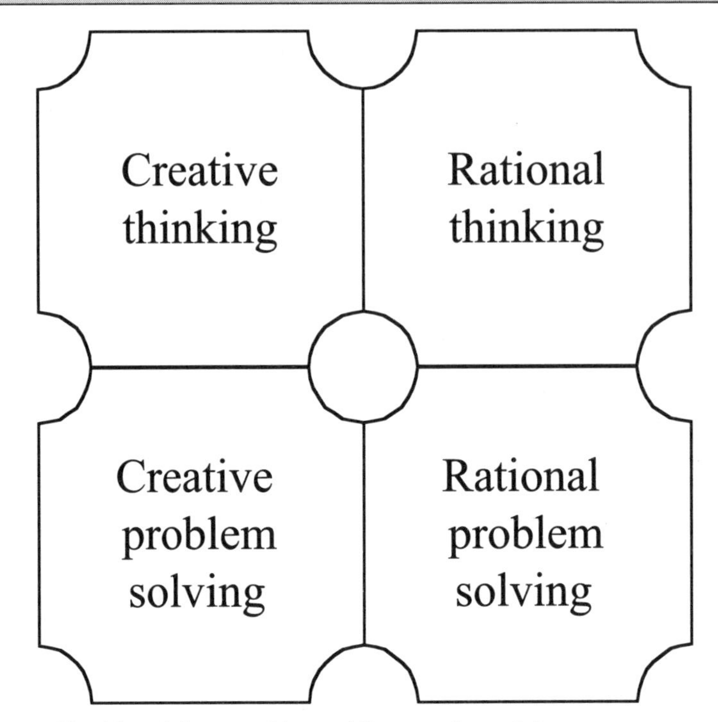

Figure 2.1: The bits of the practitioners' jigsaw of creativity

Some of the books were new to me, although most were old friends. I had some expectations that the books would help me connect up the dominant views in the popular literature of creativity and problem-solving. However, I did not have preconceived ideas in exact detail of what I would find. The sample turned out to have adequate representation of UK and North American authorship. The publication dates covered the 1970s through to the 1990s.

To my pleasure, a clear pattern of beliefs emerged from the stated and implicit messages in the books. Most authors were unconcerned about precise terminologies, writing as if their audiences of practitioners had no reason to bother about precise definitions. After some jigsaw puzzling, four regions were identified, each having a consistent theme, which I later saw as assembling into two larger themes (figure 2.2).

The four practitioner themes

The four themes repeatedly dealt with creativity as something special; personal transformation; magical and mysterious; and opposed to logical thinking and problem-solving. These ideas were subsequently combined into the two wider themes of creativity associated with a special and supercharged version of thinking or of problem-solving.

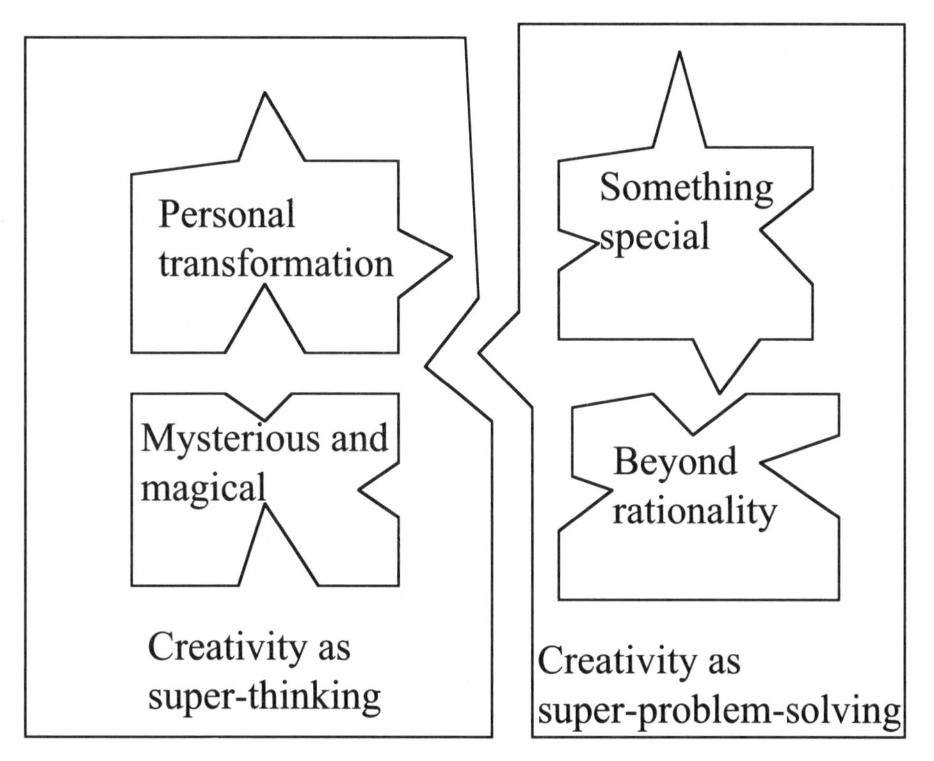

Figure 2.2: The themes in the practitioners' jigsaw

The 'something special' theme

The organizational accounts reveal a special 'something' manifest in exceptional thinking and problem-solving. The creative something special is regarded as the initiator of many great commercial achievements.

The personal transformation theme

Humanistic and cognitive psychologists have proposed a view of creativity as a human universal capacity that is more visible when it leads to great achievements. The two themes share the notion of transformation. The 'something special' tendency in the managerial ideas leads to economic and cultural transformation through personal inspiration. The universalist tendency leads to personal transformation through personal development and self-actualization.

The mystery, magic and madness theme

The popular accounts often interrelate the great benefits flowing from creativity with suggestions that the topic is poorly understood, and difficult to study. There are frequent references to its connection with inexplicable 'magical' inspiration, and to its connection with darker personal attributes of psychological instability.

Creativity opposed to the rationality of 'ordinary' problem-solving and thinking

The accounts of creativity give a further clue to its perceived nature. The primary distinction being made seems to be between everyday and rational thinking and problem-solving and exceptional or creative thinking and problem-solving. The writers imply that everyday rational thinking and problem-solving serve only to preserve existing habits of thought. The creative variants serve to break out of those existing habits of thought.

'Normal' or logical thinking and problem-solving leads to a predetermined answer which follows from the constraints of the situation. Uncreative thinking and uncreative problem-solving have no need for self-discovery and learning. This distinction fits with ideas from a growing body of writers challenging assumptions regarding the nature of management. As we will be finding in successive chapters, the old orthodoxy assumed that organizations could be studied and understood so that logically derived rules could be developed for their control. Scientific management required logical and rational thinking. More recently it has been argued that such an approach assumes that the organizational system has well-bounded and fixed characteristics that can be defined. A more convincing assumption is that organizations have ill-defined characteristics. Management involves thinking in ways that make it a reality-constructing activity.[11]

The practitioners have drawn attention to inadequacies of rational thinking and problem-solving. Within what we have called the old orthodoxy such a view has little significance, as rationality is the main defence against irrationality. Furthermore, the ideas of practitioners can always be dismissed as irrational and devoid of theoretical content. To deal with these objections we need to look at the most persistent ideas found within the creativity platform of understanding.

Creativity Theories: Reconstructing Historical Landmarks

I had already carried out many visits to the library to pore over its handfuls of books on creativity. In the interests of other explorers I did return once more to my own favoured reading list which helped me produce a short list of key stories. They can be found in both popular and more scholarly books, and collectively capture important paradigmatic beliefs. At the very least they can be said to have a cultural significance for those writing and researching creativity.

Sultan, Köhler, and the Gestalt school of psychology

Sultan, a captive ape on the Spanish island of Tenerife, became an animal celebrity and one of the first of many chimpanzee movie stars. Our story begins when a distinguished German psychologist, Wolfgang Köhler, was incarcerated on Tenerife during World War One.[12] Köhler was a Gestalt psychologist who had studied with the founder of Gestalt psychology, Max Wertheimer, at the Frankfurt Academy.

Wertheimer's earlier work had raised the questions of perception and reality. What mechanisms lead us to observe a rapid sequence of static images and see a moving picture? What leads us to construct a complete answer to a problem which had been blocking us? Wertheimer and Köhler believed the explanation involved mental structures of a special kind. These structures or Gestalten were in some way matched up with the structures presented from the outside world. The Gestalt school developed laws that they attempted to test empirically.

As Köhler watched the apes of Tenerife he found many examples of what the Gestaltists referred to as insight closure. Sultan in particular seemed able to change his behaviours consistent with Gestalt theory. Sultan was filmed when he appeared to solve problems by discovering a new use for a stick, or a box, to enable him to reach his favourite food of bananas. The process had the characteristics of a sudden unexpected discovery that the Gestaltists considered to come from a Gestalt reconfiguration or switch.

We know today that the Gestalt laws were too rigidly defined to survive close testing. However, many issues of interest to modern psychologists can be traced to the earlier Gestaltists. Furthermore, the moment of insight continued to fascinate researchers into creativity, as our next stories will show.

Even more important for later chapters are the implications for understanding sudden changes and the impact of environmental 'jolts'. Kurt Lewin's famous force field theory of change is described in chapter 8. That important theory was grounded in Gestaltist thought. It implies that change in social systems involves a weakening of a structural field or Gestalt and then a re-establishment of a new field or Gestalt.

Archimedes, Kekulé, and The Act of Creation

Arthur Koestler (1905–83) was a Hungarian-born author and journalist of exceptional intellectual powers and imagination. One of his many interests was the nature of the creative process, and he outlined his theories in a trilogy, of which *The Act of Creation* became particularly widely read and influential.[13]

When an author wants to list examples of scientific creativity you can be pretty sure she will include the famous story of Archimedes in his bath. The story has become synonymous with the act of creation, and was a central image within Koestler's analysis of discovery processes.[14] He also popularized the story of the scientist Kekulé, who, in a dream-like state, discovered a means of characterizing the chemical structure of Benzene, thereby producing a revolution in the way organic chemistry was to develop.[15]

One of the images most connected with creativity is that of the electric light bulb flashing on above the head of a cartoon character. The sudden illumination is a metaphor for insight. Within the creative problem-solving paradigm, insight is seen as the vital extra that discriminates creative discoveries from ordinary thinking.[16] In opposition to this view is that of the 'nothing new' school of psychology which regards discovery processes as producing no totally new concept. According to these arguments, all so-called discoveries are modifications or recombinations of existing knowledge.[17]

Studies of insight may provide means of clarifying the links between creativity and problem-solving. Creative problem-solving may require insights at a stage of sorting out the nature of the problem as well as at the stage of finding solution possibilities. In contrast, routine problem-solving does not require insights, and is more concerned with application of existing knowledge to arrive at problem-solutions.[18]

Wallas' four stages of creative thinking

Graham Wallas (1858–1932) was an English academic and political scientist who has been considered one of the most influential nineteenth-century social scientists. His study of near-contemporary accounts of great acts of discovery led him to propose a sequence of four stages for creativity, borrowing the first three from an earlier description.[19] The stages were preparation, incubation, illumination and verification.

Incubation is a kind of on-hold or gestation stage that can be accepted by those who believe in unconscious mental activity leading to discovery and by others who can propose some kind of recovery from a functional fixedness. The mysterious nature of creativity is mostly confined to the production of insight or discovery. Preparation and validation are in accord with orthodox scientific method. As a recent reviewer commented on his model: 'Its continued prominence after more than sixty years may be attributed to the fact that it still "rings true" to many people's experiences of creativity.'[20]

Brainstorming and the CPS paradigm

A young advertising executive, Alex Osborn, at the start of World War Two, believed he could play a part in the war-time effort for his country, if he could release the creative talent of his fellow Americans. He encouraged employees in his firm to suggest ideas for supporting the war effort. He put down his proposals in a booklet on how to dream up ideas.[21] The booklet was an immense success, and was distributed widely. Osborn had begun an interest in releasing 'everyday creativity' that stayed with him all his life. His subsequent experiments convinced him that under normal business conditions most ideas were never suggested. It was his efforts to overcome the social pressures of status that led him to develop the famous brainstorming rules of 'postpone judgement', 'freewheel', 'hitchhike' and 'quantity breeds quality'.

An enthusiastic and excellent communicator, Osborn spread his ideas widely. His later book *Applied Imagination* (Osborn 1953), which described his 'brainstorming' technique, brought him even greater success.[22] Later, he established a foundation at Buffalo, New York, in which a general problem-solving system was developed which may well be the most widely taught of all creative problem-solving approaches.[23]

Brainstorming in the 1960s was rigorously examined in large numbers of laboratory studies. These suggested that interactive brainstorming was inefficient when compared to 'nominal' (non-interactive) variants. These orthodox academic attacks were less damaging than a journalistic criticism of the technique made in a *Fortune* article.[24] The article, distorting the process, concentrating on the 'bizarre' appearance of senior executives producing irrational ideas, seemed to have a powerful impact in corporate America. Industrial support for the emerging foundation dried up almost overnight, and it took many years for it to reach its current state of pre-eminence internationally.[25]

The whole brain metaphor

Creativity researchers sometimes claim legitimacy for their field by pointing to the Nobel-prize-winning work of Bogan and Sperry on patients who had received surgical treatments severing the neural connections between left and right neo-cortical hemispheres.[26] These studies extended other evidence that speech functions are controlled via the left cerebral hemisphere and that a range of visual, emotional, and other non-verbal functions are controlled via the right hemisphere. Once knowledge of the medical work had been translated into everyday language and had reached a more popular audience it gave a name to a distinction that had been around for a far longer time period.

The original medical research showed that severing the corpus callosum to produce split-brain behaviours also led to weakening of creative performance. This has been taken to suggest that creativity involves a collaboration between left-brain and right-brain functions. A persistent theme in writings about creativity structures mental processes into two components, termed left-brain thinking and right-brain thinking. In the popular literature the expressions seem to be implying the fundamental distinction between creative thinking (right-brain thinking) and uncreative (left-brain) thinking. A rather more sophisticated approach presents left-brain and right-brain as labels for preferred thinking styles. This approach leads to a view that creative thinking is more integrative and holistic, combining the characteristics of left-brain and right-brain modes into a 'whole-brain' model.

The orthodox theories of business and science consider that 'correct' thinking is logical and analytical. The whole brain model extends this to 'rescue' kinds of thinking (intuition and metaphoric thinking for example) that would otherwise be suppressed.

Guilford's APA speech and his 'structure of intellect' model

Professor 'JP' Guilford was already a prestigious figure in the world of psychology when he became interested in creativity, hardly worthy of study by a serious psychometrician. Although he was later to be regarded rightly as one of the pioneering fathers of formal research into creativity, the story that has become most quoted is of his 1950 speech to the American Psychological Association at the time of his presidency.

The background to the speech was the launching of the Soviet satellite, Sputnik. Guilford presented the launching as an example of a loss of national technological advantage, which he attributed directly to a continued failure to encourage creativity within the education system. He called for measures to support the study of creativity as a matter of national urgency. The speech was widely reported, far beyond the confines of academic psychology. Federal funds were attracted to researching the creative phenomenon and to educational initiatives for stimulating creativity.

Guilford's academic work in the area produced a theoretical model of 'structures of intellect' within which he predicted the existence of categories of thought identifiable with creative performance which had not been previously identified. The structure of intellect model was to lead to an explosion of study into psychological processes of a divergent kind, and to the first widely applied divergent tests of creative thinking.[27]

Torrance's Tests for Creative Thinking (TTCT)

An American educationalist, Paul Torrance, took the basic concept of Guilford's divergent production of ideas, and developed a range of carefully validated measures for assessing individual creative talent. Working primarily with schoolchildren, he took on the technical difficulties in assessing and codifying originality, as well as flexibility and fluency.

His Torrance Tests for Creative Thinking (popularly, 'uses of a brick' tests) were extensively applied, and their use extended from classroom assessment of individual talent, to the assessment of the impact of specified training approaches for stimulating that talent. There is an interesting story connecting Guilford and Torrance. The impetus to creativity and space research attributed to Guilford's speech was nicely complemented when, in a symbolic gesture, a set of TTCT creativity tests subsequently accompanied astronauts into space.[28]

A modest yet inspiring educator, Torrance began his work at the University of Minnesota, and later spent many years in the institute he founded and directed, in Athens, in close collaboration with the University of Georgia.[29] His efforts to gain credibility for a method of testing for creativity ensure him a place in the history of the field. Yet the tests represent only a tiny part of Torrance's output. He published over a thousand articles on a multitude of topics. His writings on the creativity of children reveal his deep sense of wonder at the nature of giftedness and also at the more universal characteristics of creative spontaneity found in every playground.

While the story of his tests suggests that creativity might yet be captured in a universalistic way through careful measurement, the story of his life suggests something else. He has repeatedly pointed to the uniqueness of the individual, and the unique formative efforts of culture on individual behaviour. Torrance has at times felt the impact of more conventional or dominant views on work such as his own, suggesting them to be often 'questioned, rejected, ridiculed and ignored'.[30]

Rhodes' 4P Model

In the 1950s, a young educational researcher, Mel Rhodes, set out to find a definition of creativity. He collected forty definitions and analysed their contents. From this he concluded that they derived from four overlapping strands which he labelled the person, the process, the product and the press. This made up the 4P model of creativity as shown in figure 2.3. The young researcher completed his dissertation, which could have been the end of the story, for his academic thesis itself is rarely cited today.[31] However, he was to publish one paper shortly afterwards. The paper has been widely cited, and has established his reputation as a pioneering contributor to creativity research.[32] In his paper Rhodes again offered his 4P model, suggesting that much conceptual confusion was due to a failure of

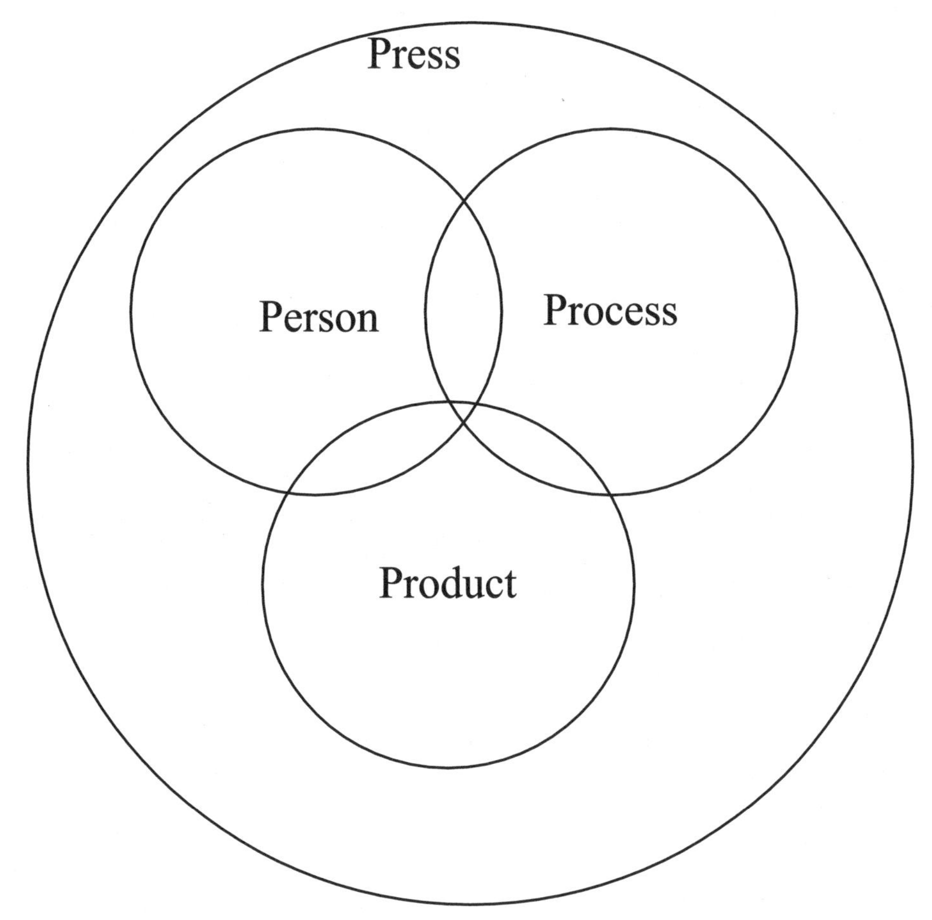

Figure 2.3: Rhodes' 4P creativity model

researchers to recognize in their definitions that 'Each strand has unique identity academically, but only in unity do the four strands operate functionally.'[33]

In August 1990, a major international conference was held in Buffalo, New York State. The conference had assembled thirty leading researchers to explore creativity as an emerging academic discipline. The conference was structured around the 4P model.[34] At roughly the same time a further series of international conferences on information systems was held annually in Hawaii. These established a creativity sub-theme, which was again organized around the 4P model. European researchers have also advocated it as a means of structuring the creative process.[35]

Edward de Bono and lateral thinking

Edward de Bono, a member of a well-known family of Maltese medical practitioners, completed his education in England, where as a young postgraduate student he popularized lateral thinking as a term for unconventional and effective thinking. The term, the author's early books and their author, all became widely known.

De Bono provided a rationale for a mechanism of mind which he popularized through easy-to-understand metaphors. Conventional (vertical) thinking proceeds sequentially like digging a hole to get to the solution at the bottom of the hole. Lateral thinking assists the process of finding a more productive hole to dig.

He has suggested that the mind is a self-structuring information surface, requiring special procedures if it is to be jolted out of its preferred patterns.[36] He is particularly well known for his invention of lateral thinking techniques. For example, he advocates escaping from vertical thinking by focusing on a randomly selected stimulus concept or word. The subsequent thoughts redirect attention so that less habitual ideas result.[37] Another technique essentially encourages the practice of wish-fulfilment – 'wouldn't it be wonderful if. . . .'.

His work repeatedly conveys the simple message – thinking is a skill that can be developed. This message has gained the widest of audiences globally. Increasing numbers of top business executives have important benefits from deliberate application of lateral thinking.[38]

De Bono has made it clear that he regards creativity as a concept that is too muddled in its various everyday usages to permit its easy study and manipulation. He appears to suggest that at the core of creativity is the form of thinking he has labelled lateral, with clearly identified cognitive mechanisms and strategies for enhancing its outputs. For many people, however, the expressions 'we need some lateral thinking' or 'we need some creative thinking' have very similar meanings.

Synectics, and Gordon's claims for psychological states within the creative process

W. J. J. (Bill) Gordon was a Harvard-trained psychologist who was co-founder of the creativity-spurring technique, Synectics.[39] Gordon became interested in the mechanisms for invention while working for a technological consultancy in the 1960s. He set about tape-recording the remarks of design engineers engaged in various invention tasks. His analysis of these recordings led him to the conclusion that prior to the period of discovery of a new breakthrough there was an observable change in the psychological state of individuals directly involved. A more professional analytical style ('cool') was replaced by a style that might be described as more regressive – Gordon called it a more metaphorical and involved style ('hot').

This gave him the basic breakthrough idea of Synectics. Suppose it were possible to increase the chances of someone getting into that intense psychological state? Might this also increase the chances of generating creative insights? He set about testing this theory by experimenting with procedures or operational mechanisms that would increase the chances of inducing psychological states conducive to the production of novel ideas. The procedures were to become a fundamental aspect of his technique system. His deliberate introduction of manipulation of metaphors was to prove particularly powerful. Thus, an engineering project for strengthening a bridge structure might be studied in connection with the metaphor of strengthening a human's handshake.

Two related streams of practical activities aimed at enhancing creative performance were to flow from Gordon's pioneering work. The first, led by Gordon himself, examined in careful detail additional means of strengthening the power of metaphoric thought in stimulating creativity. The second, led by Gordon's former co-worker, George Prince, concentrated more on the social dynamics that permit teams to operate in more creative ways. Prince's work on team processes gave the technique great applicability industrially. It also helped develop a model of creative leadership in such sessions.[40]

Teresa Amabile, and her intrinsic motivation theory of creativity

When Teresa Amabile moved from Brandeis and accepted a professorship at Harvard Business School in 1995 she gave a boost to creativity as a topic of legitimate research interest in management science. Her first influential work appeared at a time when the largely individual-centred studies of creativity seemed to be running out of steam. Her book on the social psychology of creativity became one of the most widely cited in the field.[41] It was embraced by researchers interested in creativity as a social phenomenon, and was to contribute to an upswing in research interest in social creativity in the decade after its publication.

Amabile supports a view of creativity as being driven by forces intrinsic to the individual and, in general, inhibited by forces imposed on the individual by the environment. At its simplest, the theory was anticipated by Don MacKinnon, who was fond of saying that for creativity 'the play's the thing not the pay's the thing'.[42] Amabile proposes three necessary components influencing creative behaviours: task motivation, domain-related skills and creativity-related skills. As the empirical results have been extended from controlled classroom situations to more complex organizational ones, Amabile and co-workers suggest that the intrinsic motivation hypothesis has to be more carefully interpreted.[43] It is now proposed that a broader intrinsic motivation principle still applies as conducive to creativity.

However, extrinsic factors are no longer seen as totally detrimental. The detrimental extrinsic factors are those perceived as controlling rather than informational.[44]

We are left with a rich field of theory to explore. There is a general interest in motivation among managers, and few advances have been forthcoming since Maslow's work on hierarchies of human needs.[45]

Puzzling Out the Creativity Stories

The stories make up an account that will help those readers who are happy to receive someone else's description of the platform of understanding. Those who want to go more deeply will have to study the following account of some additional jigsaw puzzling. As this is the first account of the puzzling we will go into a little detail. In subsequent chapters we will be briefer.

Unlike the task of assembling ordinary jigsaws, we have no guide to the picture we are making. To complicate things further, the new pieces may change the way the picture will turn out – even to the extent that we have taken apart some of the bits that we had already fitted together. So what we are doing is assembling our 'best current guess', always remaining open to the possibilities of changing it at a later time. If the puzzling is important enough you will return to what you have done frequently, perhaps deciding that the work is coming along nicely, or perhaps feeling there is need to take some of it apart.[46] Remember that, of the multiple combinations of the pieces possible for this kind of jigsaw, many will present you with a very similar overall picture.[47] One way of assembling the pieces from the ten stories is shown in figure 2.4.

The workers can be split into three main groupings: labellers; measurers and experimenters; and creative problem-solving change agents. Most of the examples come from figures whose reputation fits them into one category. Wallas and Rhodes are clearly labellers, with Koestler perhaps also fitting in. Bogan and Sperry, Torrance and Guilford were experimenters and measurers, widely recognized for their research methods and instruments. Osborn, de Bono and Gordon are examples of change agents who pioneered structured creativity techniques. In the work of all three of these groups, the creative individual was a focus of attention.[48]

In some contrast, Amabile represents a shift towards a newer perspective that has been gaining credibility partly through her efforts. Its essence is a belief that individuals behave under the influence of the social context in which they are embedded. Her intrinsic motivation theory requires us to recognize the influences imposed by extrinsic forces.

We now have a picture that reveals a few significant patterns. These seem consistent with the predictions of how a dominant paradigm exerts influence. What we might expect is that the dominant rational worldview influences how the researchers are recognized, as it influences their work. We would also expect that the dominant paradigm would approve of labelling, classifying and structuring behaviours. This is the aspect of the work that gets recognized. When the researcher expresses interest in things that are not so easy to fit in to the dominant paradigm, there is a risk of what Torrance described as being questioned, rejected, ridiculed

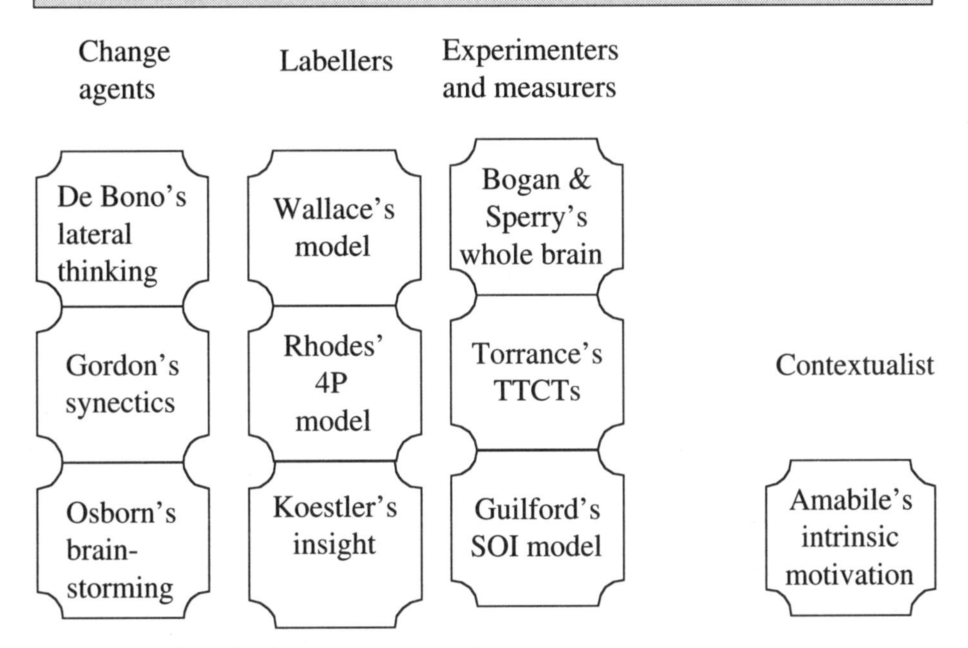

Figure 2.4: Bits of a jigsaw of creativity history

and ignored. ('What's different is dangerous.') Indeed, some creativity researchers believe that the field is being held back by its associations with 'madness, mythology and mystery' (that is to say, by one of the four themes identified).[49]

The suppressed voices of these and other creativity researchers can now be found by searching for the approaches consistent with the paradigms regarded as heresies by the dominant one (Figure 2.5). The strong radical humanist streak can be found in a shared belief that creativity exists as a universal human characteristic that is open to nurture and development. Osborn passionately wanted to liberate the creative spark that we all possess. This belief was strongly implied in the writings of Guilford and Torrance, and in the work of Gordon and De Bono with children of all abilities. Osborn wanted to change the way people related one to another so that their ideas could be liberated, and society enriched.[50]

There is also a suppressed view found in the ten stories that individual human efforts can make a difference to their futures. This more optimistic philosophy accords with the possibility of someone 'inventing' the future, rather than being in the right place at the right time in some kind of pre-determined way.

Creativity's Hidden Promise for Management Studies

This chapter has shown how creativity itself has something to say about deep human themes of self-discovery, motivation, intuition and transformation. However, we still have to return to the paradox posed at the start of the chapter. Creativity is believed to be important by many organizational practitioners and consultants, and has been endorsed by various researchers of the highest individual

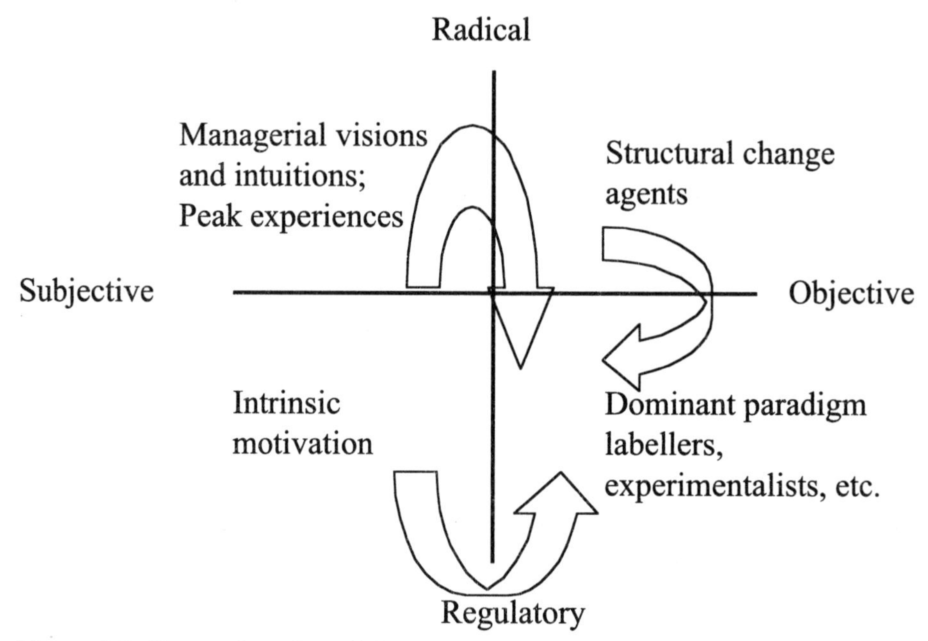

Figure 2.5: The taming of creativity

quality and reputation. Despite this, creativity still stands outside the orthodoxy of management studies, and is not taken seriously enough to make much contribution to the ongoing debate about the nature of management studies. We can approach this puzzle by addressing each of the constituent groups involved.

New insights on creativity for practitioners

Practitioners might pose the question 'why is it so difficult to show managers that creativity is important and can be stimulated in practical ways by concentrating on creative thinking and creative problem-solving?' The paradigmatic approach suggests that creativity is threatening to a deeply grounded belief in rational approaches in a great majority of educated people. This belief is reinforced within education in many technical and professional disciplines, including the most common kinds of training received by managers. Management is 'about' being logical and rational. So it is not enough to deal with managers from the assumption that creativity is 'a good thing'.

Practitioners need to develop more understanding than is expressed in popular writings on creativity about the distinctions between everyday thinking, logical thinking, and creative thinking. The various 'everyday' attempts to explain creativity in these terms have met with the opposition indicated and because the explanations leave too many points unclarified. In this chapter the new explanation is not based on the 'something special' case, rather it is based on the distinction between thinking and problem-solving appropriate where the situation permits a non-controversial answer, and the sort where new answers, and new understanding of one's own paradigm, are possible. The distinction is that of reflexivity or the capacity to renew and re-invent one's own view of the world.

New insights on creativity for business studies

Our examination is occurring at a time when old theories of organization are under intense scrutiny. Classical theories of pyramidal structures, top-down leadership, bureaucratic cultures, competitiveness are being reworked without total conviction that orthodox theory will prove satisfactory.

The treatment offered in this chapter is one that suggests that the contradictions in business studies indicate where 'deviant' possibilities are being denied. We have suggested that creativity is being ignored because of the orthodox or dominant view of aspects of human behaviour regarded as 'irrational, individualistic and subjective'. Studying creativity may help. It opens up the possibility that greater attention might be paid to what might be called the 'humanistic stuff' in business studies. The implication is that business orthodoxy has a structure that is too intolerant of the very processes that would permit it chances of challenging its own assumptions. Knowing how a dominant view does just that offers prospects for change.[51]

Next steps

The study of one 'excluded' voice has opened up some possibilities for orthodox thinking of business studies. We will continue applying this approach in the next chapter, which will deal with innovation, a topic often connected with creativity, but again one that is not well connected with the dominant disciplines of business studies.

Notes

1. Ramqvist (1994: 3). This gives a nice example of the mysterious but important role creativity is believed to play, particularly 'at the front end' of the innovation process, by practitioners.
2. Boden (1994a: 1) as editor introducing a collection of articles on *Dimensions of Creativity* (Boden, 1994b.)
3. Eysenck (1994: 200) in the same collection of articles edited by Margaret Boden as the contrary view expressed above.
4. Ford (1995: 13).
5. De Bono (1990: 218).
6. Hocevar & Bachelor (1989) give a deep critique of instrumentation difficulties. Mumford & Gustafson (1988) suggest the concept be regarded as a *syndrome* of cognitive, behavioural and environmental factors. See also Isaksen (1987) and Runco & Albert (1990).
7. I have considered for some while that the practitioners of creative problem-solving techniques have the characteristics of a paradigmatic grouping. See, for example, Rickards & Freedman (1979).

[8] A view notably supported in Sternberg (1985) and reviewed in Haensly & Reynolds (1989).

[9] I may not have wide support for this view, as textbooks continue to agonize over the lack of definitional clarity. See, for example, contributions in Glover et al. (1989).

[10] The books are written by professionals and consultants. For creative problem-solving I referred to Flood & Jackson (1991); Hicks (1991); Kim (1990); Parnes (1992) and my own work in Rickards (1973, 1990). For books on creative thinking whose titles avoided the term creative problem-solving I selected de Bono's classic text (1971) and one of his more substantial later books (de Bono, 1992); Evans & Russell (1989); Henry (1991); Van Gundy (1988); and Van Oech (1983). As texts dealing with creativity but referring only to problem-solving in the title I chose Bryant (1989); de la Bedoyere (1988); Gause & Weinberg (1982); Polya (1957); and Tarr (1973). I have also been influenced over the years by a handful of books dealing with more theoretical issues. These include Amabile (1996); Boden (1994b); Isaksen (1987); Kirton (1994); Koestler (1964); MacKinnon (1978); Stein (1974/1975); and Sternberg (1988).

[11] Benson (1977).

[12] See Ley (1990) for a fascinating retracing of Köhler's steps in Tenerife.

[13] Koestler became an iconic figure for an intellectual movement opposed to the prevailing stimulus-response school of psychology. Koestler's attack on SR psychology in *The Act of Creation* (Koestler, 1964) still deserves study as a sustained intelligent piece of writing combining rhetoric, passion and intellectual argument.

[14] The tale of Archimedes has been immortalized as the origin of the term *Eureka moment* (Koestler, 1964).

[15] Earlier writers had seized on the story. Koestler gave it its widespread currency, and maybe also paved the way to more recent interest in the role of metaphor in scientific discovery (McReynolds, 1990; Schaffer, 1994).

[16] The cooler ('objective') cognitive scientists refer to the Eureka moment. The hotter ('subjective') term is the Aha! moment.

[17] See, for instance, Weisberg (1986). This view deals with the threat to an orthodox philosophy that creativity may generate something from nothing. Nothing 'real' and 'really' new is ever created – even in the world of ideas. This denies the possibility of a 'really' new idea coming into existence.

[18] Schooler, Fallshore and Fiore (1995) described the distinction as approach-recognition and approach-execution processes.

[19] This is also now a well-instituted story. The original proposal came from 'Helmholtz . . . the great German physicist, speaking in 1891 at a banquet on his seventieth birthday' (Wallas, 1970: 91).

[20] King (1990: 23).

[21] See Osborn (1992) for a replication of Osborn's 1942 work *How to Think Up*.

[22] Osborn, an auto-didact, was intuitively attracted to the orthodoxy of scientific proof. His book contained documented evidence of commercial results using the brainstorming methods. Its style of providing meticulously documented success stories was one that was to be mimicked by later generations of technique advocates – for example within the Total Quality movement.

[23] The Parnes-Osborn CPS model. See Parnes, Noller & Biondi (1977) and Isaksen (1987).

[24] Benson (1957).

[25] From discussions with Sidney Parnes, director of the Center for many years.

[26] Technically, the operation severed the corpus callosum, the primary nerve communication network between left and right cortical hemispheres. See Bogan (1969) and Sperry (1964) for the direct accounts by the Nobel Prize winners. For excellent

summaries of the early work see Blakesee (1980); Ornstein (1975, 1986); Mintzberg (1976).

[27] Guilford identified other components of his SOI as associated with creative production, but these have been largely ignored by subsequent designers of creativity tests. For hints of the subsequently widely ignored association of convergent and evaluative skills with creativity, see Guilford, 1959; or 1970: 182.

[28] Raina (1996).

[29] An influential early book is Torrance (1962).

[30] Torrance (1991) quoted in Raina (1996).

[31] I am aware of one citation to Rhodes' dissertation (Rhodes, 1957) in studies of creativity. That was in the bibliography to Taylor & Barron (1963).

[32] The paper was published in *Phi Delta Kappan* (Rhodes, 1961).

[33] Rhodes (1987: 218).

[34] See Isaksen et al (1993a, 1993b).

[35] The Hungarian theorist Istvan Magyari-Beck advocates a new science of Creatology structured around an extended version of Rhodes' 4P model. See, for example, Magyari-Beck (1993). De Cock (1993) proposed it as a means of structuring studies of continuous improvement.

[36] The model has some similarities with recent information processing theories of a neural network kind. See, for example, Smith (1995); Perkins (1994).

[37] I still possess a 'random word generator' acquired some years ago in Canada. The plastic globe is much used on training programmes, and more than one student has borrowed it to break the hold of mental paralysis in front of impending deadlines.

[38] De Bono, like Osborn, scatters examples of impressive success stories around in his many books (Cognitive Research Trust). There can be little doubt that the anecdotal examples have some validity, nor that the CoRT system has had wide educational applications globally. See, for example, a range of reports in Dingli (1994).

[39] 'Synectics' is a term implying 'bringing together things previously unconnected'. Gordon presumably believed he had coined a neologism for the technique, although it can be found in dictionaries predating his use of the term.

[40] The split between Gordon and Prince produced two consultancy operations, each originally operating out of Cambridge, Mass.

[41] As sometimes happens, the book remained much quoted but was quite difficult to locate. An excellent updated version is now available (Amabile, 1996). See also Amabile (1982).

[42] MacKinnon (1978). He also noted that empirical research 'has shed some light on several facets of creativity, but the very essence of creativity will, I believe always elude us' (MacKinnon, 1978: xvi). MacKinnon, in reviewing his substantial contribution to the field, was signalling his doubt about the effectiveness of repeated psychometric studies for getting to the core of the creativity issue.

[43] In Hennessy & Amabile (1988) the authors seem to be implying the possibility of complicating factors in the empirical evidence for the intrinsic motivation hypothesis. Then the possibility is strengthened that 'in its simple form [the hypothesis] is incomplete' (Amabile, 1990: 75).

[44] This point is clarified in Amabile (1996) in which she acknowledges recent work by Deci & Ryan (1985).

[45] Maslow (1943) developed his famous theory of motivation and self-actualization that entitles him to a place as a pioneer of creativity research. His ideas are less comfortable for the managerial orthodoxy than theories that concentrate on more operational, and measurable aspects of human behaviour. Examples of these would include expectancy theory (Vroom, 1964; Lawler, 1973).

[46] One of the toughest bits of jigsaw puzzling faces all doctoral students. I have found that the students in management have to reach the stage of dismantling some of the pieces assembled according to their original doctoral proposal to arrive at a picture that satisfies them, and stands a chance of satisfying their examination committee.

[47] This may not be intuitively obvious. Think of a well-established theory, such as that of Darwinian evolution. If some of the evidence believed to support the theory is found wanting, the whole jigsaw may have to be reconstructed. Nevertheless, it is unlikely that the new picture will lead us to make new sense of the entire theory of evolution.

[48] Rhodes's model is a notable exception.

[49] Isaksen (1987).

[50] Maslow's work could also have been cited as suggesting that creativity permits individuals to transcend routine actions and thinking to achieve 'self-actualization'.

[51] An exciting example that shifts away from the orthodox paradigmatic way of looking at creativity can be found in Sutton & Hargadon (1996). They show that failure to examine the contextual aspects of brainstorming has resulted in a failure of academics to understand its value in practical terms. The academics chose to count ideas as their 'objective' evidence of the value of the technique. The practitioners had a range of additional criteria for persisting 'irrationally' with brainstorming sessions.

chapter 3
Innovation Revisited

One of the problems in managing innovation is variation in what people understand by the term, often confusing it with invention . . . Our view [shared by various writers] assumes that innovation is a process of turning opportunity into new ideas and of putting these into widely used practice.

***Tidd, Bessant & Pavitt*[1]**

There are few disciplinary limits as to who studies innovation. Most social scientists are interested in social change; diffusion research offers a particularly useful means to gain understandings of change because innovations are a type of communication message whose efforts are relatively easy to isolate.

***Everett M. Rogers*[2]**

Perhaps the most alarming characteristic of the body of empirical study of innovation is the extreme variance among its findings, what we call instability. Factors found to be important for innovation in one study are found to be less important, not important, or even inversely important in another study. This phenomenon occurs with relentless regularity.

***George W. Downs, Jr and Lawrence B. Mohr*[3]**

Introduction

Innovation and creativity: 'A newly wed couple?'

Once creativity has been selected as the starting point of a search for understanding of management studies, innovation is the prime candidate for the next region in which we should consider travelling. Innovation, like creativity, is more often found as an optional extra than a core business studies course. Its association with creativity is indicated by a complaint I made some years ago that the terms 'are in danger of complete degeneracy into a single blurred catch-all concept . . . Recently one finds a trend towards linking the terms creativity and innovation – a newly wed couple who hardly appear in public except as a (happily?) united pair.'[4]

The importance of innovation

Creativity and innovation may overlap in some ways. However, in one important aspect the concepts are rather clearly differentiated. As we have already seen in chapter 2, creativity is generally regarded as an individualistic and capricious process. In contrast, innovation is far more widely regarded as a process offering promise of economic advantage. This can be inferred from the willingness of governments to support research into innovation policy, and the willingness of organizational executives to take seriously consultancy packages that promise innovations in the shape of new products or processes.

The complexities and confusions associated with innovation

The widespread assumptions of the potential benefits from innovation have been challenged, albeit with muted voices. Regardless of the potential benefits, the process is considered inherently risky, as it takes the innovating company into unknown territories beyond its experience base. Suspicions have been raised that there is an innovation bias in writings about innovation. That implies attention to the benefits that might accrue from innovating, rather than taking a more balanced view of the risks also inherent in the process.[5]

The confusions of definition are probably not quite as intense as were found in the work on creativity. Nevertheless, there are well-reported failures of research studies to arrive at consistent findings and conclusions. Confusions over terminology, over-generalized inferences from empirical work and less than clear evidence for proposed mechanisms are recognized as limiting the usefulness of theoretical models and practical prescriptions.[6]

Attention has recently been drawn to the tendency of partial views of innovation[7] to be presented. Specifically, innovation has been presented as if it were only associated with technological changes. Other partial views include beliefs that only substantial breakthroughs count as ‘real innovations’. Yet there are difficulties in seeking to characterize innovation in a more comprehensive way. The innovation process, assumed as encompassing all sorts of changes, in all sorts of firms, has to justify why it differs from a general management of change process.

Overview of the bits of the innovation jigsaw

In this chapter we will once again be taking a look at the bits of a jigsaw, this time of innovation. We will concentrate first on establishing a platform of orthodox understanding, before looking deeply beyond the orthodox view.

I followed the basic approach of selecting a wide representative handful of books on innovation to form the basis of a platform of understanding of innovation studies.[8] The dozen books covered a remarkable range of human endeavours. They included macro-level economic[9] treatments and organization-level studies.[10] Some of the authors had engaged in exhaustive searches of literature of one specific aspect of innovation.[11] Others had collected together views of authorities, selected

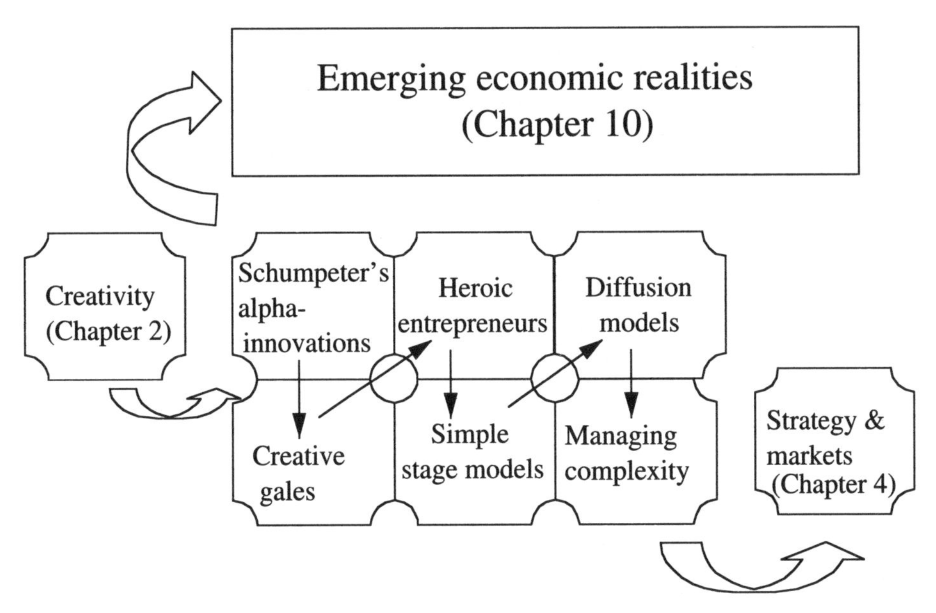

Figure 3.1: Bits of the jigsaw: innovation and its neighbours

on grounds of reputation.[12] There were also study textbooks for practitioners,[13] and popular, yet influential, 'how-to-do-it' texts.[14]

The pieces of our jigsaw will be seen to come from two related traditions, the economic and the organizational. It turned out that these groupings could be assembled into two platforms of understanding, which will be described in the next two sections. The pieces from both traditions were examined in the sequence shown in figure 3.1, which serves as a route map for the chapter.

Toward the end of the chapter we go beyond the platform of understanding (in this instance beyond the two platforms of understanding of economic and organizational studies). We demonstrate how to explore theory and practice to make more informed evaluation of the claims of each. By testing for the impact of a dominating orthodoxy we are able to show that systems for supporting innovation are based on a machine metaphor of control assuming causal links along a linear sequence of steps. This metaphor conceals the uncertainties of the process that remain as a context to be managed by the users as best they can. The analysis also shows that ultimately any structured technique will require the organizational users to deal with uncertainties throughout the process. Creativity is required beyond the more generally accepted 'front end' of discovery processes.

The Economics Platform of Understanding of Innovation

The handful of books from the economic perspective gave us the richer theoretical concepts, but fewer ideas of how the concepts might be applied in practice. An important bridging piece of the jigsaw was found in the extensive and influential work of the somewhat maverick economist Joseph Schumpeter. Schumpeter proposed that economic growth derived from the efforts of entrepreneurs. This offered economics a way of dealing with discovery processes that fell outside the bounds of their models. He later incorporated into his theories the discovery processes arising within the newly emerging technological teams within large organizations ('R&D laboratories').

Another version of entrepreneurial activity developed by the Austrian school of economists emphasized its contribution to a market-smoothing effect. These ideas were extensively taken up in studies of diffusion of innovation and new product development. These topics were themselves appropriated into marketing theory especially via work on product/market development, and so made some inroad into the business studies orthodoxy.

Schumpeter's pervasive influences

Joseph Schumpeter was a distinguished statesman in his native Austria and later settled in America where he established a reputation at Harvard as a larger-than-life academic figure and a major economic theorist.[15] Schumpeter was interested in the questions that most economists prefer to ignore. In particular, he was acutely aware that prevailing economic theories avoided the issue of economic growth, environmental uncertainties. Schumpeter was far more interested in a turbulent world he had experienced in which equilibrium was disrupted in unpredictable and violent ways. His early theorizing focused on the characteristics of the entrepreneur, someone who was to figure prominently in later writings on innovation. In one famous illustration he outlines how the discoveries of an entrepreneur trigger innovation. The entrepreneur, either through intentional search or by accident, stumbles upon gold-bearing rock. Thereafter, the conversion of gold leads to infrastructural activities: roads, guides, provisioning, refining facilities, commercial exchange and legal arrangements. The central thrust of Schumpeterian theory of entrepreneurially driven innovation is a two-step process of discovery followed by diffusion or exploitation. These two stages involved an initial 'alpha' innovation which produced the conditions favouring emergence of multiple smaller or 'beta' innovations.

In earlier literature the entrepreneur had been regarded as a person who co-ordinated resources, rather than created them. Schumpeter's basic idea offered an explanation for an empirically observed ebb and flow of economic activity, known as the economic long-waves. It also connected up innovation with technological change, a relationship that has persisted to modern times.[16] The first observed economic long-wave was associated with the rise and impact of steam power (say 1790–1804); the second (1845–95) was that of railways and the third (1895–1950) automobiles and electric power.[17]

Schumpeter later became more interested in the development of systematic innovation efforts in the form of institutional departments for discovery. He anticipated the growing influence of Research and Development (R&D) as an initiator of innovation projects within organizations.[18] He also made an important connection between creativity and innovation, describing the actions of entrepreneurs as bringing about 'a gale of creative destruction'.[19] He considered that these entrepreneurial gales would blow in unpredictable fashion, favouring some economic sectors at the expense of others.

In this world of disequilibrium, technology was identified as a major engine through which entrepreneurs created alpha-innovations and as a consequence triggered great economic changes. He had the sense of the importance of the specific and contextual that was favoured before him by the great Adam Smith. His economics concerned insight applied to detailed argument. He felt that such analyses overlooked the structural mechanisms of change that he considered of greater importance.[20] In this sense he was out of alignment with the developing body of economic theory that was becoming more statistically sophisticated and rigorous. The Schumpeterian world of heroic entrepreneurs has some attractions today for its anticipation of chaotic environments. As we will see in chapter 10, his work is located outside the mainstream of neoclassical economics, and has tended to be disregarded outside the specialized fields of those economists interested in the management of change under real-world conditions.

The Austrian school of innovation theorists

Schumpeter, although Austrian himself, had somewhat different views to those of a so-called Austrian school of economics. The important differences were summed up by one of their number as follows: 'Schumpeter's entrepreneur acts to disturb an existing equilibrium position. Entrepreneurial activity disrupts the continuing circular flow. The entrepreneur is pictured as initiating change and as generating new opportunities. By contrast, my own treatment of the entrepreneur emphasizes the equilibriating aspects of his role. I see the situation upon which the entrepreneurial role impinges as one of inherent disequilibrium rather than equilibrium. The entrepreneur, in my view, brings into mutual adjustment those discordant elements which resulted from prior market ignorance'.[21]

Schumpeter's position recognizes creativity as an unpredictable discovery process connected with the discovery of alpha-innovations. For the Austrian school, the creative processes deal with more modest challenges, and do not require exceptional personal attributes. This is the 'business as usual' school of beliefs, in which discovery is an extension of ordinary human behaviours.[22]

Less easy to classify is another influential Austrian, Friedrich von Hayek, who was able to incorporate the ideas of the Austrian school into his extensive theoretical support of free enterprise capitalism.[23]

Diffusion theories

The Austrian tradition leads naturally into diffusion theories of innovation. The theories occupy a kind of half-way house between strictly economic theorizing, and the work directly concerned with the innovation process within organizations. As the name implies, diffusion theories present innovation as a passive process. The metaphor is of a gas gradually spreading from one region to another. Diffusion

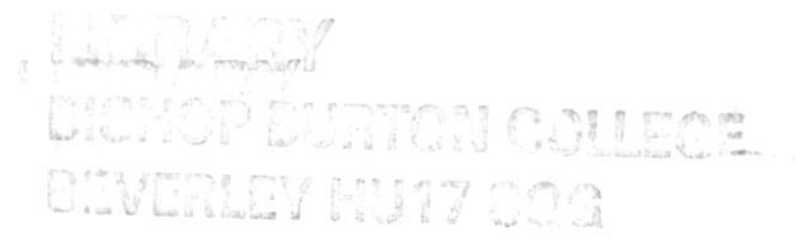

theories have favoured quantitative models that describe patterns of uptake of innovation. This tradition has its own dominant pioneer, the American Everett Rogers.

Early studies looked at the diffusion of technological innovations such as hybrid corn among farmers and new drugs among doctors. In essence the models present a world in which the changes are smooth and inexorable. We do not find any evidence of Schumpeterian jolts here. If they occur, they occur prior to the diffusion processes being studied. Nor is there much direct evidence of the entrepreneurial efforts that smooth out markets as proposed within the Austrian school.[24]

One of the favoured methods of analysis of the diffusion theorists is to construct elegant curves mapping the growth of an innovation. These can easily be turned into some version of an S-curve, typically with a slow start-up period, and steep acceleration, and a final 'tail' where the 'creative gale' of the innovation is coming to an end. An interesting practical application of S-curves is to map the decline of one innovation and the rise of the innovative replacement. The pair of S-curves can be analysed to indicate the most favourable time-window for abandoning the earlier technology and investing in the newer one.[25]

Such applications have real-world implications as they offer prescriptions of how a desired innovation might successfully be promoted. They also appeal to marketing executives, for similar reasons, at the level of diffusing a firm's new product development into its market environment. They are perhaps less appealing for managers, as they describe how an entrepreneurial innovation might penetrate the market without indicating how the entrepreneurial innovation might be discovered and shaped.

Organization-level Studies of Innovation

The books dealing with innovation at the level of the organization are found to contain a remarkable range of topics, case examples, theories and techniques. Several distinguished researchers have attempted to summarize the field, generally presenting an update or progress report. There is widespread concern over the absence of any coherent over-arching theory.

Nevertheless, by concentrating on what the authors reveal of their beliefs, important bits of the innovation jigsaw began to reveal themselves. The platform of understanding seemed to have a small number of shared beliefs that are not necessarily totally consistent. In everyday terms the beliefs can be stated as a process involving implementable novelty, associated with technology, and involving considerable levels of ambiguity and features specific to a given innovation.

It is novelty that is implemented

Most accounts of innovation describe a novel idea that appears at the start of a process and gets introduced into practice as an innovative product that can take a variety of forms. Academic studies tend to indicate the diversity of definitions, perhaps then attempting a synthesis. Researchers West and Farr, for example, offer the following as a definition: 'the intentional introduction and application, within a role, group or organization, of ideas, processes, products or procedures new to the relevant unit of adaption, designed to significantly benefit the individual group, organization or society'.[26] Another writer, offering a practitioner view, described creativity as 'the thinking process that helps us generate ideas', and innovation as 'the practical application of such ideas towards meeting the organization's objectives in a more effective way'.[27]

These views are echoed in journalistic writings, typified by a remark of Alvin Toffler's: 'Technological innovation consists of three stages, linked together into a self-reinforcing cycle. First, there is the creative, feasible idea. Second, its practical application. Third, its diffusion through society.'[28]

These examples typify a belief that the innovation process is widely regarded as connected with creativity 'at the front end'. There are important consequences flowing from isolating creativity in this way. It inexorably leads to so-called stage models of innovation in which the uncertainties of discovery are decoupled from the later stages of the system. These have dominated the pages of 'how to do it' innovation texts, as well as more theoretical treatments. The numbers and labels of the stages may differ, yet the various models do appear to be variations on a theme. An archetypal description of stages within the innovation process can be derived from Toffler's observation, namely:

(a) An initial idea generation or capture stage
(b) a development stage, and
(c) a commercialization or implementation stage.[29]

We will be looking at three practical systems for managing innovation, which are represented as stage models. We will also be looking at theoretical implications of the unrecognized divorce of creativity from later stages in the innovation models.

Innovation is essentially technological

Some authors equate innovation with technological innovation. Even if this is not directly stated, the preference is implied in the examples selected. The most celebrated and repeated examples refer to innovations that took the form of technologically advanced products. This may be something to do with the perceived focus of novelty in the innovation. Technically advanced products clearly focus on technological novelty. Process innovations tend to be mentioned with emphasis on efficiency gains rather than technological gains, and are less frequently cited. Even fewer references can be found to various other kinds of innovation where the focus is on marketing or environmental or social enhancements.[30]

Innovation is very complicated

The complexities have been treated in two rather different ways. The first way emphasizes the uncertainties and ambiguities of the process. 'The management of ambiguity' leads to the formulation of strategic responses appropriate to conditions of uncertainty. This treatment leads to material that is covered in more detail in the next chapter on marketing and strategy. We have already seen that the ambiguities can sometimes be loaded on to a front end that requires discovery of the correct recipe to be applied at a later stage in the process.

Various other strategies are also considered in managing the ambiguities of innovation. For example, one widely advocated approach is to break down communication and cultural barriers by setting up cross-disciplinary teams. Other approaches are based on developing skills of reflection and learning. 'Innovation is particularly about learning, both in the sense of acquiring and deploying knowledge in strategic fashion and also in acquiring and reinforcing patterns of behaviour which help this competence-building to happen.'[31] The simplified stage-models can be taken as starting points to the development of far more firm-specific routines arising from such learning activities. We will look at three such stage models for innovation later in this chapter.

The second way addresses the complexities of innovation by adapting what is known as a contingency perspective. Contingency theory has found favour in organizational studies generally. The term implies that outcomes of a given situation depend on or are contingent on various factors. The task for the theorist is to indicate these factors and to collect empirical examples of how the contingencies operate from case to case.

To understand the significance of a particular factor we have to remember that 'it all depends'. It all depends on sets of factors or contingencies that are specific to a given situation. For example, are large firms more innovative than small firms? 'It all depends'. The most authoritative surveys of diffusion research suggest that large firms are more innovative than small ones. Other literature recognizes that small firms might be embryo winners of the future, and that successful large firms often decline into mature and sunset states.[32] Innovative performance is said to be contingent on the size of the firm. Other frequently mentioned contingent factors include the kind of innovations under consideration: process and product innovations have to be treated differently, as they make differing demands on the innovating firms. Innovations calling for substantial organizational adjustments ('breakthrough innovations') have to be treated differently from incremental improvements ('continuous improvement innovations'). Contingency theories lead to taxonomies of innovations of the kind shown in figure 3.2. While they indicate some of the sources of complexity in innovation research, they do little to offer suggestions for managing it.

The notorious instability of factors influencing success and failure of innovation efforts was observed many years ago when it was found that factors that were established as supporting innovation in one study were found to have a different effect in other studies. This is accepted by contingency theorists who expect different contextual nuances to produce such variations in outcomes of innovation studies.[33]

From Theories to Practice: Stage Models of Innovation

Innovation has been widely studied as a series of stages. We have indicated their general format already. Now it is time to examine some examples of stage models

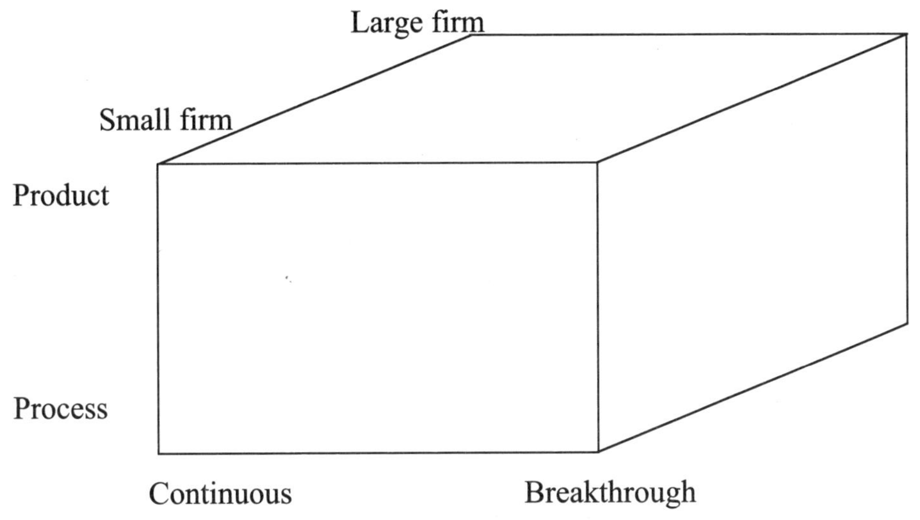

Figure 3.2: A typical taxonomy of innovations

of innovation that have been well tested in practice. The set has been selected from systems widely tested internationally.

NewProd

One of the most thoroughly tested recent stage models has been advanced by the Canadian researcher Robert Cooper. 'NewProd' incorporates into a model empirical information of factors possessed by new product projects that have succeeded and that have differentiated them from projects that have failed.[34]

The work demonstrates the benefits as well as the limitations of the orthodox research search for regularities within the subject of interest. Cooper sampled approximately 100 relatively successful and unsuccessful new products. He found that the most important success factors were that the new product was perceived as superior by users; that the organizational process had attended efficiently to market characteristics; and that the project had 'technological and production synergy and proficiency'.[35]

He later examined his own and other models of new-product development and developed a version of the archetypal model of initiation, development and commercialization. His initiation stage involved marketing, technological and production considerations, all of which contribute to a new-product proposal. The development stage incorporates assessments of market competitiveness and potential leading to a new-product launch. The commercialization stage then occurs, and is ultimately evaluated against pre-agreed criteria.

Cooper developed and tested a series of hypotheses against the model. He found that the most significant success factor was associated with product superiority. This was followed by a factor based on effectiveness of predevelopment activities and the gaining of acceptance of a strategic plan for implementation.[36] Other success factors were based on marketing and technological synergies.

An interesting conclusion emerges from these results. Cooper suggests that factors falling inside the control of the project manager and team play a significant part in the success or failure of a specific innovation project. He also indicates that the factors can be considered as check-lists to sensitize managers to the need for creative problem-solving efforts to continue throughout the innovation process.

This brings into focus a difficulty in taking results from large sample studies and seeking to infer from them action points for a specific innovating organization. The orthodoxy seeks regularities that permit predictions. The regularities are abstracted from models that assume some kind of closure or boundedness from unanticipated influences for change. However, the introduction of techniques that can make a difference between success and failure amounts to an invitation to treat the system as open to change. There is every reason for a manager to welcome this. It implies that the new-product team still has some scope for influencing its fortunes. It also implies that creativity and uncertainties will remain important aspects of any innovation project.

NewProd is a well-researched research project. It deserves study for the kinds of check-list factors it provides. It may well provide benefits to innovating teams that are seeking check-lists of factors to support their own creative efforts. However, the claims of the system to distinguish success and failure are based on assessments made on projects whose fates have already been established.

The originator points out that 'clearly if a project alters course, the link between actual and predicted results is greatly attenuated'.[37] In this accurate and honest comment we see the difficulties inherent in predicting innovation. Once those operating within an innovating system learn that the system has weaknesses that might hinder it, those workers have the power to act. Indeed, Cooper suggests that the nature of the success factors makes them open to modification. This means that however comprehensive the previous data available, there can be no precise rules predicting outcomes for a future innovation. There is a saving device that gives the model practical application. It indicates the need for creative problem-solving to 'fill in the gaps' to deal with specific contingencies.

Triz

Triz is the acronym for a Russian innovation system which in translation means Theory of Inventive Problem-solving. It is a system that is becoming better known worldwide, after many years during which it was studied in the former Soviet Union.[38] The system is based on one of the most comprehensive analyses of the process of invention that has ever been made. The innovator of Triz, Genrik Saulovich Altshuller, studied the entire set of patent applications available at the time. His search involved analysis of over one and a half million patents in order to find patterns of discovery that could then be reapplied to creating new patents. His work on Triz began in 1946. Over 7,000 people studied it during the period 1972–81, and generated 4,000 patents by following the system. Training involves studies of a classification of the invention patterns and reapplying the general principles identified.

Altshuller considers that inventive problem-solving proceeds along trial and error lines that can be substantially improved upon. The central concept is that trial and error is inefficient, especially for complex situations. Human approaches reduce the complexity, but in ways that are over-influenced by experience. Altshuller claims to have developed a more effective approach through identifying what he calls a directing mechanism. Through its use, uncertainties are reduced, and complex problems are transformed into easier ones. For situations not matching data within Triz, then the solver has to work at expanding Triz through a higher-level set of procedures known as Ariz, claimed as a systematic means of moving from the unknown to the known.[39]

Triz is interesting as a strong candidate for a means of supporting the part of the innovation process that is most widely regarded as least manageable – the creation of technological novelty. In doing so Altshuller appears to reconcile the apparently irreconcilable. He does so by departing from the strict canons of scientific orthodoxy.

Within the former Soviet Union the political system of Marxism-Leninism also incorporated its own scientific orthodoxy of dialectic materialism. Triz was founded on this philosophy, which presumes a reality or objectivity which can be studied and understood through dialectics.[40] A fundamental aspect of dialectics is the tension and struggle between opposites within all systems. The resulting contradictions are resolved as the system develops.[41] From this theoretical starting point the objective nature of creativity reveals itself in evolution and development of natural and man-made systems. The creativity exists of itself, waiting to be discovered through objective analysis. The creativity of human beings may be seen as having a subjective character, although in time the objective evolutionary process will increasingly reduce the subjective elements of the process. Discovery will become more purely scientific and objective.

Scimitar

Substantial claims have been made for Scimitar as a means of generating new products.[42] I worked with the inventor of the Scimitar system during its development, and was co-author with him of the first book describing it.[43] The original work was conducted in the United Kingdom during the late 1960s and early 1970s by a new-products manager, John Carson, then operating within a medium-sized chemicals conglomerate. By the late 1980s he could claim that the system had been used by over 700 companies in 200 different industrial settings, and had generated over half a million new business ideas. Carson's experience in new-product development had included technical training and employment in major chemicals organizations in America and the United Kingdom. He had also studied extensively the popular literature of entrepreneurship and technological innovation. He concluded that in-house innovations could be more successful if the team deliberately followed the principles unconsciously applied by entrepreneurs who founded and built up their own businesses.

Carson had grasped the importance of the in-house entrepreneur as proposed by Schumpeter, and then sought to minimize the risks of adapting the change to the organization, in the spirit of the Austrian entrepreneurs.

He constructed a scheme for systematically evaluating business opportunities and for developing them into working prototypes, and then into new products. Carson found a way to model the company and its environment so that 'systematic creativity and integrative modelling for industry, technology and research' (Scimitar) became more routine.

At the heart of the systematic analysis was the Scimitar box, a three-dimensional cube, physically constructed from clear plastic sheets and struts. Each box was composed of cells indicating a unique combination of materials, processes, and markets relevant to the company. The systematic search involved a cross-discipline team examining each cell, armed with information from the market, especially user needs. All possible ideas dealing with a perceived need were noted and allocated to the appropriate cell. Special attention was paid to cells in which the organization had no existing product. In this way, project teams generated large numbers of promising new product ideas.[44]

Screening of ideas is based on rather well-known quantification approaches involving check-lists, risk assessments, and criteria evaluation. Through these screens, the numbers of promising ideas are whittled down to front-runners for investment as new-venture proposals.

Scimitar offered a structure for idea search and development that had wide face-validity for users. These included the explicit proposition that a deliberate and systematic search process for new ideas was more likely to succeed than their previous approaches. The formation of a cross-disciplinary Scimitar team also made sense to users. The screening approaches encouraged decisions based on available best-judgement across the firm.

The blueprint for a Scimitar project indicated a start to the idea search once the corporate go-ahead had been received. There is a very important rite of passage that occurs at some agreed point, marking the beginning of the commercialization stage. The short-listed set of ideas, each with a tangible output, and commercialization justification is presented to the corporate sponsors of the project. The ceremony involved the Scimitar team and senior corporate executives. Some senior-level commitment is required for the concepts to receive further corporate support. Those projects that are accepted acquire corporate legitimacy and the necessary resources to proceed to the marketplace.[45] The reported evidence showed that teams following the Scimitar approach consistently generated ideas believed to be new and valuable to organizational clients at the time of its application.

A large number of ideas are generated systematically within a domain identified by participants from the client company. The agreed selection criteria favour ideas that are relatively easy to convert to prototypes. Furthermore, the ideas that fail to reach the prototype stage in a given agreed time are shelved. Thus, many ideas which have been over-optimistically rated are taken out of the game early on. Adequate numbers of ideas progressing to plan reduces the likelihood of team members transferring energy to rescuing their favourite ideas. The process acts to screen out rather than select in. The process can be seen as one in which the more quantifiable risks are articulated and minimized as far as is practically possible. Furthermore, the ideas have high acceptability for the strategic decision-makers involved in the process. In principle, the decisions can reflect a firm's willingness to back higher risk projects in search of higher rewards.

Carson went on to develop more refined search models for strategic studies. These retained the basic three-dimensional structure of Scimitar models, as well as many of its operational components.

Beyond the Stage Models of Innovation: Thinking Outside the Box

The handful of books approach reveals innovation studies as sharing a set of beliefs and assumptions that we will now look at in a little more detail. They are of interest for the paradoxical reason that they are rather taken for granted and ignored. As creativity can be regarded as the challenging of self-imposed constraints, these themes may be a good starting point for some creative thinking about innovation.

Front-end loading of creativity

Many of the innovation stage models have an initial stage in which creativity is said to occur. This front-loading of creativity means that the whole tricky question of discovery processes has been got out of the way so that the subsequent stages can be presented as rational and logical sequences of activities. Creativity, if addressed at all, is isolated and controlled.

Concealing the learning requirements within the process

As with the creative problem-solving systems, innovation models tend to permit learning, while concentrating on the learning of task-related 'data'. In Cooper's NewProd, for example, its interest lies in the possibility of the system predicting outcomes of innovation actions. However, as we have seen, the check-list of success factors can at best serve as a sensitizing device through which users focus their learning efforts.

Until recently, innovation as a learning process was a minor theme in innovation studies and even more concealed within technique systems. More recently, far more attention has been paid to organizational learning. Indeed, a whole learning school may be emerging within innovation studies.[46] A good question for examining techniques for innovation is: 'how is learning managed within the technique's structures?'

Deterministic claims for the techniques

Uncertainties can be denied if processes are claimed to be deterministic. We have seen how placing creativity at the front end of an innovation process was one means of isolating the uncertainties and presenting the rest of the process as highly plannable. Triz claims that discoveries are objective, and can be objectively reached. This is asserting determinism for the discovery process. Other models also imply determinism in implementation. The claims in a technique of predictable outcomes is one that aligns the technique with the implicit assumptions of the dominant managerialist orthodoxy. A good practical question of techniques becomes 'how do they address the issues of openness of systems to unpredictable events?'

Excessive reliance on empirically claimed knowledge[47]

The dominant orthodoxy of managerialism requires hard evidence before accepting a new theory or system. Its requirements are for empirical evidence. This evidence turns out to be hard to collect in ways that satisfy independent evaluations. This explains the reluctance of more theoretical management researchers to endorse complex systems for enhancing innovation. It also explains the efforts of technique advocates to present convincing empirical evidence of its successful utilization in practice. Yet all such efforts fall short of answering the most important question for would-be innovators: 'What will happen when I use this technique under my particular set of circumstances?' To break out of this box the innovating manager has to go beyond the empirical evidence and consider the kinds of ways the system is proposing for overcoming the complexities of innovation.[48]

Procedures claiming to manage risk

If innovation is generally accepted as inherently risky, how might risk be managed in the innovation systems? We might expect that the systems would indicate ways consistent with those acceptable to an orthodox view of management. If so, we might also expect risk to be controlled by procedures involving the acquisition of 'reliable' information and subsequent rational treatment of that information. Inspection of the proposed model will reveal whether the system has been designed to conceal risk or manage it! Techniques that claim to deliver low-risk innovation are denying or concealing risk. To break out of this box, the innovative practitioner might ask the question 'what is the system doing to manage risk?'

Denying complications of the innovation process

The models conceal complexities in various ways. For example, the platforms of understanding recognize that innovation is highly context dependent.[49] A pointed question might be 'how does the model deal with situational or contextual factors and their varying significance?'

Where the Innovation Jigsaw Puzzling is Taking Us

We can now discern where our jigsaw puzzling is taking us. Schumpeter historically developed his economic theory of alpha-innovations or revolutionary discoveries. Here the whole process generated change in a creative gale of destruction generated by heroic entrepreneurs.[50] These ideas are too threatening for the dominant managerialist perspective and, not surprisingly, have hardly been given a voice in courses on innovation. More acceptable to the orthodoxy would be the Austrian school, in which entrepreneurs are 'smoothing' agents assisting regulation and equilibrium. The Austrian ideas and the diffusion models of innovation are far easier to examine using well-developed mathematical models.

Listening to the hidden voices

We can look more systematically for heresies using the grid proposed in chapter 1. According to the theory, the heresies are silenced or tamed by being forced into the conceptual box occupied by the orthodoxy. Figure 3.3 shows how creativity might be tamed within innovation models. At the same time, innovation is itself tamed. Schumpeter's creative gales of destruction have been ignored as unmeasurable and unpredictable. The novel structures or technique systems for innovative change have been accepted because they have tamed and confined creativity to 'the front end' of the process. The dangerous subjectivity of sense-making and learning within innovation processes has been made safe by concealing the learning needed within the stages of the innovation techniques.

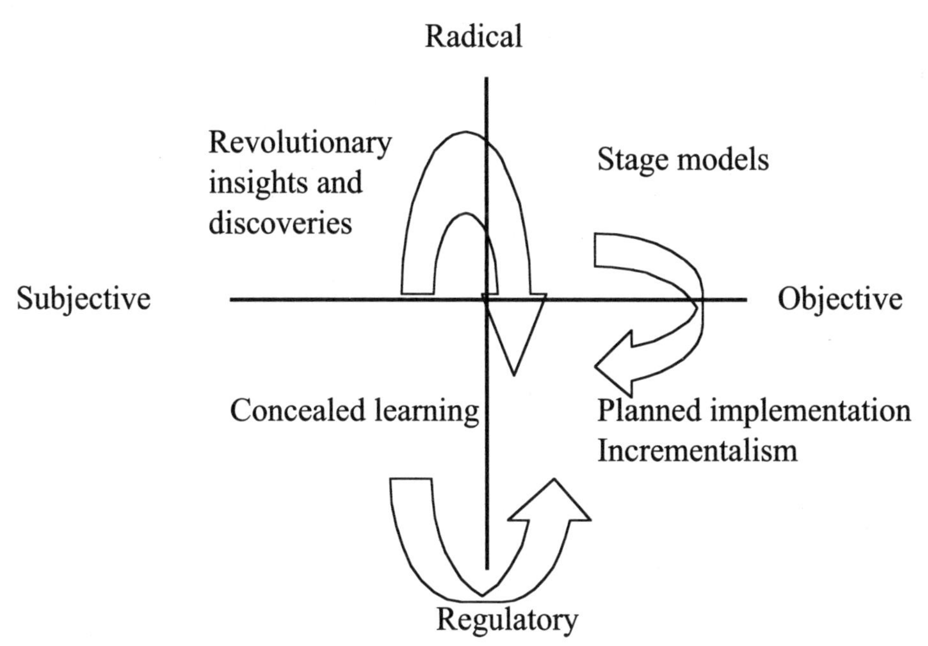

Figure 3.3: The taming of innovation

The machine metaphors revealed

Our examination of theory and proposed techniques suggests that the dominant view of innovation has been a process operating in a closed system. Progress is presumed to be made step by step in a linear and causally connected way. These are characteristics of a famous dominant metaphor for organization, the machine metaphor. This metaphor has been seen as capturing the classic bureaucratic organizational form. Our description of a dominant kind of managerialism is also one that accords with the machine metaphor. The metaphor is increasingly considered to be inadequate for dealing with the uncertainties of organizational life. The search is on for ways of thinking that help us escape from that machine metaphor.

Conclusions

We have found that innovation studies offer ways of understanding and influencing organizational change processes. We have also found various claims made for technique systems that deserve to be taken seriously. However, the more theoretical ideas have been resisted by processes we have connected to a dominant managerialist orthodoxy that denies the uncertainties and ambiguities in which innovation flourishes.

The technique systems are in some way aligned to such beliefs, in that they conceal the uncertainties and confine creativity to a special place at the front end of the innovation process. This means that uninitiated managers have no direct means of assessing the merits of techniques from the managerial orthodox perspective. We have shown that an assessment can be made by puzzling out the assumptions of techniques and of dominant platforms of understanding of innovation. This learning process helps to combine 'what they teach you at business school' and 'what you need to put ideas into practice'. It will lead the way to more powerful ways of thinking about organizations and organizational change.

Notes

[1] Tidd et al. (1997: 24).
[2] Rogers (1995: 98).
[3] Downs & Mohr (1976: 700).
[4] Rickards (1991: 97–8).
[5] Once the notion of a pro-innovation bias is pointed out it becomes visible on inspection of samples of popular and more academic literature. It is revealed by the general stance of authors, together with the absence of comment regarding possible disadvantages arising through innovation efforts. For a more thorough analysis see Abrahamson (1991).
[6] These criticisms were raised powerfully in Nelson & Winter (1977) and have never been particularly well rebutted since.
[7] Tidd et al. (1997).

[8] For this study I identified approximately thirty texts from *Stimulating Innovation* (Rickards, 1985) and revisited the contents of the journal *Creativity and Innovation Management* (1992–7) published by Blackwell. Editing this journal had helped me keep up with new texts dealing with innovation, of interest to our readership of practitioners, consultants and academics.

[9] Freeman (1982); Kingston (1984); Swann (1993).

[10] Nyström (1990); Pettigrew & Whipp (1991).

[11] For example, Everett Rogers (1995) in his fourth edition, examined over 4,000 publications that he considered comprised the field of diffusion studies. Tidd et al. (1997) provide a wide-ranging critique of the literature of innovation management.

[12] West & Farr (1990); Grönhaug & Kaufmann (1988).

[13] Henry & Walker (1991); Rickards (1985); Twiss (1992).

[14] Drucker (1985); Foster (1986).

[15] I have drawn this picture of Schumpeter from a wide range of sources, especially Cheah (1993), Freeman (1982), Kingston (1984) and Manimala (1992).

[16] See, for example, Freeman for a brief account of the so-called Kondratiev cycles.

[17] It makes for a neat story to link James Watt with steam power, Stephenson with railways, and Ford and Edison with the third wave. This kind of 'spot the pioneer' is not without problems. Trevethick might be acknowledged as an earlier pioneer of a steam condenser or, still earlier, Hero of Alexandria. Benz might claim priority for the first internal combustion engine and so on.

[18] Schumpeter also pointed to the significance of non-technological innovations. His categories were those processes introducing a new 'good' or product, or a new quality of a known product; a new method of production; the opening up of a new market; the 'conquest' of a new source of supply; and the achievement of a new form of organization that shifts the industry structure through setting up or breaking a monopoly position (Manimala, 1992).

[19] Schumpeter (1947: 83).

[20] Freeman (1982).

[21] Kirzner (1973: 72–3), in Cheah (1993: 245). Extensive applications of a continuous improvement model have been developed by Bessant and co-workers (e.g. Bessant, 1991, Bessant et al., 1993).

[22] However, Schumpeter (1947) makes the sharp distinction between the inventor and the entrepreneur, who exploits another's invention. See also Cheah (1993: 244).

[23] Among Hayek's admirers can be numbered Tom Peters, who was himself a powerful influence on a generation of practising organizational managers. See Peters (1992) for his notes on Hayek's 'liberation' economics.

[24] In Rogers (1995) the chapter on organizational innovation is a minor part of the work. In it, there is a model of organizational innovation in which the first stage is some kind of mutual adjustment of the incoming innovation and the organization. The general impression, however, is that the process is not particularly influenced by individual or organizational competencies.

[25] See Foster (1986).

[26] West & Farr (1990: 9).

[27] Majaro (1988).

[28] Toffler (1972: 28).

[29] King (1990) mentions six overlapping stage models. Among these I would consider Zaltman et al. (1973) and Rogers (1995) to be particularly worth studying.

[30] Tidd et al. (1997) warn that a strictly technological view is inadequate to characterize innovation. Easingwood (1986) is an early study of new service products; Surdbo (1998) is a more recent one. Even in this sophisticated treatment, however, there is no challenge

to the importance of the technological dimension, but a reminder that we should also consider other non-technological ones.

[31] Tidd et al. (1997: 19).

[32] Rogers (1995) favours the large-firm thesis. Most small-firm literature claims the opposite. This confusion is partly explained if we consider that Rogers is interested in uptake of innovations, whereas the small-firm literature tends to accept a product life-cycle approach.

[33] Downs & Mohr (1976) give a thoughtful analysis.

[34] Cooper (1992) summarizes a range of studies on the NewProd system.

[35] Cooper & Kleinschmidt (1987). This dichotomy is less problematic, the more closely the success–failure pairs are matched.

[36] Cooper adopted the term protocol for the strategic plan, after Crawford (1984).

[37] Cooper (1992: 121).

[38] I am indebted to information provided by Professor Phan Dung (Dung, 1994, 1995), who studied the Triz system extensively in Moscow, before introducing it into Vietnam at HoChiMinh City University, as a course for developing inventive creativity.

[39] Triz should also be compared with the systems of creative problem-solving in chapter 3. Ariz as a self-learning, creative, problem-solving system has some similarities with Creative Analysis (Rickards, 1973).

[40] In the paradigm classification of chapter 3, this would be seen as an example of a *radical structuralist paradigm*.

[41] Hegel's laws of dialectics are sometimes summed up as thesis and antithesis leading to synthesis. Marx was at first influenced by Hegelian thinking, only to evolve his own ideas from it. At one level this seems a natural development, according to the laws of contradiction and resolution.

[42] Carson (1989); Carson & Rickards (1979).

[43] My personal involvement in the development of this technique helps me in a 'gamekeeper turned poacher' role. My objective in this work is to illustrate how such systems can be evaluated more effectively by potential users.

[44] The system can be reapplied to other corporate projects of diversification, strategy formation, import substitution and so on, by changing the dimensions of the box (Carson, 1989).

[45] In practice the negotiation will reflect the situation and requirements of the strategy-forming individual or group. Deadlines, resources, and financial requirements tend to the desired at the expense of the realistic. The process may have the appearance of rationality concerning factors that enter into the shared discourse within the decision-making. However, the process is open to political influences and concealed agendas.

[46] Nelson & Winter (1982) give a good early account of innovation as a learning process. The importance of tacit knowledge in the process has also become recognized (e.g. Nonaka & Kenney, 1991; Leonard-Barton, 1995).

[47] When empirical evidence is equated with the only reliable source of theoretical proof, we have abstracted empiricism, outlined in chapter 1 as a means of taming voices that opposed the dominant orthodoxy.

[48] Here is a sharp distinction between world views. Social scientists are generally convinced that empirical evidence from past social events cannot predict the outcomes of future social events. The managerial orthodoxy generally assumes the opposite. Perhaps the more pragmatic issue is whether the knowledge derived from past journeys serves as an adequate map for future voyages.

[49] Downs & Mohr (1976: 700). The old assertion remains a challenge for a new generation of managers and theorists.

[50] If we assume a preference for the dominant rational and regulatory beliefs, we might assume that Schumpeterian ideas would be difficult for the economic orthodoxy to accept. It would probably be more acceptable to those who consider radical humanistic modes of change as good descriptions of the real world.

chapter 4 Marketing and Strategy Revisited

Because it is its purpose to create a customer, any business enterprise has two – and only these two – basic functions: marketing and innovation. They are the entrepreneurial functions.

Peter Drucker[1]

The word marketing is often used loosely and vaguely . . . Scores of definitions exist, ranging from the high-flown – 'the delivery of a standard of living' to the pedestrian American Association version, 'the performance of business activities that direct the flow of goods and services from producer to consumer or user'. No single definition is adequate, except for limited purposes.

R. J. Lawrence & M. J. Thomas[2]

Unfortunately, defining strategic marketing and/or marketing strategy has been confused by the seemingly endless use of the terms strategy and strategic . . . everyone seems to have his or her own definition.

H. Thomas & D. Gardner[3]

It turns out that strategy is one of those words that we inevitably define in one way yet often use in another.

Henry Mintzberg[4]

Strategic success cannot be reduced to a formula. Nevertheless, there are habits of mind that can be acquired through practice to help you free the creative power of your subconscious and improve your odds of coming up with winning strategic concepts.

Kenichi Omae[5]

Introduction

From creativity and innovation to marketing and strategy

Over the years, I had searched for those business disciplines with affinities with my own interests in creativity and innovation. These unsystematic efforts tended to point to marketing and strategy as the most promising of the core business disciplines. Marketing courses incorporate information on innovation and product development. Strategic management courses touch on the benefits deriving from creative strategic insights. In the absence of evidence that favoured other business topics, I decided to continue my journey of exploration with a visit to the regions of business orthodoxy known as marketing and strategy. These topics are often taught as distinct yet related topics within business courses. By visiting both regions in a single journey, we are better able to discover similarities that are generally concealed.

The journey of exploration

The journey began with the construction of the platform of understanding of marketing orthodoxy. The expected dominance of a rational or managerialist view was found, including a rationalistic treatment of innovation processes. However, a connection with creativity was also established particularly in the shift to relationship marketing, where intuition and 'market sensing' is being rediscovered. The journey continued into the strategy territories. Again, a rational orthodoxy was found that dominated over other voices. Here the more heretical voices of the strategy practitioners (including business owners and top executives) had been supported by the influential academic voices of Henry Mintzberg and supporters. These voices suggest strategy also benefits from intuitive, creative approaches. The route map to the journey is shown in Figure 4.1.

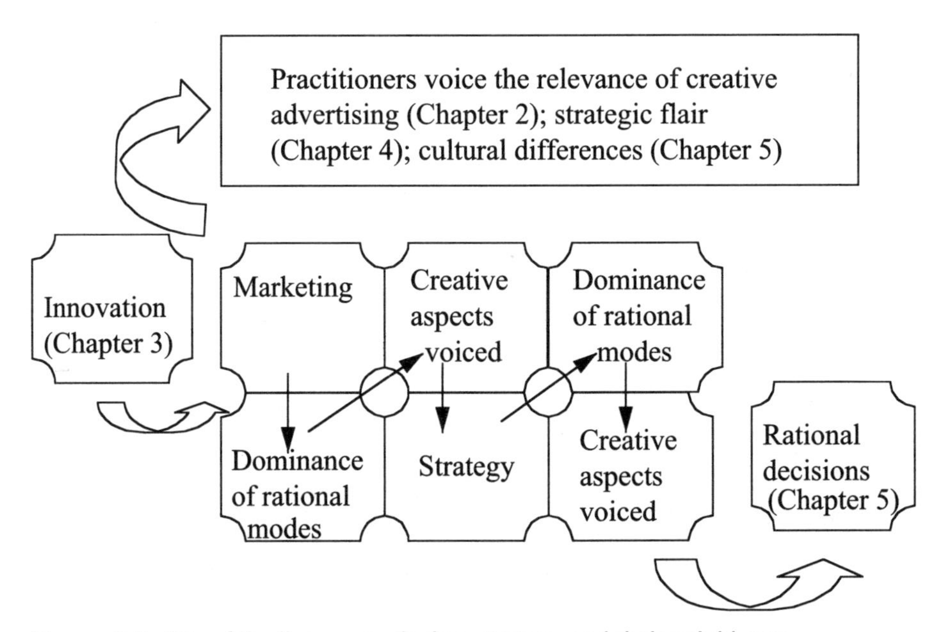

Figure 4.1: Bits of the jigsaw: marketing, strategy and their neighbours

In Search of the Bits of the Marketing Jigsaw

Philip Kotler

To enter these territories I was in need of guides who would be able to speak for the business areas, helping me to approach their platforms of understanding of marketing and strategy. It became a relatively simple matter to identify the essential figures and themes according to the shared platform of understanding of researchers and teachers in these subjects. Among these, I found a wide consensus accepting the views of the American academic and influential author Philip Kotler as a reference point for teaching marketing orthodoxy. The dissemination of his ideas by others makes him a sound starting point for building a platform of understanding of the field. His co-authored textbook, *Principles of Marketing*, had passed a sixth edition as I began my search. It provided a master guide from which to approach the subject.[6]

The platform of understanding for marketing

At the start of the chapter can be found the widely asserted view that marketing – whatever it is – is not easily pinned down in a widely accepted definition. We can assume that Kotler's treatment will be a good starting point from which to depart. Kotler recognizes multiple definitions, suggesting that they reflect different emphases on marketing 'as a process, a concept or philosophy of business or an orientation'.[7] The same text offers a working definition as 'a social and managerial process by which individuals and groups obtain what they need and want through creating and exchanging products and value with others'.[8]

In my subsequent journey into the marketing literature I found handfuls of books that extended and enriched the basic ideas in Kotler's writings. The shapes of new sub-disciplines became clearer, such as brand management, retail marketing, and relationship marketing. Yet there was little that directly contradicted the main premises provided by my guide. To puzzle out the essential features of marketing beliefs, a thematic rather than a discipline approach was followed, as described in the next section.

Puzzling out the themes in the platform of understanding

Key themes in such writings from the 1960s and 1970s have become important – obligatory – components for today's marketing practitioners and theorists all over the world (although later we will have to take cultural differences far more into account). More recent introductory texts have carried over the themes, reworking them to meet changing circumstances and fashions. Six recurrent themes go a long way to building a platform of understanding of contemporary marketing thought and its historical antecedents: the marketing concept; the marketing plan; marketing mix and the four Ps;[9] branding and positioning; marketing communications theory; and the newer theme of relationship marketing.

The marketing concept

This gives the field its philosophic basis. It captures the earliest rationale for marketing as an orientation which puts the market and the customer centre stage, where before it was the organization's products and production that were centre stage.[10] From it, the other issues all flow. We can begin with the marketing concept proposed by Kotler in one of his earlier writings.[11] Its similarity with the marketing definition is evident. '[Marketing orientation is] a management orientation that holds that the key task of the organization is to determine the needs, wants, and values of a target market and to adapt the organization to delivering the desired satisfactions more effectively and efficiently than its competitors.'[12]

Note that the marketing concept as defined suggests an overlap with everyday understanding of what might be called the strategy concept. Determining the needs and wants of a target market are tasks that are closely connected with the marketing function; adapting the organization to deal with these market requirements involves corporate level responsibilities.[13]

The marketing plan

Here we have another highly significant term. The marketing plan stands for the most visible organizational symbol of marketing orientation. Any formalized record of intentions of matching a company's products and markets can be taken as a marketing plan. From that basic starting point has developed a global industry of advice and consultancy on how to prepare the plan. Such knowledge is an important output from formal professional studies of marketing such as the qualifications of the Chartered Institute of Marketing in Europe.[14]

The specific steps in the marketing plan can still vary. In this respect, we have the marketing parallel with the structures or techniques for 'doing' innovation or creative problem-solving. What the market plan implies is that marketing is manageable through systematic planning.

Marketing mix and the multiple Ps

By an increasingly time-honoured convention, the process of managing the marketing function has become equated with managing the four Ps of product, price, promotion and place.[15] The important feature of a mix is that the ingredients have to be adjusted according to circumstances.

The notion that marketing deals with a 'mix' of factors is an important aspect of a marketing orientation.[16] The original four factors have been extended in various ways – it is the concept of mix, rather than the precise number of its ingredients that matters. They should be factors over which marketing activities have some control, and which make a difference to the outcome of those efforts. The marketing mix seems suited to a systems design approach, with the challenges of integrating (managing) the various components. It also indicates that marketing will require a knowledge of detailed information differentiating one set of circumstances from another. Here we have an indication of why case studies are so valued as an educational tool in marketing.

Branding and positioning

Brand marketing has taken on its own professional significance with the rise of brand managers as important members of marketing departments. We can again begin with Kotler. 'Perhaps the most distinctive skill of professional marketers is their ability to create, maintain, protect, reinforce and enhance brands. A brand is a name, term, sign, symbol, design, or combination of these, which is used to identify the goods or services of one seller or group of sellers and to differentiate them from those of competitors.'[17]

Branding has its own influence leaders, who have helped indicate the combination of the intangible and tangible aspects in commercial terms. David Aaker, in a series of influential books and articles emphasizes the intangibles that are associated with brand image.[18] In some contrast he also writes about brand equity – the added commercial benefits deriving from successful brands, and describes ways in which brands can be positioned.

The tangible aspect of brand equity or commercial value and the intangible aspect of brand image may appear to be distinct. There is some ambiguity about this, neatly summed up by another leading researcher into branding, Jean-Noel Kapferer. 'It is only recently [referring to the 1980s] that we have realized that [a company's] real value lies outside the business itself, in the minds of potential buyers.'[19]

Marketing communications theory

As implied in the marketing mix, marketing requires a theory of communications. Speeches from marketing executives sometimes include the homily that marketing is all about communications. Within the marketing mix we learn of the 'communications mix'.[20] This includes decisions on the appropriate mix of advertising, promotional activities, and which media should transmit the information about the product. What implementation is to creative problem-solving, communication is to marketing.

Relationship marketing as a new paradigm

In general, earlier marketing theory had a focus on getting new business. This is a traditional view. Later, its connections with strategic operations became appreciated. More recently, the emphasis in both theoretical and practitioner work has moved towards building relationships with customers. The shift is one from one-to-one transactions to both short-term and long-term relationships in networks. The shift has been described as a third marketing paradigm after traditional and strategic views.[21] Within it, the developing ideas of brands and brand equity are being extended to deal with the intangible values of a company's brands.

Making Sense of the Marketing Platform of Understanding

The dominant rational paradigm

From these points we can construct a first impression of the core beliefs within the marketing paradigm. The marketing plan, brand equity theory, brand positioning, communications theory, and the marketing mix fit very nicely into a rationalistic worldview. Marketing students generally accept the received wisdom that marketing is progressing from a dangerously unpredictable art to a discipline grounded in scientific principles. The new relationship marketing theme offers promise of a break that may yet be unfulfilled because of the persistence of the old orthodoxy of rationality.

The marketing plan is offered as a professionally certified approach to young marketing trainees. The dangers of human intuition and bias are firmly held in check.[22] Branding is strongly connected to the idea of adding to the value of a company's equity. This is in principle measurable in an objective no-nonsense way as a contribution to the bottom line. Brand positioning is presented as a logical analytical approach that provides an objective result.

The taming of a new paradigm

The shift towards relationship marketing suggests considerations that are less tangible. More sophisticated commentaries warn of the need to move away from strictly financial analyses to behavioural considerations. They warn that the shift may be trivialized by a widespread use of the term relationship marketing.

'That would be a pity; it is a revolution in marketing thinking. The term "relational paradigm" is more precise . . . The traditional micro-economic paradigm is no more "wrong" than early astronomers were "wrong". Paradigms are just different ways of understanding. The challenge of the reformers is that it [i.e. the traditional paradigm] is too mechanistic, too transactional, too internally focused on the company's actions, too rational and too financially oriented.'[23]

Creativity in marketing

Where does this leave creativity in marketing? The rational and formalized perspective leaves some space for creativity, but sets it aside, leaving it to professionals to work to a brief that accords to a rationally derived plan. This is not overtly stated in the most widely used texts. Rather it is implied. For example, the emphasis on communication theory suggests a high level methodology for 'filling in the gaps' between plan and implementation. If the plan fails, the analysis is as likely to identify poor communications as poor creative ideas or poor implementation.[24] In texts that are more popular there are some claims that marketing provides the creativity for corporate change efforts. Even in these texts there can be found criticisms that marketing people 'tend to concentrate too much on the role of advertising and creativity, which at first sight is very glamorous, and focus less on analytical or strategic marketing, which is so important for the future'.[25]

Marketing and innovation

Marketing texts do claim product development as an aspect of market development. Yet, its relationship with innovation is ambiguous. Some marketing theorists such as Nyström make a discriminating contrast between innovative and marketing strategies. In this sense, he takes the rather restrictive view of innovation as technologically oriented. Peter Drucker had a rather different discrimination: 'Marketing aims at satisfying customers today; innovation focuses on satisfying tomorrow's customers.'[26]

Summary of marketing orthodoxy and the heresies

We can pull together these considerations using the now familiar idea of marketing heresies or suppressed voices (figure 4.2).

The marketing orthodoxy has developed to protect marketing from unscientific and irrational approaches. As a direct consequence, great benefits have accrued through the informed efforts of countless thousands of people who have contributed to more structured approaches within marketing practice. However, creative thinking has been largely left to advertising 'creatives'.

The perceptual aspects of branding, for example, might suggest the importance of studying sense-making.[27] Instead, the methodology of brand management has

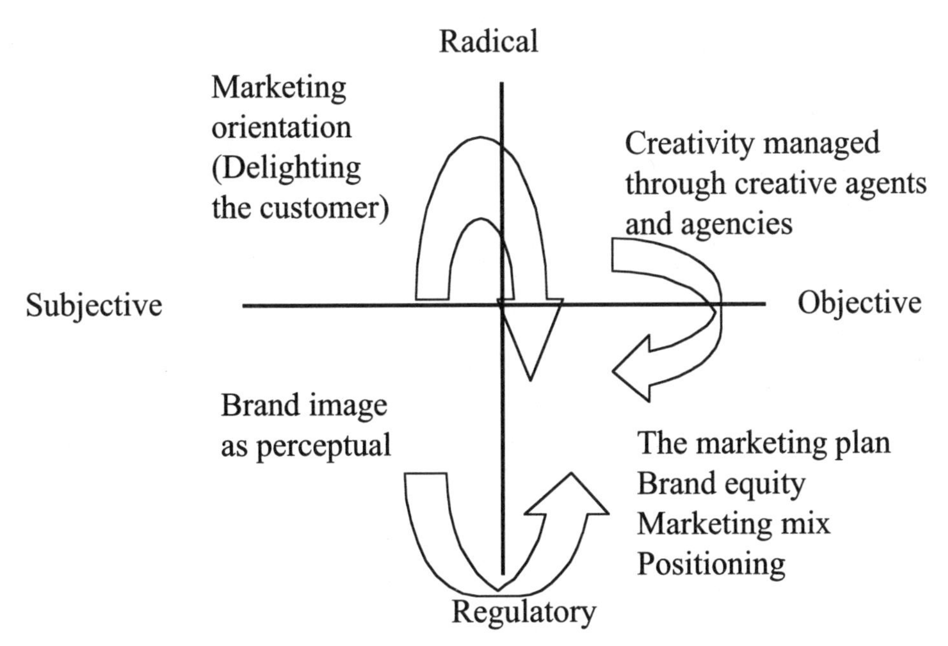

Figure 4.2: The alternative marketing voices

largely given priority to the functional requirements of communicating effectively. Finally, and most radically, we have to ask where is there space for inspired ideas? How do we explain what Tom Peters describes as a wild obsession with delighting the customer?

It might seem that the answer lies in combining the two paradigms into a hybrid, to achieve both the benefits of rationalistic analyses and of more humanistic and creative approaches. The future lies in approaches that recognize the benefits of both rational planning and intuitive judgements. In the vocabulary of chapter 3 we are favouring both left brain analysis and planning, and right brain intuiting and judgement. In the next part of the chapter, on strategy, we will find a very similar conclusion can be reached.

Pioneers of Strategy

Building the platform of understanding for strategy

Strategy has a range of influential figures whose work we are about to encounter. One high-profile figure, Henry Mintzberg, something of a heretic himself, has, more than anyone, surveyed the field and explored the nature of its orthodoxy. His work made a promising, if somewhat dangerous, starting point. For the purposes of establishing, not evaluating, strategic ideas, Mintzberg stood out. We assemble the platform of understanding from the work of two giants of the field, Ansoff and Porter. Mintzberg then provides a way of revealing less orthodox possibilities.

Ansoff's reconceptualization of management

Various American writers have laid claim to pioneering the modern business subject of strategy. Igor Ansoff is perhaps most widely regarded as a pioneering figure in the field in Western studies.[28] Ansoff's conceptual grounding can be best appreciated by an examination of his earliest and probably most influential text entitled *Corporate Strategy*. In it he indicated that his work departs from the dominant theory of organizational decision-making which derives from micro-economics, and which, he argues, is an inappropriate model for strategy formulation because it operates within a surprise-free environment.[29]

'Over the past ten years, a number of writers have provided partial analytical insights into strategic business problems. The purpose of this book is to synthesize and integrate these into an overall analytic approach to solving the total strategic problem of the firm . . . Methodologically, the 'scientific' method of operations research and management science is not wholly applicable to the strategic problem. In fact, the method falls short in several important aspects. A partial result of this book, therefore, is a new methodology, which appears more suitable for problems of the type considered here.'[30]

He points out that prevailing decision-making models derived from micro-economic theories assume that the decision-maker has access to the complete set of decision options. Ansoff indicates that the stages of perception and option formulation are both difficult yet critical.[31]

Ansoff distinguished between strategic, administrative and operating decisions. He defined strategic as 'pertaining to the relationship between the firm and its environment',[32] and considered strategic decisions to be particularly concerned with external marketing issues: 'specifically with the selection of the product mix which the firm will produce and the markets to which it will sell'.[33] Both administrative and operational decisions are seen as subservient to strategic decisions.[34]

His system involves the formulation of objectives and strategies, which were to be treated as provisional, and mutually interactive. This process permits a requisite element of designed-in flexibility.[35] Conceptually, Ansoff had succeeded in locating the weaknesses in prevailing micro-economic theories for practitioners seeking to survive and grow. His analysis remains relatively unchallenged.[36] However, the challenge of operationalizing the objectives, strategies, and decision-rules proved enormously difficult. Ansoff supplied numerous check-lists, techniques, and suggestions to help the planner work through the model. In his efforts Ansoff discovered and popularized many powerful decision-support concepts. His proposals for deriving objectives and strategies included the concept of gap analysis. His proposals for evaluating goodness of fit for a proposed strategy incorporated the concept and terminology of synergy, which for a while became one of the best-known bits of jargon associated with strategic planning.

In his idealized model, this process turned out to require over fifty boxes, of which nearly two dozen required managerial decisions. In recognition of the provisional nature of objectives and strategic ideas, he had incorporated numerous options for iteration within the model. For example, a sequence of activities might have identified an opportunity or performance gap. An objective might be set, and a strategy derived for achieving the objective. The model permits a review of the objective and of the strategy as further information becomes available. In his second edition, his models had become even more complex, the numbers of little boxes of activities even more numerous.[37]

Porter's position

In the 1970s, a common sight in business schools was that of students heading for class, each carrying a little volume of Ansoff. In the 1990s, an equally common sight has been that of students heading to class with several rather larger volumes written by Michael Porter. Professor Porter is a Harvard-based researcher, consultant and international advocate of the benefits of his ideas on competitive strategy. His books reveal a lucid and authoritative style that pulls the reader along with him. His work derives from the orthodoxy of economics.[38] Specifically he has attempted to deal with the nature of competition. We will examine the key features of two of his most important works.[39]

In his first major book Porter looks at the structure of industries and proposes an elegant way of classifying their competitive characteristics. Two important ideas are those of the five forces or drivers contributing to the dynamics of competitiveness and the three generic strategies of firms competing effectively within the influences of those five forces. Two of the five forces are represented by the bargaining powers of suppliers and buyers respectively. Two others arise through the threat of new entry into the market of rival firms, and of substitute products or services. The final and fifth force is the dynamics of rivalry among firms already competing in the marketplace.[40]

The significance of components within the five drivers differs according to industry sector. Thus, the strength of each driver for a specific organization has to be estimated through an analysis of these components. Porter has derived several powerful concepts in his work on this system, including the notion of entry barrier and bargaining leverage of buyers. It is Porter's contention that such an analysis can indicate the financial attractiveness of an industry.[41] Armed with such information, a firm can then examine its chances of earning profits above the industry average. This requires knowledge of Porter's second contribution to the field, his typology of generic strategies. He is emphatic that there are only three viable generic strategies for a firm seeking competitive advantage. These arise as follows: 'The significance of any strength or weakness a firm possesses is ultimately a function of its impact on relative cost or differentiation. Cost advantage and differentiation in turn stem from industry structure. They result from a firm's ability to cope with the five forces better than its rivals.'[42]

Organizations can strive for cost advantages or differentiation advantages. These may be directed across a wide range of industry segments or restricted to a narrow and focused industry segment. Porter identifies the strategy of wide-ranging cost advantage as *cost leadership*. He describes the wide-ranging strategy as the differentiation strategy. He then combines two versions of narrow-range strategies as a focus strategy (with cost advantage and differentiation characteristics respectively).[43] Porter explains that such strategic analyses can produce healthy and orderly market conditions, with firms competing, but not so as to weaken the mutual set of arrangements financially. This avoids the destructiveness, for example, of a battle for cost leadership, which tends to produce 'a protracted and unprofitable battle'.[44] It is to deal with such undesirable results that the author turns, in his next book, to the means of gaining a sustainable competitive advantage.

In his later book on competitive advantage, the organizing structure is that of the value chain. It is probably from this work that added-value has installed itself into everyday business-speak. It is also a concept of importance to marketing theory, as it indicates a way of approaching delivering customer value and satisfaction. The elegant representation of the value chain has the shape of the flight feather of a broad arrow. The lower portion of the arrow is divided into horizontal sequences of production activities, each feeding into the next. In his own terms, Porter has represented the classical flow of inputs to a firm, leading to production operations, distribution, marketing and servicing. The upper part of the arrow has three vertical bands, which show activities running across all the operating stages. These represent the firm's infrastructure, and comprise the categories of human resource management, technology development and procurement. Margin earned is represented at the head of the arrow.[45]

The value chain is an imaginative way of analysing components of a firm's activities that might produce competitive advantage. To take a specific example, technology is recognized as a potential means of gaining competitive advantage through innovation. Yet most innovation literature is weak on explaining how technology development can be assessed in the context of a firm's corporate strategy. By considering technology development in the context of Porter's value chain, it is easier to appreciate possible strategic connections with logistics, operations, marketing and so on.[46]

The writing and associated illustrations are of exemplary clarity, and logical persuasiveness. For much of the writing, there is a sense of comforting determinism for any organization that follows his prescriptions. Yet Porter does acknowledge the complications of organizational uncertainties, admitting that strategic planning largely keeps quiet about situations of high uncertainty.[47] His recommended technique is that of Scenario Generation. This is offered as a technique for improving creative performance. 'They [scenarios] cannot insure (sic) creativity,' he notes, 'but they can significantly raise the odds.'[48] Creativity is considered to be of increasing importance for strategy formulation under conditions of uncertainty, and may be supported with what must be classed as a technique for enhancing creative outputs.

The platform of understanding indicated by Ansoff and Porter

Porter and Ansoff stand for many of the shared values within the strategy paradigm. Both authors have taken an economic view and have developed innovative and coherent models for studying the nature of corporate strategy. They also provide practitioners with techniques to support the general process of strategy formulation. The general tenor of their writings is that strategy can be approached in a rigorous and scientific manner, albeit in a field in which uncertainties and complications abound in practice. Ansoff and Porter also recognize, perhaps more implicitly than explicitly, that the complexities of organizational life require imagination and creativity.

Mintzberg's Guerrilla War on Strategic Orthodoxy

As a young researcher, Mintzberg carried out observational studies to establish what executives really do with their time. The received wisdom among academics at the time was that top managers were there because they epitomized the highest skills of scientific management. In practice, he found that the managerial life was one of frenzied actions, interruptions, and short-term attention to a multiplicity of issues. It was what we might today call parallel processing. It was far more to do with short-term trouble-shooting and unreflective actions than to do with rational economic reasoning and long-term planning.

The significance of the research lies in its implications for the dominant theoretical belief in scientific management. Mintzberg had not so much discovered something no one else knew, but spoken up in public so that a dreadful and concealed secret could no longer be successfully denied by academic researchers.[49]

The prevalent notion of management as captured by a rational economic model could no longer be taken for granted.

In one of his often-cited writings, he took the whole-brain metaphor to polarize the activities of planning from the activities of managing. The message was clear – that much that passes for planning (and by implication strategy) presented itself as 'left-brain', rational, and arriving at decisions of a rational, and logically determinable kind. In contrast, management, as Mintzberg had found by observation, was 'right-brain', which involves operating under uncertainty, with leaps of intuition and judgement. In as many words, Mintzberg was suggesting that strategic planning was ignoring important components of managerial activities.

According to Mintzberg, the literature of strategy can be divided into no less than ten schools. He clustered three schools in his planning category, considering them as prescriptive in emphasis, outlining what strategic planners should do. The other seven schools were more concerned with describing the nature of planning, based on their particular assumptions and beliefs. This is how Mintzberg summarized the three prescriptive planning schools.

'The first I call the "design school" which considers strategy-making an informal process of conception, typically in a leader's conscious mind. The design school model, sometimes called SWOT (for internal strengths and weaknesses to be compared with external opportunities and threats) also underlines the second, which I call the "planning school" and which accepts the premises of the former, save two . . . that the process be informal and the chief executive be the key actor . . . The third, which I call the "positioning school", focuses on the content of strategies (differentiation, diversification, etc.) more than on the processes by which they are prescribed to be made (which are generally assumed, often implicitly, to be those of the planning school). In other words, the positioning school simply extrapolates the messages of the planning school into the domain of actual strategy content.'[50]

He goes on to list the seven schools that are less prescriptive: the cognitive; entrepreneurial; learning; political; cultural; environmental; and configurational.[51] Mintzberg sees the descriptive schools as less influential among practitioners and consultants.

In his view the cognitive approach includes intuitive ('right-brain') or judgemental components required to deal creatively with the uncertainties of strategy formulation. The entrepreneurial school has strong connections with innovation-seeking. The learning school treats strategy as a means of sense-making through a mix of planning, acting, and revising one's plans. The cultural school examines the significance of culture in supporting or disrupting social beliefs. The political school places its emphasis on conflict and exploitation, while the environmental school regards organizations as responding passively to the pressures of outside forces. Research assumes that the efforts to change are no more than forced adjustments to environmental signals. Finally, the episodic or configurational school reflects the so-called contingency view. This approach is sometimes called the 'it all depends' philosophy. The outcome of an event – let's say the occasion for considering what a firm's strategy might be – all depends on factors highly specific to the event.

Mintzberg indicated that the fragmentation into schools gives rise to many definitions. The most widely accepted definitions, however, were consistent with strategy as a plan which was essentially Ansoff's view, and strategy as a position, which was Porter's view. This provides us with reassurance that '[N]o single definition is adequate, except for limited purposes'.[52] Mintzberg then undertakes a dazzling refutation of expecting one definition to stand for a concept found in so many different contexts or schools. We have to settle for partial definitions, which indicate 'what work the definition is expected to do'. For planners, strategic implies plans that are longer-term and corporate in range; for positionists, strategy implies positions that are long-term and corporate in range.

Mintzberg's main target is the planning school epitomized by Ansoff's work, although he sometimes broadens his attack to cover all three prescriptive schools. The main thrust of his argument is that the schools consider that strategy is discovered, unique and full-blown. Implementation is not considered of consequence. None of the variants of the prescriptive kind indicates how strategies are discovered. In the design school the process is regarded as a kind of art, which develops through practice. Inasmuch as the process is formalized, and aims at a best-fit between environmental and organizational features, Mintzberg considers that it reduces scope for creative and imaginative strategic thinking. There are far greater levels of formalization found in models such as Ansoff's in the planning school, and Porter's in the position school, so that the restrictions to creativity in strategy formulation are greater. Furthermore, a preference for generic strategies in these systems seems again to reduce scope for creativity.

A school which equates strategy with planning, he argues, can never yield effective strategy. He suggests there are three sets of assumptions (he calls them fallacies) in the approaches. These are the fallacy of predetermination; the fallacy of detachment: and the fallacy of formalization. The assumption of predetermination permits planners to believe in a stage of implementation independent of the strategy formation. The assumption of detachment justifies the existence of strategic managers without line authority, and inevitably without the kinds of procedural expertise held by those with line authority, regarding the chances of implementation of any strategic idea. The assumption of formalization is perhaps the most damning. It regards planning as characterized by sequences of routines that have been analytically derived, made explicit, and of a demonstrably rational and objective nature.[53] For Mintzberg, planning under these conditions is essentially analytic, and can make few claims to support processes of synthesis necessary if strategic thinking is to lead to imaginative breakthroughs.

He suggests that planned strategy can never be formalized to the degree that uncertainties are removed in the planning stage. Thus, any plan should be regarded as provisional or intended. This leads to his preferred definition of strategy as a pattern of realized behaviour over time. He considers that within an intended strategy there will be unanticipated actions which in time will be identified and honoured with the term strategy. This is emergent strategy. Emergent strategy may be the unintended result of some other intended strategy. It is not predetermined, and for that reason permits a kind of learning associated with creative discoveries, innovation and change. Mintzberg argues that strategy as a discipline is in need of a major shift of values away from the dominant planning paradigm, and towards new kinds of thinking that enhance creativity. Interestingly, support for a creative approach to strategic thinking comes from eastern cultures, in writings by authorities such as Kenichi Ohmae.[54]

Mintzberg on Prahalad

A wave of interest has developed from an influential article on core competencies by Prahalad and Hamel which appeared in *Harvard Business Review* at the start of the 1990s.[55] The original article indicated how firms gained a persistent manufacturing advantage attributed to technological know-how, which translated into innovative new products. The concept has been extended to core competencies in service organizations. The strategic importance of competencies became 'what they teach you at business school' in the 1990s, adding to the orthodoxy of strategy and technology management. Mintzberg has rather briefly dismissed it as an extension of the position school, and an old idea. His objection remains that competencies – as the term is being used – remain essentially undefinable in adequate detail to provide effective guidelines for predicting strategic outcomes.

Strategy and Marketing Revisited

Adding creativity to strategic and marketing structures

The familiar handful-of-books journey confirmed Mintzberg's view that the dominant Western approaches to strategic and marketing planning constrict creativity and imagination.[56] The literature of marketing has many parallels with the strategy literature. It too is preoccupied with multi-stage planning systems. Its techniques seek the kind of formalization that Mintzberg suspects, and have considerable overlaps with the elements of the techniques found in books on strategy.[57] If the case for injecting more creativity into strategy is accepted, it can be applied similarly to marketing.

Creativity was typically presented without explanation of how it might have occurred. I could not find any suggestion that executives with responsibilities for strategic decisions actively and deliberately used creativity techniques in achieving some spectacular marketing or strategic concept. Neither did I find many proposals for the use of creativity techniques to support aspects of strategy formulation. Porter's reference to Scenario Generation, hardly a common technique, was one of very few examples.[58]

I found other researchers who shared some of Mintzberg's dissatisfaction with results from various strategic approaches. However, the discontent tended to be defused by a view that the approaches had not been sufficiently rigorous.[59] In other words, the remedy was seen to lie in pursuing even more vigorously the general approaches already espoused.

Yet the processes of strategy formulation are rather easily supported through deliberate use of creativity-spurring techniques. Jim Leonteades, a former colleague of Ansoff, who became Director of the Cyprus International Institute of Management, has demonstrated this in his work with MBAs over a period of years. Leonteades incorporated creativity techniques into one of Ansoff's structures, SWOT analysis. The creativity techniques help users to be less rigid in their classification of strengths and weaknesses, and more able to find unexpected ways of turning weaknesses into strengths, and threats into opportunities.[60]

There are other opportunities for introducing creativity techniques into strategy-seeking exercises. An imaginative proposal was recently made by Masafumi Ise, an executive of the West Japan Railway Company.[61] He showed that the various kinds of innovation originally identified by Schumpeter could be incorporated into Porter's value chain diagram. The result is to make visible how innovation and, by inference, creativity, within the innovation process, run throughout the functions of the firm.

Other silenced voices

Both strategy and marketing have admitted some level of self-criticism from within their most dominant circles accompanied with calls for more attention to social constructions of reality.[62] Our simple efforts at jigsaw puzzling help us understand the various tensions in these fields. Mintzberg's classification, for example, can be fitted into a map of a rational orthodoxy and various heresies (figure 4.3). The map parallels the tensions in the field of marketing shown earlier as figure 4.2.

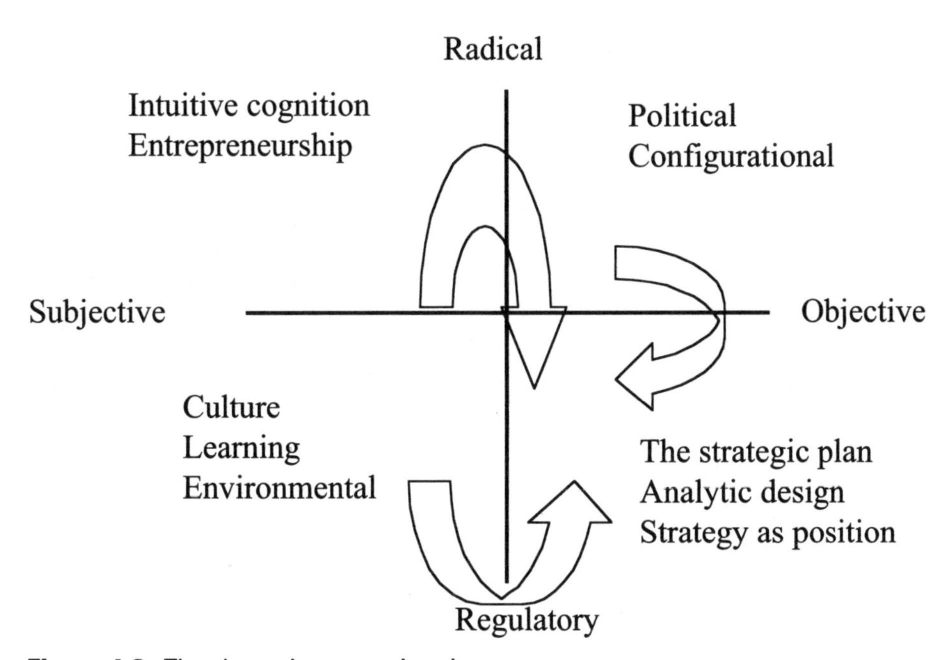

Figure 4.3: The alternative strategic voices

An inspection of figures 4.2 and 4.3 is instructive. In general terms, we can see how creativity can be tamed (even dispensed with) if plans are made that imply their subsequent guaranteed implementation. The defence mechanism available for those who believe such things might run as follows. If the plan fails – the failure may be due to inadequate planning or inadequate implementation.

Both rationality and creativity

We have seen how dominant or orthodox views of strategy and marketing suggest a rational approach to complicated business issues. The dominant views may have underestimated the importance of features requiring creativity, learning, entrepreneurship and trial and acceptance of uncertainties (emergence of unplanned possibilities). Perhaps reinforced by a fear of a return to naive management practice, the orthodoxy rejects these features as too irrational to be incorporated into the orthodoxy. To choose between orthodoxy and any one of the heresies is to confront a dilemma. The future may lie in greater willingness to accept that there is a case for taking some of the currently unfashionable themes far more seriously.

Next steps

Strategy and marketing began as efforts to rescue management from a sort of unthinking and unreflective state. In gaining orthodoxy for rational views, they retained the essential feature of an older orthodoxy of rationality. The journey into the nature of management studies now takes us even deeper into that territory of rationality within the management processes of decision-making (chapter 5).

Notes

[1] Drucker (1955: 53).
[2] Lawrence & Thomas (1971: 7).
[3] Thomas & Gardner (1985: 5).
[4] Mintzberg (1994: 23).
[5] Ohmae (1982: 277).
[6] I followed the European version of *Principles of Marketing* (Kotler et al. 1996) based on Kotler & Armstrong (1994). I doubt if I could have arrived at a single text by the traditional academic method of comprehensively cross-checking the various candidate texts. There is no clear winner. I relied on a judgement based on many informal discussions with those who had taught and/or received marketing education. Having completed the journey, I have no cause for regretting the choice.
[7] Kotler et al. (1996: 29).
[8] This does provide us with a theory of marketing. It suggests we will share some of the theory of the economic sciences to be covered in chapter 10.
[9] Not to be confused with the four Ps of creativity (See Rhodes, 1961, in chapter 2), although the two models have some systems similarities that have never been examined

seriously as far as I am aware. There is yet another different four-P or five-P model of strategy (see Mintzberg, 1994).

[10] The concept came to life for me in one of the most quoted articles of all time, 'Marketing Myopia' (Levitt, 1960), and one of the most quoted questions 'what market are we in?'.

[11] No doubt Kotler would repay far deeper reading for shades of meaning. Remember, it is only the general sense of an important concept that we are after here.

[12] Kotler (1976: 14), also quoted in Biggadike (1981).

[13] George Day claims that 'progress is being made in identifying market-driven businesses' (Day, 1994: 37).

[14] One of the best-selling European texts of all time, sponsored by the Chartered Institute of Marketing, is organized around the premise that 'doing' marketing can be synonymous with effectively preparing and using marketing plans (McDonald, 1995).

[15] 'Place' deals with aspects of placing the product for ease of access. Doyle (1994) glosses it as distribution and adds service and staff to the mix. The mix seems to me best treated as a sensitizing structure for insights about marketing in specific contexts.

[16] See Biggadike (1981) for an insightful overview.

[17] Kotler et al. (1996: 556) drawing on Bennett's *Dictionary of Marketing Terms* (Bennett, 1988).

[18] Aacer (1991; 1996).

[19] Kapferer (1997: 15).

[20] See, for example, Doyle (1994); Lawrence & Thomas (1971).

[21] For example, in Ambler (1997) and Buttle (1996).

[22] 'The plan . . . permits a rational debate about the potential and chances of success' (Doyle, 1994: 81).

[23] Ambler (1997: 179).

[24] Compare the political analyst on an unpopular policy who says 'there's nothing wrong with our policy – we just haven't communicated it to the people'.

[25] Group chief executive of Rentokil Initial, Sir Clive Thompson, in *Marketing Business* (1998: 11), 'Top Table' March, pp. 11–14.

[26] Quoted in Doyle (1994: 215). Simmons (1986) is one of the few theorists who suggests a closer connection between marketing and innovation. Nyström (1990a, b) has developed theory and obtained empirical evidence of the relationship.

[27] Day (1994).

[28] Drucker (1985) claims to have written the first text using the term and dealing with it in its modern business context (Drucker, 1964). He also indicated that Chandler (1966) was the first modern business book to have used the term strategy in its title.

[29] I have returned to his first edition (Ansoff, 1965). He is referring to capital investment theory which does not recognize the possibility of potentially conflicting objectives. He seeks to extend the newer behavioural theory of the firm (Cyert & March, 1963) to incorporate strategic kinds of decision.

[30] Ansoff (1965: 10).

[31] He cites Simon (1960) in support of this.

[32] Ansoff (1965: 18).

[33] Ansoff (1965: 18). Here he points out that he does not intend the term strategic to differentiate those decisions that are important, as operational decisions may have more immediate claims on importance, from time to time. He does, however, suggest that operational decisions are inevitably recurring and routine, whereas strategic decisions are not.

[34] Ansoff approvingly quotes a well-known dictum in Chandler (1962) that 'structure follows strategy'.

[35] This is his departure from capital investment theory, which is based solely on criteria for financial maximizing of capital. His proposal for preserving internal flexibility is to build in a level of liquidity or financial slack, based on appropriate experience. His proposal for external flexibility is to sustain some diversity – perhaps the maxim is 'don't put too many of your eggs in one basket', although the numbers of baskets, and numbers of eggs in each, again cannot be theoretically determined.

[36] Even Mintzberg, his most vociferous critic, recognizes the merits of his analysis of the concept of strategy (Mintzberg, 1994: 44).

[37] In preparing this material, I was reading Ansoff's book in an airport departure lounge. I fell into conversation with a fellow-passenger, who turned out to be an aeronautics engineer. We began talking about Ansoff's book and I explained how some critics thought his main ideas were too structured to reflect any convincing real-life situation. I showed him the infamous decision-flow diagram of the strategic planning process. 'That's just like the blueprints you get in the Aerospace industry,' remarked the engineer. Ansoff had spent his formative working years at the Lockheed Aircraft Corporation.

[38] Pettigrew & Whipp (1991), Porter (1980, 1985, 1990). His third study examines macro-economic forces (Porter 1990).

[39] I have based my remarks on Porter (1985). This, the second of his three major works, includes a concise summary of the salient features of earlier work (Porter, 1980).

[40] Porter represents the rivalry driver as a curved arrow in a box in the centre of a diagram, with the other four forces around the box threatening to invade it (e.g. Porter, 1985: 5).

[41] Porter does not distinguish between financial attractiveness and overall attractiveness (see, e.g. Porter, 1985: 4).

[42] Porter (1985: 11). The terms are explained by Porter in largely self-evident ways.

[43] It is not clear conceptually why there should be three rather than four generic strategies.

[44] Porter (1985: 22) persisting with the familiar military metaphor of strategy.

[45] The bottom line has been transformed into the leading edge in this model.

[46] Although not influencing his main argument, he uses the term technology development, considering it less limiting than the term research and development. This overlooks the overlapping nature of the two concepts.

[47] 'Uncertainty is not often addressed very well in competitive strategy formulation' (Porter, 1985: 446).

[48] Porter (1985: 481).

[49] Mintzberg (1987). The story demonstrates how an orthodoxy, in this case the rational manager paradigm, is reluctant to look for disconfirming evidence, and is strongly critical of those who do.

[50] From Mintzberg (1994: 3–4, *original emphases*).

[51] These labels are reasonably self-explanatory with the exception, perhaps, of the configurational school, which 'seeks to put all the other schools into the contexts of specific episodes in the process' (Mintzberg, ibid.: 4).

[52] Lawrence & Thomas (1971: 7).

[53] 'Formalization here would seem to mean three things: (a) to decompose, (b) to articulate, and especially (c) to rationalize the processes by which decisions are made and integrated in organizations' (Mintzberg, 1994: 13).

[54] Kenichi Ohmae, *The Mind of the Strategist* (1982: 277). I was unable to find such a positive endorsement for creativity in strategy within serious texts written by American or European authors.

[55] Prahalad & Hamel (1990). See Nonaka and Takenchi (1995) for indirect support.

[56] I will spare the reader the complete detail of the journey here as it would add little to the accounts provided earlier. My contention is that any reader following the approach outlined is likely to be reconstructing a common platform of understanding – the actual sample of books will reflect the dominant orthodoxy.

[57] Ansoff matrix; competitive strategies; SWOT analysis; objective setting are all prominent in, for instance, McDonald (1995). Ansoff, Drucker, and Porter are well cited in Doyle (1994).

[58] The practical accounts of Scenario Generation in the Royal Dutch Shell group would be one additional contribution. These are summarized in Schwartz (1996).

[59] Thomas & Gardner (1985).

[60] Similar and subsequent work with owners and directors of small firms gave similar encouraging results, reported to a conference on applications of lateral thinking (Moger, 1994).

[61] Ise (1995).

[62] For example, in the excellent special issue of the *British Journal of Management*, vol. 6, December 1995.

chapter 5
Decision-making Revisited

It would be interesting to know in how many cases where decision-theoretic techniques have been used, and published as having been used, an exact numerical solution was both obtained and precisely applied to real life. Let us be bold and say: this very rarely happens.

Stafford Beer[1]

In teaching decision-making, most business schools concentrate on analytical approaches and techniques; the intuitive aspects of decision-making are downplayed or ignored . . . It is enigmatic that intuitive thinking is virtually absent from the business-school curriculum; not only philosophers but scientists have for centuries recognized the importance of intuition.

J. Daniel Couger[2]

In a culture where only workaholics get to the top, the chairman of Granada is an oddity. He works about thirty hours a week, devoting most Fridays to golf with his eldest son . . . Running a business, even one that stretches from broadcasting to rentals with a stop *en route* at motorway service stations, is so simple that if he were to write a book on the subject 'it would only fill three pages,' he said. 'Most business books are full of gobbledygook.' In his opinion, an executive who has made a dozen clear decisions has had a good week.[3]

Introduction

In the world of management theory, we have already seen the hallmarks of a dominant world-view, or paradigmatic set of beliefs. A fundamental characteristic is the respect in which rationalistic approaches are held. One field of study epitomizes the rationalist orthodoxy in its aspirations, claims, approaches and basic beliefs. That field is concerned with the processes of decision-making.[4] Decision-making has acquired academic credibility as a 'proper' discipline. This happens to coincide with the beliefs expressed by managers generally – that their role is intimately connected with their performance as rational decision-makers.

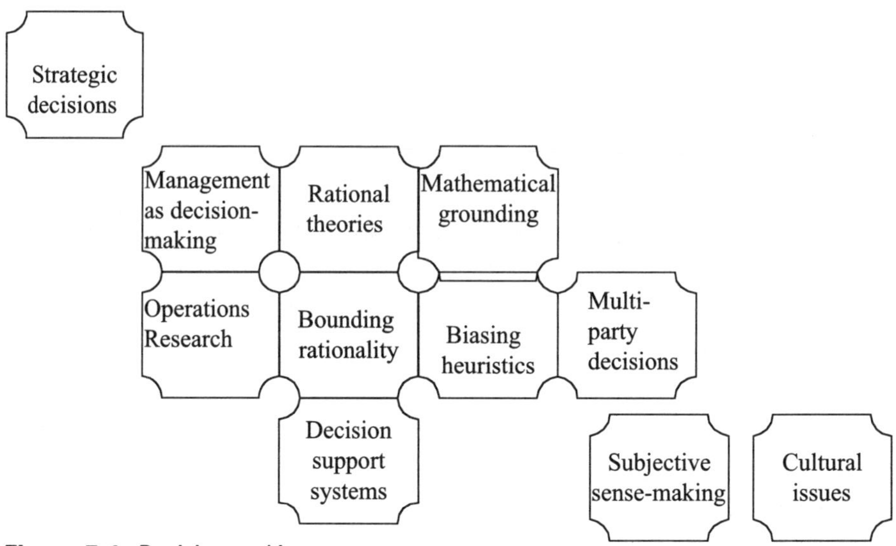

Figure 5.1: Decision-making

The bits of the decision jigsaw

The journey of exploration to find bits of the jigsaw had some features within the process setting it apart from our earlier exercises. The explorations of creativity and innovation were made easier because of prior knowledge of many of the main bits of jigsaw. Marketing and strategy regions also offered short cuts: the handfuls of books observed to be in wide current circulation among managers and students were helpful indicators.

In some contrast, the decision-making territory seemed more remote from the concerns of managerial professionals, for example. In further contrast, the field had a richer set of historical antecedents. Therefore, when the handful of books exercise was conducted, pieces of a jigsaw emerged that assembled into a picture with historical content. This was to be the basis of the platform of understanding of the decision-field.

Eventually the bits of the jigsaw were assembled as shown in figure 5.1. The historical view suggested a family tree, a Darwinian tree, if you like. The tree revealed the rationalistic origins of the subject, including the start of the so-called scientific management school. Among modern developments, the work of Herbert Simon was easy to locate as a most authoritative guide.

The Darwinian tree of decision science

The bits of the jigsaw were assembled into a Darwinian tree of decision science as shown in figure 5.2. The earliest decision-making approaches sprang from the soil of contemporary economic theory, especially at a micro-level of the theory of

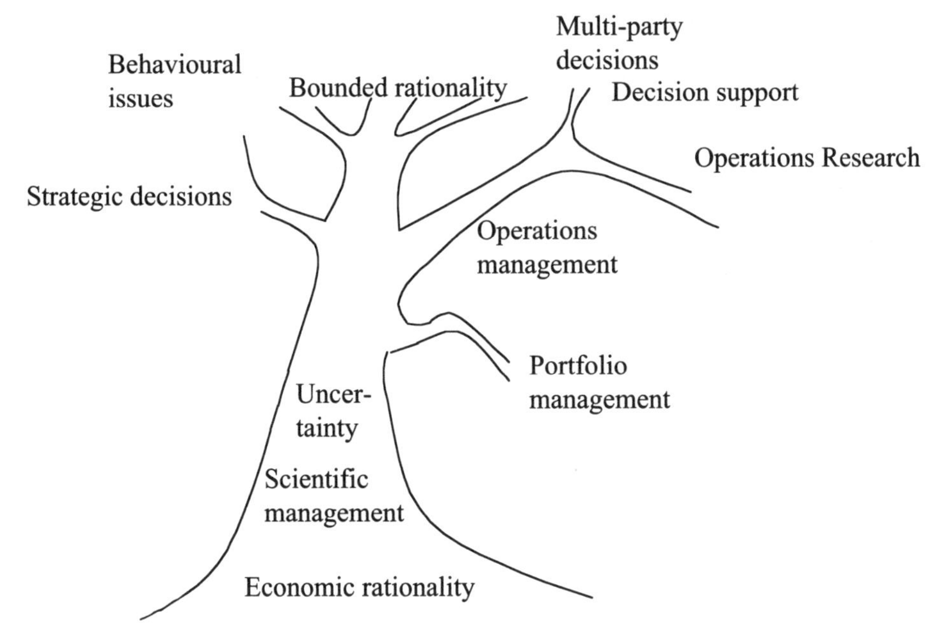

Figure 5.2: Darwinian tree of decision theories

capital investments and portfolio selection theory. Drawing on these traditions, decision theorists set about solving problems under circumstances with less certainty in available information. This gives the tree its first large branch. Theories of risk and uncertainty management emerged. From those theories descended strategy and marketing as further outcroppings. The general evolutionary movement was pushing out to produce 'species' equipped to dealing with increasingly uncertain situations.

An adjacent branch includes organizational operations. The field became known as operations research. At first, its techniques were restricted by the calculating limitations of manual methods. They turned out to be particularly suited for electronic computation methods. Both financial and operational branches, however, were strongly associated with providing the best possible answers or decisions.

A third branch was one that incorporated new theories of organizational decision makers as hybrids descended from rational economic creatures. The behaviours of the species on this branch aspired to rationality while being constrained or bounded by the limitations of human memory and informational processing.[5] They became known as individuals or groups who operated under conditions of bounded rationality in decision-making behaviours. Newer work, of great practical importance, deals with multi-party decisions.

Historical context of decision-theory

The history of organizational decision-theory stretches back to the early attempts to understand and codify the practices of managers in organizations. I have chosen three figures whose work is still widely acknowledged in contemporary accounts.[6]

In the nineteenth century, the principles of a professional approach to management were established particularly through the writings and work of civil engineer Henri Fayol, and Colonel Lyndall Urwick. Fayol has been regarded as the founder of the theory of those processes necessary and sufficient for effective control of organizational systems.[7] His ideas gained greater influence when translated into English, late in his own life. One of his popularizers was Lyndall Urwick, who had attained the rank of Lieutenant-Colonel in the British Army and who later became an academic administrator, and a founder of an influential management consultancy.

These Europeans were aware of the work of an American engineer, Frederick Winslow Taylor, who proposed a way of running companies on scientific lines.[8] His principles in their pure form implied that all the thinking work resided with the manager, who then had to specify unambiguously the precise operations that the workers had to carry out.[9] Taylor's ideas were influential in the rise of measurement and control techniques leading to clipboard and stopwatch methods of time and motion studies.[10]

These ideas were to dominate thinking about management. They had the benefit of high face-validity to early managers and administrators who could connect the theories to the workings of the great military and commercial enterprises of the nineteenth century.[11]

Taylor, Urwick and Fayol were in their day the advocates of a new orthodoxy. The old orthodoxy, we might speculate, was considered to be the approaches of the day to the management of the work force and the organization. Was it not unthinking, and irrational, when compared with the gains made by rational and scientific thinking in the natural sciences? What was missing was general understanding of principles of managerial behaviours, so that the many could learn from the few who had discovered and studied such principles.[12] Taylor was particularly concerned with the inefficiencies produced through lack of application of scientific method to managing work practices.

The emerging orthodoxy rejected managerial behaviours considered irrational and unthinking, and proclaimed the virtues of science in management. Like other sciences, the subject would be amenable to principles that had been derived from conceptual thinking and confirmed in practical experience.

Fayol and his supporters codified principles which even today have some credibility.[13] The principles emphasized the vital importance of a clear line of authority, and co-ordination of interests by function. The principles stood as evidence of management as science, and managers as applied scientific investigators. Taylor and the other early advocates of scientific management did not make a central issue of decision-making. However, once their work had become the accepted orthodoxy, a theory of decision-making was needed. The impetus came from the dominant figure within decision theory, Herbert Simon.[14] Simon provides a thoroughly reliable guide to the vast subject of applied decision-making, through his intellectual dominance and scholarship.

The Impact of Simon and his School on Decision-theory

Herbert Simon

Herbert Alexander Simon was born in 1916, and served with great distinction at Carnegie-Mellon from 1949. He has had the recognized advantage of longevity in a range of fields, some of which he has come to dominate. His writings presented a picture of human decision-making that became the orthodoxy. In essence, he set the agenda for decision-making to be regarded as a rational computational process, helping to popularize a new field of computer science. Among the recognitions and awards, he received the Nobel Prize in 1978 for 'pioneering research into the decision-making process in economic organization'.[15]

Simon had common cause with Taylor, Fayol and Urwick, in seeking to replace mystery and flair in management with rationality and science. His own analysis, however, led him to mistrust the management principles being proposed. His opposition was based on a belief that specific managerial situations required skills at decision-making. More general principles could serve at best as a background to such analysis. He showed that the proposed principles, far from being straightforward guidelines, were somewhat akin to proverbs. While they pointed to widely accepted ways of behaving, these ways had little power to help a manager in a specific situation. Indeed, a close study reveals inherent paradoxes in them. For example, one principle encourages managers to keep to a minimum the number of direct reports. This principle came into focus with much of the corporate flattening and de-layering of the 1980s and 1990s. However, following this principle works against a second principle that advocates the efficiency of fewer rather than greater numbers of direct reports. To flatten the organization is to increase the span of control.[16]

Simon's work put decision-making firmly at the centre of the new orthodoxy. At one point he wrote memorably: 'I shall find it convenient to take mild liberties with the English Language by using "decision-making" as though it were synonymous with "managing"[17] . . . Executing policy, then, is indistinguishable from making detailed policy. For this reason, I shall feel justified taking my pattern for decision-making as a paradigm for most executive activity.'[18]

In this work Simon distinguished between two types of decision, programmed and nonprogrammed. He also contrasted traditional with modern approaches to decision-making. Programmed decisions are found in clerical routines, or habitual responses. Judgement, intuition, creativity and rules of thumb traditionally took nonprogrammed decisions.[19] He argues that the modern approach to routine and programmed decisions involves the newly developed mathematical methods of Operations Research, backed by the power of computation of the developing electronic computers. For nonprogrammed decisions he proposes even more sophisticated computer decision support systems. Here the computer does not provide the correct answer but rather supports a discovery process.

The combination of the interests in human decision-making, and computer support to decision-making, was to prove a fruitful one. Out of it, Simon and co-workers developed a comprehensive theory of information processing. Here is Simon, referring to the basic principle, in one of his most revealing short papers – on computer programs that solve scientific problems. 'No sparks of genius need be postulated to account for human invention, discovery, creation. These acts are acts of the human brain, the same brain that helps us dress in the morning, arrive at the office, and go through our daily chores, however uncreative most of these chores may be. Today we have [evidence that thinking, solving problems and being creative are all based on the same process] . . .

1. Thinking is information processing that involves reading symbols, writing symbols, assembling symbols in relational symbol structures, storing symbols, comparing symbols for identity or difference, and branching on the outcome of the comparison. Intelligence calls for these and only these processes.
2. The processes required for creative acts are the same as those required for all intelligent acts.'[20]

The impact of Simon and his various colleagues and admirers can be detected throughout the decision-making literature. We can look at three particularly significant contributions in the fields of economicsm management and computer science.

Simon's impact on economics and non-optimizing theories

Decision-science was able to claim its orthodoxy through its similarities with that other and longer established orthodoxy, economics. The newer discipline stretched and extended the older one in a way that suggested modifications to it, rather than outright rejection. This part of Simon's work is now widely captured in the term managerial satisficing. It is in this way that Simon's contributions have been recognized in economic texts. Mainstream economic theories assume that managerial decisions are essentially directed towards profit maximizing.[21] Simon drew attention to the distinction between the classical entrepreneurs of economic theory, and managers within large firms. The latter were primarily concerned with satisficing their own needs in the processes of making decisions, which resulted in less than optimal results on a purely economic calculus.

Simon's impact on decision science, behavioural factors, and bounded rationality

The work on satisficing was developed into a more substantial theory of how behavioural factors influenced managerial decisions.[22] Under unprogrammed decision-making conditions, managers are ill-equipped to process all the required information. Even when they seek economically rational results, they are forced into an approximate form of rationality. Decision-making is modelled essentially as a computational process, which explains why the rational laws of economics are replicated within social systems even at the level of individual choices. However, the human mind is not designed in a way that permits full rationality and we have to settle for a limited version. Human frailty requires it. Rationality is the intention, but a restricted or bounded rationality is the operating reality.

Rationality is made more problematic by the recurring structures in firms of sub-units or departments each of which tends to produce its own different sets of goals. From such a starting point, the decision-making found in firms is inferred to be requiring attention to internal factors of which the struggles and coalition-forming politics are always present, and usually important.

This means that mechanisms develop in organizations through which conflicts are hidden away unresolved, in the processes seeking to preserve localized interests.[23] Uncertainties are ever present, and typically are avoided, perhaps by structuring decision-making to make the processes appear rational.[24] The satisficing nature of search is attributed to pressures on executives within a sub-unit to concentrate on solutions that are within their immediate range of experience and competence.[25] The theory presents learning as occurring in a somewhat reluctant way, as the inefficiencies of the decisions force adjustments of goals.

> In summary, organizational goals change in response to the sub-goals or interests of those who form the coalition, to a minimum level of what will be accepted all round, after restricted examination of a limited and selective range of information. In this way, the full complexity of decision-making is reduced to what is practicable, and uncertainty is absorbed.[26]

Simon's impact on computer science and cognition

Co-workers of Simon also developed ideas of human information processing in terms of computing theories.[27] The architectural features proposed for mental activities were described as if they were identical with processes occurring in the functioning of electronic computers.[28] Such a theory gave a sense of direction to research into 'computing' and helped in the rise of artificial intelligence studies. It became much easier to justify computational research if the work could also offer insights into those other little computers, the human brain.

The inter-disciplinary innovation of Operations Research

One of Simon's proposals was for a new science, which improved on decision-making processes of a routinizable kind. He explicitly nominated Operational Research for the job. Operational Research, or OR, had, by the 1980s, like Strategy and Marketing, developed into a professional body with branches in countries all over the world. OR departments were to be found particularly in industries requiring complex analysis of production and logistic processes.[29] More recently, OR departments are transforming themselves into Information Technology, or IT, departments. OR can be seen as a natural accomplice to Scientific Management. The official definition of the OR Society used to appear in each edition of its journal as follows:

> Operational research is the application of the methods of science to complex problems arising in the direction and management of large systems of men, machines, materials and money, in industry, business, and defence. The distinctive approach is to develop a scientific model of the system, incorporating measurements of the factors such as choice and risk, with which to predict and compare the outcomes of alternative decision strategies or controls. The purpose is to help management determine its policy and actions scientifically.[30]

OR, according to one of its leading figures,[31] emerged as an applied scientific discipline under the pressures of the Second World War. One of its novel features was the application of science not within a particular discipline, but essentially in the gaps across disciplines that could only be bridged by a multi-disciplinary team. The first war-time team worked with high impact on tasks such as effective application of the newly discovered Radar technology, and the operational principles of submarine warfare. The interdisciplinary team was headed by a Nobel Laureate in Physics, Professor (later Baron) Blackett. Other members contributed mathematical, medical, military and astrophysics expertise. At such times, when major breakthroughs are called for, 'The scientific description of the whole situation has to be rewritten, which is a job for operational research.'[32]

After the war the new approaches were transferred to peace-time industries and made major operational contributions to steel mills and car plants, chemical refineries, airlines, supermarkets, hospitals, and a host of other complex organizations. The approach established its own dominant techniques with a bias towards mathematics of linear programming yielding theoretical analyses of hypothetical and closed systems.[33] In time, the developing new subject began a serious re-examination of its approaches and achievements. The restlessness within the field led to criticism of the formal and bounded mathematical approaches and an espousal of systems approaches, which we will cover in a later chapter. One systems theorist summed up the discontent, claiming that 'The future of operational research is past'.[34]

At a conference in the late 1980s, the OR community met with social scientists to examine the links between the two. One keynote speaker, a psychologist, suggested that linkages between the two remained rather weak. He also noted that the original ideal of exceptional scientific talent deployed in an interdisciplinary way had faded away 'in favour of a view of OR as a discipline in its own right, with applied mathematics, modelling, and optimization as its substantive and methodological core'.[35]

Judgemental Heuristics in Managerial Decision-making

A major contributor to knowledge of unprogrammed decision-making comes from Max Bazerman, who had tested his ideas with large numbers of managers and business students in two major institutes, first at Boston University, and subsequently at the Kellogg Graduate School of Management of North Western University. Bazerman began with questions posed by the work of Simon's school on bounded rationality. If managers deviate from rationality, how, and under what conditions, might this departure occur? And how might decision processes be improved? He identified an influential series of papers by the research team of Tversky and Kahneman. Their work suggested that Simon's theories of bounded rationality could be confirmed through empirical experiments. People do find ways of limiting the efforts of searching for information, and generally simplifying decision procedures. The simplifying strategies were termed heuristics.[36]

Following Tversky and Kahneman, Bazerman summarized the most common classes of heuristic. Two general biases, and three types of more specific kind of heuristic, were identified. Bazerman went on to explore the consequences of heuristic-driven or judgemental decision-making, with the intention of improving unconsciously applied managerial approaches.

The general heuristics

The first general heuristic is the confirmation trap. It arises because of widespread inclinations for individuals to seek reinforcing evidence for what they believe to be the case.[37] The second general heuristic has overlapping characteristics with the first but is more associated with hindsight. It manifests itself in the way in which we tend to be wise after the event. Once some uncertain event has happened, we tend to forget just how uncertain the outcome had been in advance. In both heuristics, I am forcibly reminded of variations of Murphy's law – 'what can go wrong will go wrong'. While every engineer will be prepared to explain mishaps by invoking Murphy's law, this belief tends to be an after-the-event phenomenon.[38] A related version of the heuristic may be demonstrated by the inability of experts to write manuals remembering what it was like to be a non-expert, and sometimes even to communicate with non-experts. One of the folk stories of the 1990s is of a generation of users unable to reprogramme their video-recorders, who were largely dependent on computer experts such as young children.

The availability heuristic

Items that come to mind vividly are treated more seriously than instances that are not so easily recalled. This heuristic has enormous practical implications in the advertising and marketing professions. Other practical aspects are the consequences of first impressions in or outside recruitment interviews. We can easily find examples of the availability heuristic in the human tendency to assume that if an event tends to be followed by a second event, the former is the cause of the latter.[39]

The representativeness heuristic

These groups of biases have been largely tested to assess individual judgement of statistical events. In general, the biases seem to arise from a failure to appreciate the basic principles of statistics. This is regrettably widespread in the eyes of statisticians.[40] It may well contribute to the behaviour of gamblers in many occupations, including entrepreneurs and innovators. As even unlikely events can occur sometimes, such decisions infrequently produce a spectacular return. Each big hit reinforces the behaviours that produced it. In the long term, entrepreneurs, innovators and casino gamblers vulnerable to the representativeness heuristic will mostly lose out to those who are less vulnerable.

Anchoring and adjustment heuristics

In essence we use these heuristics in a range of everyday decisions which lead to an accept or reject decision. Take the purchase of a car, for example. We may consider other factors, but in some way, we have to answer the question in a way that satisfies ourselves: 'is it worth that much more than the last one I bought?' If we try relating the price to that of our previous car, we are using the earlier experiences to anchor our judgement.[41] This process may appear to be similar to the one followed by a surveyor comparing the location of one point in reference to another. However, the longer the time, the more adjustments we need to account for changing circumstances. The general process seems to be one of insufficient adjustment. We act as if anchored too closely to our past position.[42] Such anchoring is one way of understanding reactions of sellers and buyers of houses, and widely held ideas about bargaining.

Other kinds of decision that can be explained in these terms include economic judgements which ignore the possibility of the unexpected. Sometimes the consequences can be profound, as in the underestimation of decommissioning costs of nuclear power stations. More regularly, the uncertainties are ignored in assessing how to implement new technology.[43] The bias seems to be accompanied by an unjustified confidence in the accuracy of the decisions taken.[44]

The Behavioural Edge of the Platform of Understanding

Simon argued that wherever possible these human biases are best controlled through support from the unbiased information processing of computers. Bazerman interpreted the implications in a more behavioural way. He suggested that, through study, individuals could discover the nature of their heuristic biases, which would lead to more effective judgemental decision-making.[45] Some workers might challenge the place of the more behavioural ideas on the orthodox platform of understanding of decision theory. We suggest the ideas were only peripheral to the platform of understanding of decision science in the 1990s. Some extend the basic concept of bounded rationality. Others suggest a bridge with domains such as creativity. We look briefly at bits of the jigsaw from everyday treatments of risk; the dynamics of escalating commitment to a decision; and a potential role for creative processes in escaping from heuristic biases.[46]

Everyday treatments of risk

Studies of risk and its management pervade the decision-making literature. Once we are aware of the biasing effects of everyday judgements, we have every possibility of a more informed approach. In particular we reach an appreciation of the gap between the declared rationality of decisions and the limitations imposed by assumptions that would otherwise remain unchallenged.

The evidence seems to support the view that managers, without appropriate instruction, share with most other people a need to deal with the uncertainties of life by denying their existence.[47] The informal ways we deal with risk will be strongly influenced by our ways of simplifying the situation. In betting parlance we only gamble on horses we believe might come into the frame. More generally we only attend to information partially and selectively in order to frame a decision. We make sense of our world through less than rational assumptions.

The dynamics of escalating commitment

A fundamental principle of risk assessment is the acceptance of lost or sunk costs. In some contrast, there is a powerful influence in decision-making coming from effort and investments of economic and psychological kinds. The appropriate aphorism for the behaviour might be 'in for a penny, in for a pound'. The dynamics need not be competitive. Many managers and, even more strongly, politicians have a fear of appearing weak and inconsistent. A need to present such a public persona contributes to escalating commitment to publicly expressed views. Bazerman comes up with four forces that may occur singly or in various combinations to reinforce commitment. These are perceptual biases, judgemental biases, impression management and competitive rationality.[48]

The role of creativity in escaping decision biases

Theories of decision-making use a vocabulary of framing, which can be carried over without difficulty into the vocabulary of creativity, blockbusting and paradigm switching. Knowledge of the irrationalities produced through the biasing effects of heuristics can be discovered and perhaps adjusted for. The approach can be supported by approaches for stimulating creativity.[49] Bazerman illustrated the connection between creativity and decision-making by placing them in the context of research investigations. At one end of a continuum, there are routine or highly predictable activities. In contrast, there are people engaged with ideas and activities that are so much to the far side of orthodoxy as to be considered absurd. Research in the middle ground, where new ideas are valued and rated as creative, has been described as essentially intriguing and interesting.[50] In that region, assumptions are effectively challenged, so that the unconscious biases of decision-making heuristics are revealed.[51]

Multi-party Decision-making

The complexities of decision-making are compounded when we consider those real-life decisions within which there are various parties who do not necessarily have the same needs and requirements. Every family has experienced situations which concern who eats what when, how loud is too loud for music to be played, and so on. Boards of directors, and project teams have to find ways of dealing with the different views of their memberships. In principle, these social groups have the basis of a shared set of values, and a desire for decisions to be mutually beneficial. Even these groups are often baffled at the difficulties that can lead from disagreements to disputes to highly charged conflicts, to irreconcilable breakdowns of the group. Yet, within the world of economic groupings, there are situations in which the disputes are even more central to the interpersonal dynamics. These include formal and informal negotiations ranging from the personal to the global.

Game theory[52]

Game theory has concerned itself with developing understanding of processes and outcomes of decision-making involving more than one individual. The great applied mathematician Von Neumann helped codify the theory in the early days of Operations Research. Thanks to game theory, we have become sensitized to some of the most important issues facing social groups. These include the tensions between self-interested action and altruism; co-operation and competition.

In its most familiar form matrices are set up which reveal the choices of players. One of the best known is the prisoners' dilemma matrix. Imagine two prisoners kept in isolation. The authorities are concerned only with getting prisoners to confess. Each prisoner may incriminate the other, say nothing, or confess. What happens after each prisoner has chosen depends on the decisions both have taken. If each prisoner remains silent, the authorities find a way of giving him or her a minor sentence. If one prisoner remains silent and the other makes an accusation, the accuser is released immediately and the other prisoner gets a heavy sentence. If both prisoners make accusations, they each receive a moderate sentence. The prisoner contemplating what to do becomes aware of a dilemma. So do players of the game as an intellectual or learning exercise. What is the course of action destined to produce the best result for the individual? The best result, and a possible one, is immediate freedom. However, this only happens if one prisoner accuses the other, who has chosen to remain silent. As it happens, your freedom also results in the other prisoner receiving the worst of sentences.

The simplest game is a once-and-for-all event. In that case, the dilemma is evident. If each prisoner could be confident that the other would collaborate, each would receive a minor sentence. If each were expecting to be accused by the other, the best that would happen would follow from following the accusatory line. The moral implications are that mutual trust is to be preferred, although it may not be possible. The game gets more interesting if it continues over a large number of trials. Now the hypothetical prisoners have to take into account the possibility that earlier decisions will influence subsequent ones. It turns out that players spend less of their infinitely long lives in jail if they work out the benefits of collaborating. Even in this game, the immediate rewards of selfish behaviour may lead to a switch from collaboration to a break for freedom. The first to switch to accusation can be pretty sure that the other has continued to collaborate. This is a version of getting your retaliation first, a tactic not unknown in many confrontations.

One well-known version involves groups of managers and management students in a version of the prisoners' dilemma game. Teams are invited to bid for blue or red counters. If teams both bid blue, they win moderate amounts; if one team bids red and one blue, the red bidding team wins all. If both teams bid red, each wins smaller amounts. Teams play several rounds and may consult between rounds. Regardless of the team's backgrounds, the team-climate within the game usually becomes very serious.[53] Teams want to win. Team discussions quickly reveal the dilemma. The genuine desire to be collaborative usually loses out as fears grow of being suckered.[54] Almost all teams (even if some of the players are experienced) produce lose–lose results. The main winner is competition over collaboration.

Such experiences illustrate the tensions between self-interest, competition and collaboration in managerial contexts. They provide powerful evidence that self-interest may produce lose–lose outcomes.[55] We must be careful not to extrapolate the results too far. Game theory suffers from the limitations of its pre-set assumptions. There tends to be a whiff of a rigged game about the initial conditions. The players have no scope for reshaping the rules of the game through their creativity or persuasiveness. Negotiators concerned with resolving disputes in the real world have argued that the constraints make the whole subject unhelpful for their needs.[56]

Raiffa's bounded rational approach to negotiations

Raiffa has made many contributions to a rational theory of decision-making. He has also sought to find ways of making the subject more accessible to practical decision-makers, including negotiators. He has mapped out sticking points or alternatives to settlement that might play a part in the negotiations, the interests of the parties, and the relative importance of each party's interests.[57]

The approach moves away from the game theory in which assumptions are accepted as constraints, and information as essentially accurate and unchanging. Exploring the interests of the parties can be a highly creative process in which the acceptability zone is defined and redefined. Whereas the decision-makers in game theory are passive searchers for the biggest share of a fixed pie, Raiffa has provided us with means of searching for ways of enlarging the pie to the greater satisfaction of the parties involved. These approaches depart from the economic constraint assuming that one party gains only at the expense of another party. One researcher summarized the process as follows: 'Integrative agreements [often] involve the development of novel alternatives. Hence, it is proper to say that they usually emerge from creative problem-solving.'[58]

A simple example from political negotiations arises in the need to bring hostile groups together. One group refuses to talk in the presence of the other. Various means of making progress have to be tried. They might involve creatively redefining what is meant by 'talks'. So there arise talks about talks. Or maybe pre-talk talks. In common with other creative activities, an impossibility is treated as a state of mind rather than an absolute logical statement of proof that no progress can be made. By such means have the bitterest conflicts sometimes been resolved, in boardrooms and battlefields.

Electronic decision-support systems

Ever since Simon's pioneering studies, computerized decision-support systems have attracted practical and theoretical attention. Purveyors of computerized management systems have claimed a range of practical benefits. One leading research team summed up the rationale: 'GroupWare is [a] new breed of computer technology that targets the trouble spots for team productivity. Besides supporting information access, GroupWare can radically change the dynamics of group interactions by improving communication, by structuring and focusing problem solving efforts, and by establishing and maintaining an alignment between personal and group goals.'[59]

Electronic decision-support can be conceived as operating at the level of the individual, team or organization. Its evaluation is therefore as complex as assessing the impact of major technological change at all organizational levels.[60] It seems likely that attention to date has concentrated more on means of enhancing communications than on enhancing decision-making and information processing.[61] As in any emerging field, the available empirical evidence is open to interpretation in more than one way. Enthusiasts are already claiming that electronic brainstorming can enhance the efforts of a group to reach effective decisions.[62] Other workers have begun the trickier issue of working out the contingencies within any specific application, so that managers in organizations will receive more precise and accurate advice regarding which systems help which decisions, and why.

Among the contextual issues is the influence of the medium on the process. Some media, such as face-to-face video conferencing, appear warmer and more intimate. Other media appear cooler and less intimate.[63] It seems likely that the computerized decision-support systems will achieve their stated intentions in helping overcome the inadequacies of humans in processing large data sets within decision tasks. The challenges will be in helping the individuals and social groups to challenge their frames in decision-making and thereby lead to reframing and creative insights.

Decision-theory Revisited

The platform of understanding, while deriving from multiple sources, was presented in simple format in the Darwinian tree of figure 5.1. A more 'scientific' decision-making has helped rescue managers from the excesses of irrational decisions. This orthodoxy was itself supported through the great influence of the founding fathers of scientific management. A similar respect for scientific methods was found in the development of the Operations Research movement.

Yet there was also evidence that the scientific approach to decision-making was not completely satisfactory. Simon and his successors emphasized the limitations of human cognitive capacities. These limitations became more acute as the most critical decisions had to be taken under conditions of high environmental

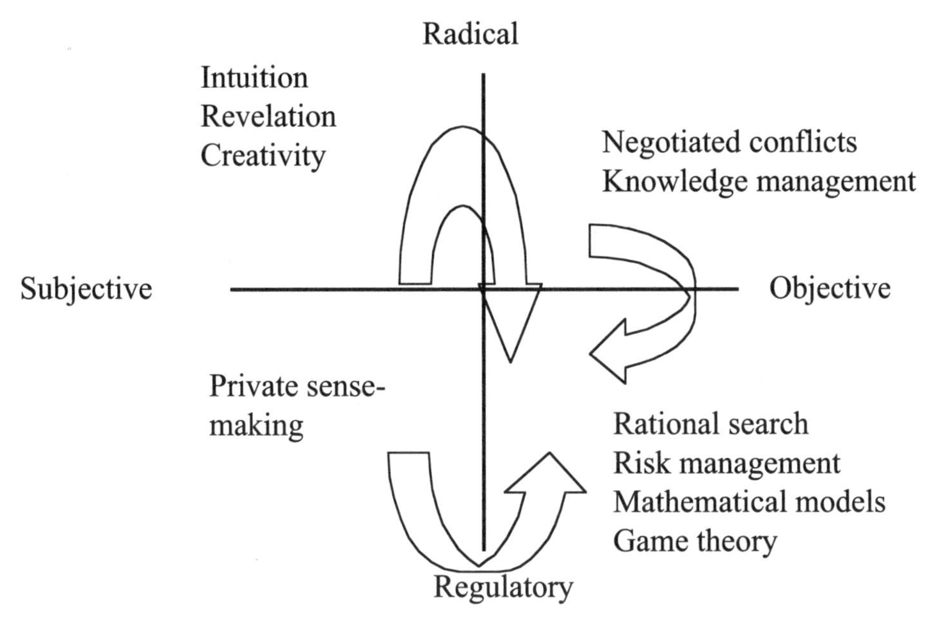

Figure 5.3: The alternative decision voices

uncertainty. We have consistently found the theory of paradigmatic dominance instructive at this point to explore these tensions. We might expect to find that unorthodox views have to be rejected or 'tamed'. This is what seems to have happened within decision studies. These views are shown in figure 5.3. The taming processes are variants of those considered in earlier chapters.

Simon recognized the need for creativity in non-routine decision-making. It became important for him to develop theoretical explanations for creativity as something that could be left to computers. [64] Bazerman seeks to introduce more behavioural dimensions into decision-making, but in a way that accommodates creativity in a 'safe' bit of a spectrum of decision possibilities. The intuitive and outrageous decisions of business tycoons are also tamed by the argument that these are exceptional people with exceptional talents. A more scientific approach gives the rest of us a chance to compete with the wunderkinder.

Superstitions, divination and other heresies

It is consistent with orthodoxy to treat alternative beliefs not just as different, but as wrong, inadequate, misguided, and perhaps even evil. A better approach might be to examine those heresies perhaps because they may lead to a complete personal transformation of belief. Or, more likely, because such a study helps us become sensitized to aspects of our own beliefs that are influenced by dangerously concealed assumptions.

An Experiment with a Decision Approach of Non-Western Origins

What happens if we choose to take seriously a form of decision-making that does not fit the dominant norms of Western culture? The results may be surprisingly relevant. I will illustrate a specific form of divination, the ancient Chinese approach involving consultation of an oracle, the *I Ching*. This approach has been selected for the simple reason that the dominant rationalistic view we have been exploring is increasingly a world-wide perspective. Therefore, the *I Ching* may be increasingly considered outmoded – not unlike the way Simon considered traditional Western decision-approaches to be intuitive, unpredictable in outcome, and outmoded.[65]

The *I Ching*, or the *Book of Changes*, is believed to have its origins in methods used 3,000 years ago in China to provide leaders and state officials with advice in their affairs. In essence, the *I Ching* provides a set of procedures for studying present circumstances, contemplating changes, and planning the future. The preliminary stage of study involves a way of selecting the description of the present, and the components within it that are to be studied, for their change significance. The present and the changes lead to the identification of the future to be studied. The future is therefore made up of the components of the present treated as unchanging, together with components that have changed. Each possibility, present or future, has six facets, and may therefore be thought of as a hexagram. Each facet may be represented in one of two ways, giving sixty-four possibilities. Thus, the *I Ching* contains information on sixty-four hexagrams. Within each hexagram there is a description of the implications of six change possibilities, one for each of the six facets.[66]

The procedure involves extracting two of sixty-four possible states, one representing the present and one the future. There follows a study of the changes indicated in both present and future states. The changes are given within the procedure for identifying the present state.

The oracle is approached with a question to which a decision is required. In one trial, I asked 'How might modern decision-making be improved?'[67] The appropriate rituals led me to an instruction to concentrate on modest certainties, which will be the basis for future success. For management of decision-making: 'Keep everything simple, straightforward, rational and strictly accountable. Boring but imperative.' As for creative judgement, 'In the field of everyday business your creative judgement is out of focus and misaligned. In the realm of imagination it is best kept quiet. Better still, shelve the whole lot and get on with something safe and relevant to the here and now.'

The overall note of caution and staying close to what is current reality is strongly advised throughout the present hexagram. Its one change or link with the future again urged that 'Your wings are not strong enough to undertake that kind of flight. Do not attempt it. Stay with convention for the time being.'

Turning to the future hexagram, the oracle instructed me to see the change as taking me into unfamiliar territory. Now the time is auspicious for creative judgement. 'This is a time you will come into contact with many new ideas. Be open-minded and receptive. Share information and ideas. The possibility for future creative judgement is auspicious. Recognize you are a guest in somebody else's "home" in every sense. Be prepared to take your shoes off, as it were.'

I Ching *as a way to reveal new decision-making possibilities*

The experiment with the *I Ching* is a way of challenging the orthodoxy. Our intention is to understand why *I Ching* is ignored by the orthodox paradigm. It stands for other 'heresies' such as Edward De Bono's discovery model of Lateral Thinking. The first point to be made is that in use it seemed to lead to rather evocative and valuable ideas. Discovery processes seem to be as productive when supported by the *I Ching* as when supported by more orthodox decision support systems. If, then, such systems are indistinguishable under some conditions from more reputable ones, are there benefits to be gained from their study? How and why have they been superseded by the new 'rational' scientific modes of decision-making? Are managers any more 'scientific' when following a more orthodox set of principles (Ansoff's for example)?

Here we are certainly approaching things they don't teach at business school. Yet, once we become aware of other possibilities we might become more aware that orthodox decision-support systems conceal the uncertainties and unknowables. By remaining open to the rationale for such systems we increase the scope for a deeper understanding of currently 'silenced' voices in decision-making. Creativity can be reintroduced, not as a computer output, but as a vital form of managerial intuition, for example.

From dominant culture to multicultural perspectives

The *I Ching* experiment serves an additional purpose. Our studies of aspects of managerialism have revealed a dominant view of the world that at times excludes all other possible views. *I Ching* reminds us that there are other cultures, other views. The silenced cultural views are not just those from geographic regions, but from earlier times. The old may be rejected as having outdated cultural norms. In our next chapter, we approach more closely to the nature of cultural differences, with particular emphasis on corporate cultures.

Notes

1 Beer (1966: 225).
2 Couger (1995: 386).
3 *Independent on Sunday*, 3 December 1995, p. 5.
4 Strategy might be seen as an alternative candidate. However, strategy has tended to confirm its own legitimacy by reference to decision-theory.
5 Specifically the limitations of short-term memory.

[6] Pugh (1971) provides an excellent set of readings on the founders of classical management theory and Thomas (1993) offers a readable sociological account.

[7] Gray (1984) provides a revised English language text of Fayol's *General and Industrial Management.*

[8] Morgan (1985) gives a nice account of Scientific Management and Taylorism.

[9] See Pugh (1971).

[10] Associated particularly with Frank and Lilian Gilbreth (Gilbreth, 1911).

[11] The systems were not simply applicable to Western capitalist organizations. For example, Marx chose to justify his case for the ultimate destruction of capitalism on the economic superiority of communism, and the scientific inevitability of its revolutionary triumph.

[12] Fayol points out that business deals with economic matters, so that more general moral and religious rules, while not to be contradicted in business affairs, offered insufficient guidance.

[13] Thomas (1993) traces a subtle shift in emphasis over time. Fayol emphasized what today would be described as both structural and behavioural aspects of management. Later, perhaps through Taylor's influence, the principles became more structural. Fayol's ideas of 'esprit de corps', initiative and equity were quietly dropped.

[14] Simon (1997) is an outstanding summary of his later work, with more than adequate accounts for the serious researcher of his extensive interests.

[15] *Chambers Biographical Dictionary*, 1990 edn.

[16] See Thomas (1993) for a recent and clear account of Simon's attack on the classical principles.

[17] Simon (1960) quoted from Pugh (1971: 189).

[18] Simon (ibid.: 193).

[19] Simon's own terms (ibid.: 196).

[20] Simon (1986: 4). The first of these two hypotheses should be considered the major one in setting the scene for the computer model of human information processing. The second gives insights into Simon's beliefs about creativity.

[21] Or towards optimizing on other economically computable variables such as sales revenue (Baumol, 1959), growth (Marris, 1963) or managerial utility (Williamson, 1963). See Gough & Hill (1979) for a clear and brief summary of these theories.

[22] The original work, of stunning intellectual power, can be found in *A Behavioral Theory of the Firm*, by Simon's colleagues at Carnegie-Mellon, Richard Cyert and James March (1963).

[23] One of the explanations for the existence of ambiguities within organizational life.

[24] March & Simon (1958) proposed that in bureaucracies the behaviours of sub-units reinforce and sustain the sub-unit perspectives, thus reducing the capability of the entire organization to act in a more comprehensively rational manner.

[25] An interesting experiment supporting the theory of limited search procedures has recently been reported (Wood & Gaston, 1996).

[26] Cyert & March (1963), quoted in Pugh, Hickson & Hinings (1971: 84).

[27] Notably Allen Newell, with whom he collaborated for many years. Newell & Simon (1972) is a particularly important contribution.

[28] The mind is treated as a serial system consisting of an active processor, input (sensory) and output (motor), and internal long-term and short-term memory and externalized memory. Symbol manipulation occurs by 'writing' processes etc. Whatever the intent, the outcome seems to be a comprehensive acceptance among later computer scientists that the mind *computes*: 'computation, and all that it entails regarding rule-governed transformations on intentionally interpreted symbolic expressions applies just as literally to mental activity as it does to the activity of digital computers' (Pylyshyn, 1979: 435).

[29] It is significant that decision-making has not become institutionalized as a professional body.

[30] Quoted in Dando & Sharp (1978: 940), and Willmott (1989: 67).

[31] Stafford Beer, a colleague and mentor for many years. I have reconstructed this account in great part from many discussions with him, and from his work, especially Beer (1966, 1979).

[32] Beer (1966: 41).

[33] This view can be found in influential books by pioneers of the subject (e.g. Churchman, Ackoff & Arnoff, 1957).

[34] Ackoff (1979), who was exploring the importance of creativity in problem-solving at the time (Ackoff, 1978; Ackoff & Vergara, 1981).

[35] Burgoyne (1979: 4).

[36] The term implies some kind of discovery process. It comes from the same Greek work that provides us with the exclamation 'Eureka!'. Simon had referred to heuristic problem-solving as the modern replacement for judgement, intuition and creativity in non-programmed decision-making.

[37] In the popular creativity literature a similar effect is often mentioned under some such term as the self-fulfilling prophecy, mindset, or perceptual blind spot.

[38] In Wales it is said that after a rugby defeat, every supporter (most of the nation) believes he or she could have done a better job in picking the team than the 'Big Five' (selectors). The hindsight heuristic afflicts sports fans all over the world.

[39] *Post-hoc, procter-hoc*, as the illustration of this classic non-sequitur used to be taught.

[40] Perhaps more people would be able to avoid the representativeness bias if statistics teachers were more aware of the hindsight bias in their teaching methods.

[41] Benchmarking is a form of anchoring.

[42] It may be prudent to beware the dangerously seductive metaphoric nature of this description of *anchoring, adjustment, position* and so on, which provides a description of the heuristic without adding understanding of the mechanisms involved in the process.

[43] Subsequently the process leads to accusations of incompetence by others not directly involved, often in terms suggestive of the hindsight heuristic, and denial by those involved. See Bazerman (1994), Tversky & Kahneman (1974) and Perrow (1984) for more detailed accounts based on heuristics of judgemental decision-analysis. Psychological explanations have been offered by Festinger (1957) and Argyris (1990).

[44] In groupwork the phenomenon of group polarization can sometimes lead to *the risky shift* or its converse in decision-making. *Groupthink* (Janis, 1972) seems a related phenomenon.

[45] Bazerman drew on Lewin (1947), a model considered in part three as the most influential in the change literature, based on the three steps of *unfreezing, changing and refreezing*.

[46] I have drawn particularly from Bazerman (1994) in this section. His most significant contribution in the context of this book is the connection he draws between judgemental decision-making and creativity.

[47] There is plenty of evidence that seems to build a coherent picture of the biases of uncertainty reduction. However, I find many of the laboratory experiments contrived and difficult to connect with practical managerial decision-making. A similar accusation might be made regarding the demonstration of mindsets within creativity training, of which the famous nine-dots problem (Scheerer, 1963) is a representative example.

[48] I note that the model has similarities to a well-known one on the dynamics of short-term memory (Atkinson & Shiffrin, 1971). The model led to an empirically derived taxonomy of blocks to creativity (Rickards & Jones, 1991).

[49] Rickards (1990).

[50] 'That's interesting' is a well-known theme that can sensitize researchers towards productive research endeavours (Davis, 1971). Bazerman successfully 'tames' the less orthodox categories for acceptance within the orthodox decision paradigm, a nice example of 'abstracted empiricism' as a strategic weapon.

[51] Robin Hogarth, another major researcher into decision theory, has also identified the importance of creativity within human judgemental processes. However, in one of his most influential non-technical texts (Hogarth, 1987) he does not attempt any integration of the two domains. Bazerman (1994) takes a first step towards this integration.

[52] My handfuls of books directed me to synoptic summaries of game theory in Barnes (1995); Bazerman (1994); and Zartman (1976).

[53] Mostly from professional business groups or business students. The literature suggests a similar pattern of behaviours across many other kinds of teams.

[54] Presumably there is projection of one's own less admired impulses on to others. Teams justify deceit to themselves by inferring signs of deceit in the other team's actions.

[55] Barnes (1995) gives a particularly clear account, albeit from outside the game-theory paradigm.

[56] Zartman (1976) contains several interesting articles, of which the one by Bartos is particularly instructive.

[57] Raiffa (1982).

[58] Pruitt (1983) quoted in Bazerman (1994).

[59] Nunamaker et al. (1996: 418).

[60] Nunamaker et al. (1996) identified four categories of support system: idea generation (including electronic brainstorming); idea organization; prioritizing; and strategic or policy development. Lim & Benbasat (1996) argued that the taxonomy should recognize the importance of judgement, and proposed information exchange, idea-generation and problem-representation.

[61] Benbasat & Lim (1993).

[62] Gallupe & Cooper (1993), drawing on the much quoted review by DeSanctis & Gallope (1987). A cautionary note was sounded in Rickards (1994).

[63] Daft & Lengel (1986).

[64] His early concern seems to have been that creativity as manifest by intuitive business leaders was capricious and not easily managed with respect to its timing or risk evaluation.

[65] Damian-Knight (1986). As far as I can recall, I was sent a copy of the book by the author, some years ago, after a telephone discussion about decision-making and creativity. I am grateful to my graduate colleague Frederick Hsu for additional guidance.

[66] I found it easy to understand, but only after I had worked through a few trials.

[67] A kind of decision about decisions. I also found the system instructional for more practical decisions such as 'How can I market this product?' The results, being personal, did not seem to have the same illustrative impact as a more general question relevant to the chapter's theme. The selection gave me hexagram 62 with change in the sixth (top) line for the present (the preponderance of the small). The future was given as hexagram 56 (travelling business people).

chapter 6
Culture and Climate Issues

There is a theory that internationalization will create, or at least lead to, a common culture worldwide. This would make the life of international managers much simpler. People point to McDonald's or Coca-Cola as examples of tastes, markets, hence cultures, becoming similar everywhere. There are, indeed, many products and services becoming common to world markets. What is important to consider, however, is not what they are and where they are found physically, but what they mean to people in each culture.

Fons Trompenaars[1]

Organizational culture researchers do not agree about what culture is, or why it should be studied. They do not study the same phenomenon . . . No wonder, then, that research on organizational culture has sometimes been dismissed as a 'dead end', as unrelated to mainstream theory, or as a fad that has failed to deliver on its promises.

Peter Frost[2]

Climate affects organizational and psychological processes such as communication, problem solving, decision-making, conflict handling, learning, and motivation, and thus exerts an influence on the efficiency of the organization, on its ability to innovate, and on the job satisfaction and well-being that its members can enjoy.

Göran Ekvall[3]

Corporate creativity is highest not where self-styled geniuses advertise themselves vociferously, but when a flow of original ideas encounters intelligent and constructive feedback, along with people willing to push these ideas through and complete every last detail of their implementation.

Charles Hampden-Turner[4]

Introduction

I carried out a handful of books study of popular culture in the course of preparing this chapter. The experiment can be repeated by visiting any bookshop with a general management section. Look through recent examples of the 'how to transform your company' kind. Each of the books shares a format of promising a route to corporate excellence. The book is likely to contain examples of successful organizations with details of their corporate cultures. It will also indicate how you will be able to benchmark the culture of your own organization. Follow some simple check-list and you will be able to locate your company into one of several cultural types. There may follow advice on 'choosing an appropriate culture', and on moving from less desirable to more desirable cultures.

The repeated claims of a new answer from a proliferation of books may be enough to arouse suspicions. But how should we evaluate such claims? For that, we need to take a closer look at the platform of understanding of culture, and at material that is rarely included in the more popular texts.

Culture and climate as important bits of the organizational studies jigsaw

Culture has become a widely discussed concept with practical managerial implications. At the corporate level, successful companies are popularly believed to have special cultures of excellence. At this level, efforts are being made to understand culture in order to find ways in which poor cultures may be transformed into excellent ones. At a more global level there is growing interest in national cultural differences and how these differences impact in multicultural environments of international organizations. Each of these reasons makes culture an important piece of the organizational studies jigsaw. Fortunately, the practical interest can be connected to a body of more academic knowledge from a range of disciplines including anthropology, social and cognitive psychology and sociology.

Organizational climate has received less attention in organizational studies, and is sometimes considered to be an aspect of culture. Furthermore, climate is a topic that has attracted more attention than culture among researchers into creativity.[5] These reasons justified a journey of exploration to gain a deeper understanding of both constructs.

The bits of the culture and climate jigsaw

Each of our journeys of exploration had its unique features. For the studies of climate and culture I had already collected pieces of the jigsaws from earlier journeys in areas such as creativity, outlined in chapter 2.[6] These experiences helped me as I set about collecting handfuls of books during a visit to the business school library.[7] From these books, the culture and climate jigsaws became clearer. The two topics were far from distinct, and it was possible to see that the pieces could be split into two jigsaws, or seen as a more complex larger puzzle, as shown in figure 6.1. It is still easier to treat the pieces as coming from two jigsaws, although the journeys might be seen as criss-crossing adjacent territories.

Our first bits of the culture jigsaw deal with the definitional confusions. The next sections will cover the materials on culture. These will be followed by sections on corporate climate. The culture work is more sociological in its grounding, and feeds through to a related body of work on transformational leadership in the next

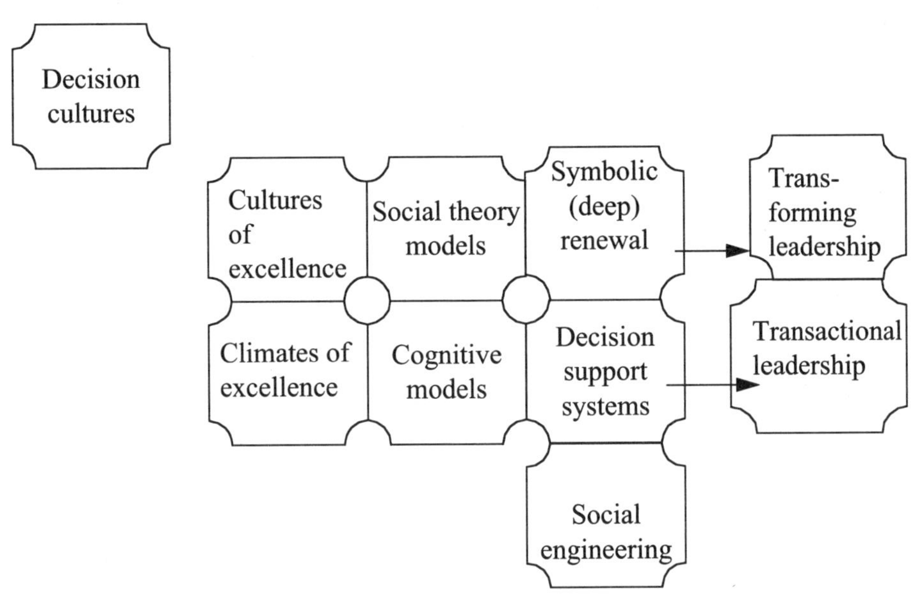

Figure 6.1: Cultural bits of the jigsaw

chapter. The climate material is closer to the orthodoxy of cognitive psychology, and again has a connection with features in the chapter on leadership, namely those of a cognitive psychological orientation. We will be better able to see that culture studies have come from more sociological research traditions, and therefore have had poor alignment with the dominant managerial orthodoxy. The climate studies have come from a branch of cognitive psychology that is closer to that orthodoxy. By searching for the assumptions behind the claims, we have a means of evaluating the popular books on culture transformation. It seems likely that the proposals will be better at identifying and labelling cultures than in providing specific rules that any organization can immediately apply to good effect.

Defining culture

The handfuls of books gave a variety of definitions of culture. One study catalogued over a hundred definitions and then suggested this comprehensive summary: 'Culture consists of patterns, explicit and implicit of and for behavior acquired and transmitted by symbols, constituting the distinctive achievements of human groups, including their embodiment in artefacts: the essential core of culture consists of traditional (i.e. historically derived and selected) ideas and especially their attached values: culture systems may, on one hand, be considered as products of action, on the other, as conditioning elements of future action.'[8]

Subsequent definitions have not added to such a comprehensive description.[9] Ed Schein is an influential change practitioner and theorist. We will come across his work again in chapter 8. His definition reveals his own preference for a more psychologically oriented view:

'Culture is:

1. A pattern of shared assumptions,
2. invented, discovered, or developed by a given group,
3. as it learns to cope with its problems of external adaption and internal integration,
4. that has worked well enough to be considered valid, and therefore,
5. is to be taught to new members of the group as the
6. correct way to perceive, think, and feel in relation to those problems.'[10]

Schein has also been associated with a less formal definition of culture that amounts to 'the way we do things around here'.[11] This is a wonderful condensation of the complex construct of culture. Its simplicity makes it a good starting point for managers asking the question 'what is this culture thing all about?'. Unfortunately, the definition immediately illustrates a difficulty. It is almost identical to a definition of climate that has been suggested by other workers.[12]

Other simple definitions have been offered. One of the books that drew attention to the importance of culture is *In Search of Excellence*, by Peters and Waterman. Culture is defined once, and extremely tersely, in two words, 'shared values'.[13] Another brief yet evocative definition comes from a pioneer of culture research, Geert Hofstede,[14] who suggested that culture is 'software of the mind'.

Overall, the proliferation of definitions reminds us of the state of research in the other topics we have explored. We can expect some of the confusions to become clearer as we see more of the way in which the definitions are put to work.

Historical Influences in Culture's Platform of Understanding

Geertz's thick descriptions

A dominant influence on organizational culture has come from anthropological field studies. Thus, the approaches were those of the intrepid pioneering researchers who sought out understanding of tribal practices by immersing themselves in native cultures. The approaches were observational and participative.[15]

An important influence, still frequently cited in organizational literature, is the American Clifford Geertz. His fieldwork led to theories of comparative religion, environmental issues, and particularly theories on the nature of culture. In essence, Geertz replaced the collection of 'objective' facts with interpretations of the symbolism of observed actions as a major product of research investigations. One of his most influential papers suggested that cultural studies require the construction of 'thick' descriptions. This has inspired a generation of organizational researchers to experiment with anthropological studies, with organizational 'tribes' as the focus of the field trips.

Deal and Kennedy

Allan Kennedy, who had been a colleague of Peters and Waterman at McKinsey's consulting organization, had been cited in *In Search of Excellence*. Together with Terrance Deal, he helped popularize the term corporate culture. Although sharing *ISOE*'s enthusiasm for the benefits of a strong culture, their work was a more conceptual examination of modern management as essentially the development and sustaining of desired cultural conditions, including shared values, through symbolic actions. Their ideas have remained influential.[16]

A symbolically sensitive manager seeks to achieve goals indirectly rather than directly. Motivation is subtle and permitted to arise through skilful use of stories, images, and consolidating shared values needed for achieving the goals. Their ideas read today as a cultural expression of the American dream of individual autonomy and entrepreneurship, aligned with corporate visions and goals. They can be found re-expressed in many consultancy and popular books on culture change and business transformation.[17]

Schein's interventions

Edgar Schein has developed an approach to cultural analysis that sits somewhere between the cognitive symbolic approaches.[18] Schein, by discipline an organizational psychologist, has written extensively and lucidly about procedures whereby external agents can intervene. His methodology is that of process consultation. The process consultant is recognizable as an investigator engaged in building a conceptual model of the organization's culture. The prevailing belief systems within the organization are studied and explored.[19] The approach helps the organizational players to uncover important and possibly unhelpful assumptions on corporate life.[20] Schein describes simply the operational procedures associated with process consultancy, as well as its underlying rationale.

Harrison and Handy

In the 1970s, the Irish business theorist and philosopher Charles Handy wrote an unusual and influential book on management.[21] Handy took an issue-centred approach. The upshot was a rather loosely organized grouping of topics, connected to more mainstream thinking through the author's knowledge of theory and practice.[22]

Among the issues that Handy introduced was the notion of organizational cultures based on the work of Roger Harrison, an American-domiciled researcher and consultant. Harrison identified and classified four cultures using self-reports of organizational actors. Each culture was associated with an organizational structure. The basic cultures were the role culture, the task culture, the power structure and the constellation or atomistic culture.[23]

The role culture is associated with the classical pyramid or hierarchy of control. Its rules are enshrined in its numerous codified statements and policies. The task culture is that of the project team or task-force. The power culture is that of the powerful chief ruling by edict, and dispensing power to lesser chiefs, operating in a spirit of fierce rivalry and no little fear. Unlike the role culture there are few written rules. The constellation or atomistic culture can be found where a group of like-minded individuals can operate relatively independently and without hierarchies. Such informal networks appear within firms of partners in consultancy or service businesses.

Role cultures have highly formalized and centralized structures. Task cultures are highly formalized but are less centralized in structure. They have been associated with research teams, and industrial innovation projects. Power cultures are relatively low on formalization, but highly centralized, so that the powerful leader can keep in close contact with what is going on. Finally, the atomistic culture is relatively low both on formalization and on structure. The culture seems appropriate for fast-moving advertising agencies and management consultancies. Their individual members are often proud of the creativity demonstrated within the culture.

Hofstede's contributions

Hofstede was a personnel manager within IBM, who later became a distinguished academic. He found a rich source of data from self-reports of IBM managers collected from all corners of the world. He realized that the coherent nature of IBM culture globally would help in extracting differences across national cultures. The application of the inventory in the same language, English, across nearly a hundred different national groupings was justified in the long-established tradition within the company of treating American English as its universal business language.[24]

Hofstede was able to collect and store electronically an enormous database of responses and other biographic data from over 112,000 employees from nearly 100 countries.[25] From subsequent analysis, Hofstede concluded that four major cultural factors differentiated the respondents. They were leadership distance, uncertainty avoidance, individualism, and masculinity.[26]

Leadership distance indicates the level of general acceptance of inequality between individuals. In some cultures the acceptance of leadership distance is rather low. Countries found to have low leadership distance scores were non-Latin parts of Europe such as the Nordic region, Great Britain and Ireland. Cultures manifesting a higher leadership distance were found in Asian and African countries and Hispanic-Latin countries.

Uncertainty avoidance is the degree to which individuals in a culture feel threatened by uncertain or unknown situations. High score cultures are found in Latin countries, Japan and South Korea. Lower scores were reported in other Asian countries, non-Mediterranean countries and African countries.

Individualism indicates the priorities of individual rights over those of the social or cultural group. The individualistic frontiers mentality at its strongest can be found in US, Australian and British behaviours, attitudes and beliefs. Asian and South American countries generally place the needs of the corporate or social group over that of the individual.

Masculinity indicates the social significance of gender, and subsequent allocation of roles between males and females.[27] The most masculine cultures are found in Japan, followed by Austria, Venezuela, Italy and Switzerland. Moderate cultures include North American countries, Great Britain, Jamaica. The most feminine, or least masculine-biased, cultures were Sweden, Norway and the Netherlands.[28]

Hofstede had provided strong empirical evidence that organizational behaviours could not be explained in universalistic generalizations. The work was enthusiastically embraced by social scientists who were quick to point to its practical implications for international management.[29] His subsequent work has had a less sensational reception, but nevertheless is more directly concerned with corporate culture. He analyses cultures as having increasingly deeper levels. Deeper can be taken as the most deeply installed, and the hardest to recognize and change. The deep level of culture involves values. Shared cultural values are manifest in shared rituals, at a second layer of cultural characteristics. In organizational terms, the rituals often involve heroes and symbols. Thus, the symbols observed in social actions are at best the surface level indicators of cultural processes. His approach to diagnosing and influencing organizational culture shows some similarities to Schein's process consultation methods.

Recent Reframers of Culture: Identification of Three Paradigms

An international network of researchers of organizational culture developed around a series of conferences in the 1980s. One of the leading figures is Peter Frost, a Canadian researcher into organizational symbolism, culture and innovation processes.

Frost traces the origins of the network to North American researchers who had become interested in ambiguity and change, and who had met at various locations, including the University of Illinois at Urbana, University of California, Santa Barbara, and the university of British Columbia.[30] He recalls his impressions that the ideas would be too unorthodox for acceptance in the most influential management journals although the group included distinguished academics, and others who were to gain distinction subsequently.[31]

The network has proposed that, despite the variety of views and approaches, much of culture research can be given a shape in terms of three broad paradigms or frames of reference. Most researchers have interests and beliefs that dispose them to one or other of the integrationalist, differentiation or fragmentation perspectives.

The integrationist perspective

The integrationist emphasizes the significance of shared values that make up a strong culture. Some of the best-known of the culture writers have followed an integrationist perspective, including Peters and Waterman; Deal and Kennedy; and

Ed Schein.[32] The perspective is a strong candidate for a managerially dominant one, and matches the simple definitions of climate as 'shared values', (Peters and Waterman) and 'the way we do things around here' (Ed Schein).

The differentiation perspective

The differentiation perspective draws attention to the differences in culture that can be found, even within a single organization. This idea has an intuitive validity for employees who are accustomed to inter-departmental rivalries. Work from this perspective draws attention to the way that each sub-culture can have a coherent yet different view to other sub-cultures. Thus, each group has a world view that is largely self-consistent and unambiguous. Only when the views are compared can inconsistencies and paradoxes be detected.[33] The differentiation perspective directs attention to sources of conflict and possible means of resolving them.

The most obvious evidence of differentiation of cultures can be found at the level of national and ethnic groupings. This is the level that interested Hofstede in his most famous study. He can be seen as speaking with the voice of the differentiation paradigm in his definition of culture as software of the mind.[34]

The fragmentation perspective

The fragmentation perspective regards the cultures of organizations to be even less coherent than those proposed by a differentiation perspective. From this view, ambiguities and uncertainties are believed to pervade all organizational activities and beliefs.[35] However, we have repeatedly found a dominant view of organizations, in our studies of decision-making, strategy, marketing, to be that of rational human behaviours channelled towards rationally established goals.[36] It might be expected that the cultural perspective of coherence is most easily accommodated by the dominant view or orthodoxy, whereas the fragmentation view is less easily accommodated.

The significance of the three perspectives

The culture networkers have succeeded in making a case for culture, and for identifying some of the ways in which the broad church can itself be seen to be made up of sub-cultures. What they share, however, is a belief that culture is significant, and that its significance lies in the symbolism of actions and events, rather than in the tangible characteristics of artefacts. Culture exists not so much as a phenomenon that can be objectively measured, but as a story that can be experienced and retold, in ways that sustain its mythic meaning.

The culture reframers were in no doubt that their work was speaking up for the voices silenced by a dominant or orthodox voice. One leading figure described culture as 'the code word for the subjective side of organizational life [rebelling against] the dominant functionalist or "scientific" paradigm'.[37]

For the first time in our journeys, we meet up with other travellers who signal awareness of the importance of going beyond the voice of the dominant orthodoxy. They have also indicated the nature of that orthodoxy as rooted in the classical scientific approach to discovery and change.

Cultures of Excellence

Peters and Waterman awaken popular interest

In the more popular literature there has always been a reverence towards the unusual, perhaps unique, aspects of successful organizations. Interest in culture change is an indication of how practitioners and consultants see excellence. It represents a shift from a 'less excellent' culture to a 'more excellent' one. Peters and Waterman helped set off one wave of interest by claiming that excellent organizations were characterized by various features, among which 'shared values' and a strong culture were important.

The visionary culture of excellence

A recent study picked up the notion of visionary companies.[38] These researchers demonstrated that companies nominated as visionary were likely to outlast and outperform matched control companies. Their founders had a vision that acted in the long term to sustain the firm in times of hardship and environmental buffeting. How to explain such differences? There is no easy explanation according to rational theories of organizational behaviour. We may well say that the visionary firms have a visionary culture, or even a survival culture. In such statements, we have the rationale for studying culture. It is a term to begin dealing with things that orthodox business theories cannot deal with. However, that does no more than suggest culture as a mysterious factor of successful firms. It does not get us any further in understanding what is the essence of a successful culture.

Porras and Collins concluded that their visionary companies differentiated themselves by a persistent emphasis on a core ideology. It is a nice way of reviving a term that has had negative connotations for some while. Ideology was a term originally proposed around the time of the Enlightenment to describe a project for a new science – the study of ideas and feelings. Napoleon supported the project at first but later undermined it and its adherents as a political threat. For the next two centuries the term acquired negative connotations of closed and rigid beliefs or dogma. More recently, the term has been losing some of its negative connotations.[39]

Porras and Collins do not give a formal definition of core ideology.[40] Their writings are rather consistent with the ideas popularized by Peters and Waterman. Overall, these concepts relate to the notion of stable long-term belief systems of the kind studied by earlier culture researchers. These beliefs transcend simplistic economic considerations. In the case of an economic culture of excellence, the core ideology is aligned with, but not identical to, economic success. In other words, it has economic survival value.

They found this one of the clearest differentiators of companies – with seventeen out of eighteen visionary companies 'more ideologically driven and less purely profit-driven than the comparison companies'.[41] They were careful to point out, however, that great companies do not survive by ignoring profit. Yet profit is a necessary condition for the furtherance of long-term goals that are enshrined in cultural or ideological beliefs. The content of the ideology differed from company to company. For Johnson & Johnson, the customers were central; for Hewlett Packard and Marriott, concern for employees was a prominent component of their ideology; for Motorola and 3M, innovation was central. The unifying feature was not the content. It was the dedication to the core ideology. The core ideology acts in some way to instil and retain commitment of employees to the well-being and survival of the company. In the language of the culture reframers, visionary companies represent the integrationist perspective. They have strong shared values. 'The way we do things around here' is what gives them their long-term economic success.

The assumptions behind cultures of excellence

The journeys have helped shed light on some of the confusions within the culture literature. The dominant voice of popular writings has emphasized shared values. This is clearly an integrationist view. The implication is that objections to a proposed corporate vision are aberrations. What if some individual or group does not share the values? 'Debate is healthy,' one corporate leader announced shortly after his appointment, 'but we no longer have time for anyone who thinks we are sailing in the wrong direction.' The statement captures much that is implicit in organizational writing about shared values. Creative challenge of top management's views risks being opposed as disloyalty or worse. Shared visions may well be important attributes to achieving corporate excellence. The approaches required for achieving shared excellence still have to confront the implications of cultures in which the values are not shared.

Puzzling Out Organizational Climate

The development of the climate concept

Climate research can be traced to the work of social psychologists. A particularly important early influence was Kurt Lewin, whose work will be covered in chapter eight as a pioneer of social psychological research. Lewin's famous Force Field theory required empirical evidence of the forces. Since Lewin, climate has been regarded as a candidate for exploring the forces that give social groups their coherence.

These ideas were brought into experimental studies by Litwin and Stringer, in the 1960s, and their factors of climate have been influential in subsequent climate studies. We get some indication of the problems of studying the field from the kind of factors they examined, such as structure, warmth, support and conflict.

Later researchers struggled with measures of individual attributes or perceptions, and of organizational attributes.

The culture–climate confusion

Some researchers have coupled the words together, as if culture and climate were not easily separated.[42] The most apparent, but generally unstated, distinction was that the early work on culture came from a sociological or anthropological perspective, whereas the climate studies derived from a psychological perspective. A recent development is to study culture using the kind of quantitative methodology previously found in climate studies. Hostede was perhaps the most celebrated example.[43]

Climate has tended to be regarded as a more short-term indication of individual moods and feelings, whereas culture captured more permanent characteristics of a group's beliefs and philosophy.[44] Because culture has been mostly studied in qualitative ways, and climate in more quantitative ways, even that distinction is not one that can be simply established. A recent thoughtful review pointed out that both climate and culture could be regarded as ways of exploring the 'social context'.[45] We are some way from a consensus that climate and culture are distinct phenomena.

Payne and Pugh's resolution

One of the most thorough early examinations of the climate literature was carried out in the 1960s and 1970s by a team of British management theorists and psychologists.[46] Roy Payne and Derek Pugh proposed a general model for studying organizations, in which structure and climate were major categories. In a range of studies in the UK, and subsequently the USA, the researchers claimed that work patterns were most strongly associated with technology and size. The climates, however, showed a more complex set of relationships with structural measures. The work helped toward a recognition that climate was open to various interpretations. Of particular significance was a distinction made between organizational climate, which implied the existence of something that was consistent throughout an organization, and psychological climate, associated with an individual's view, from his or her particular organizational position.[47]

Payne and Pugh concluded their influential review with two possible interpretations of the prevailing research into organizational climate. The more pessimistic view was that climate research had fallen into the trap of extrapolating simple data to explain the nature of complex organizational systems.[48] In which case: 'This chapter's research, then has been performed by the unwary. Future research can ignore most of these studies and utilize a completely different approach. We need deep involvement from the members of a complex system to gather meaningful data which accurately reflect these people's experiences.'[49]

The researchers then presented the positive case, with which they were more in sympathy. They suggested that their own clarification of the nature of climate, and subsequent development of better methodology, would lead to more valued results through future climate research. The thoroughness of Payne and Pugh's analysis has served subsequent workers well. However, the difficulties they indicated for studies of climate have been more fulfilled than their hoped-for advances in methodology.

Ekvall's analysis

Göran Ekvall is a Swedish researcher into the nature of industrial work. In a review article he reached much the same conclusions as Payne and Pugh regarding the need to discriminate between psychological climate and organizational climate. He also recognized the potential of climate as a means of connecting up organizational-level features with individual behaviours. Furthermore, he supported studies aimed at making clearer the nature of variations across work groups within organizations.[50] This interest led him to concentrate on one particular manifestation of climate that he termed the climate for creativity. Ekvall makes it clear that he treats climate as a metaphor for exploring organizational perceptions.

Ekvall developed a creative climate questionnaire (the CCQ). With this instrument he identified a range of factors associated with a creative climate. In an important series of studies of the innovativeness of Scandinavian firms,[51] scores on the CCQ were found to be predictors of the innovative performance of the firms. Subsequent studies have collected additional evidence that the CCQ is a simple-to-use inventory that discriminates between reported organizational environments.[52] His factors were similar to those found in earlier work by Litwin and Stringer, incorporating trust, idea support, risk, as well as the negatively scored conflict dimension.

KEYS

Teresa Amabile, in collaboration with the research group at the Center for Creative Leadership, Greensboro, NC, has extended earlier climate work. The measures are again of the self-report kind, and again derive from the earlier studies.[53] Additional factors of barriers or impediments to creativity have been added. Data were collected by asking respondents to recall contrasting high and low innovative projects of which they had direct experience. The results confirm the broad pattern of earlier work. The high innovation projects were associated with high creative climate scales, and with lower inhibitory factors. Furthermore, the high innovation projects were associated with high (perceived) effectiveness of the projects. The scale of the project (over 12,000 response sets for the validation study) provides a strong base on which to build further work.

Making Sense of the Culture–Climate Confusions

Are culture and climate different phenomena?

Culture and climate are very much still in the background of business orthodoxy. Yet the concepts do not go away. The unresolved issues include the relationship between culture and climate; how such concepts alien to the economic business orthodoxy persist; and how they might be taken more seriously within business studies. Two obvious possibilities suggest themselves. First, culture and climate are two distinct phenomena – the former of a 'deep' symbolic form; the latter more superficial, and accessible to psychometric measures. The second possibility is that culture–climate contains aspects of a dualism. Culture and climate are interrelated constructs which deal with the organization's environment.

In a thoughtful recent review, it was pointed out that both climate and culture could be regarded as ways of exploring the 'social context'.[54] There is a relatively simple explanation for the existence of the two constructs, dealing with a deeper unitary concept, if we return to our ways of thinking about a dominant orthodoxy and the suppression of heretical approaches. The climate construct derives from the dominant orthodoxy, with its attention to carefully validated quantitative questionnaires, and concerns about the objectivity of its measures. In contrast, the historical tradition from which much culture research derives is qualitative, and seeks to explain features in organizations such as shared values that are hard to pin down. We might expect it to be suspect from the rational orthodox perspective in management studies.

The treatment of culture and climate

According to our theory of multiple voices, we might expect culture and climate treatments seeking to address real-world issues to be influenced by the dominant managerial orthodoxy.

The predicted 'taming' and denying of these unorthodox voices is shown in figure 6.2. Culture's original theoretical roots were well-equipped to deal with

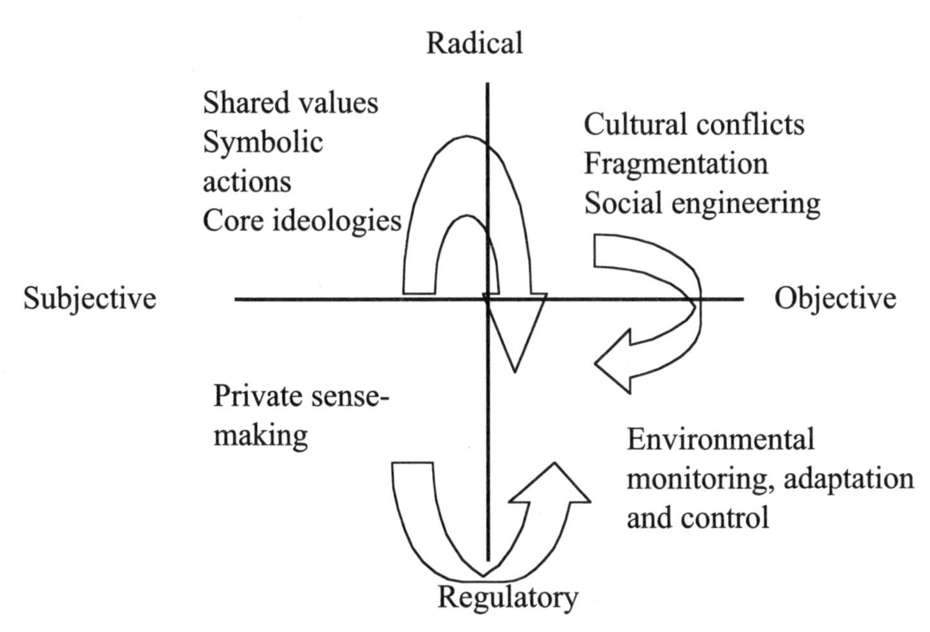

Figure 6.2: The alternative culture/climate voices

radical and subjective notions of shared values, symbolic actions and core ideologies. Managerial authors have tended to import such concepts into recipes for corporate transformation by finding ways to measure and predict their characteristics. This is the approach in which a company identifies its culture using self-report inventories, for example. This is the 'taming' of an approach through abstracted empiricism. The various traditions would not put emphasis on measures in this way. A humanistic and radical treatment would place more emphasis on symbolic actions. A sense-making approach would encourage dialogue.[55] The more thoughtful work acknowledges the extended and skilled work inherent in such efforts. Only if we are able to look out for such clues are we in a position to appraise the claims of the managerial texts claiming corporate transformations through diagnosis and change of corporate culture or climate.

Notes

1 Trompenaars (1993: 3).
2 Frost et al. (1991: 7).
3 Ekvall (1987: 183).
4 Hampden-Turner (1990: 16).
5 Ekvall (1991) connected climate and culture.
6 Hofstede (1980, 1991) and Frost et al. (1985, 1991) have been widely cited for contributions to culture. Payne & Pugh is particularly well-cited in climate studies. Goran Ekvall has an unrivalled tenure as an authority on creative climate, although his English language publications are rather difficult to locate. Amabile et al. (1996) is a recent important review.
7 My handfuls of books that had influenced my earlier thinking came from Handy (1976); Graves (1986); Ekvall (1987); Hampden-Turner (1990); Adler (1991); Lessem (1990); Hofstede (1991); Frost et al. (1991); Trompenaars (1993) and Linstead et al. (1996). Amabile (1996) was a late addition to the list. I came across the collected volume of essays on organizational climate and culture later (Schneider, 1990). This would have been a valued 'piece of the jigsaw'. The handful of books sampling technique risks missing such excellent guides from time to time. The robustness of such sampling is based on the assumption that any missing piece will contribute by strengthening the broad platform of understanding being assembled, rather than altering it substantially. This is some comfort to anyone undertaking research in organizational studies!
8 Kroeber & Kluckhohn (1952) quoted in Adler (1991).
9 See Graves (1986) for a representative set of definitions.
10 Schein (1991).
11 For example in Schein (1985).
12 See Reichers & Schneider (1990).
13 Peters & Waterman (1982: 75).
14 Hofstede (1991).
15 Perhaps Margaret Mead (1887–1948) became the most celebrated in the public eye for her total involvement approach in remote regions such as Samoa and New Guinea, and her theories of gender as cultural conditioning.
16 Deal & Kennedy (1982) is particularly well-cited. A useful summary can be found in Lessem (1990).

[17] There are cross-cultural differences here. An English colleague at an American conference remarked on the number of people that had been honoured or celebrated before dinner. 'In Europe we don't have to do that sort of thing,' he remarked thoughtfully.

[18] Schein's classic writings on process interventions (Schein, 1969, 1979) deserve attention by anyone interested in influencing organizational change.

[19] Lessem (1990) gives a useful summary of Schein's approach to culture analysis.

[20] I have noted that technically trained executives find Schein's ideas appealing and easy to relate to their own scientific mind sets. However, the competent process consultant requires a grasp of the emotional sensitivity of cultural dimensions that is acquired slowly and painfully through a process of personal learning. Schein not only has a conceptual scheme carefully worked out, he is (by repute) an exceptionally skilled practitioner. Exceptional means rarely encountered.

[21] *Understanding Organizations*, Handy (1976).

[22] Handy was a long-time Shell executive who had also held a visiting position at London Business School.

[23] Harrison derived the four ideal cultures from two important structural dimensions of organization, the degree of formalization and the degree of centralization.

[24] I found that working with such groups in IBM in the 1970s revealed not much more than some token English speakers within some countries. In the absence of head-office influences, the language of business reverted to the language of the locals.

[25] Hofstede (1980, 1991).

[26] Hofstede (1991) notes that the dimensions fitted closely to those proposed theoretically in Inkeles and Levinson (1969). This supports Hofstede's point that the methodology is not too weakened because respondents were all from IBM. If anything this reduces the variations in corporate cultures that would be found in wider ranging sampling.

[27] Interestingly (and unlike individualism), masculinity is not in any way associated with a country's degree of economic development.

[28] There is one footnote to the work, wryly acknowledged by Hofstede himself (1991). A team of Chinese researchers set about looking for a cultural dimension they had expected to find, and which had not appeared in Hofstede's analysis. A careful reworking of the earlier results, and further investigations, revealed evidence of the kind they were looking for and which was labelled *Confucian dynamism*. This fifth dimension has been suggested as a component in the economic rise of Japan and the South Asian Little Tigers.

[29] See, for example, Nancy Adler's (1991) excellent text on international dimensions of organizational behaviour, and also Adler (1983).

[30] Frost gives a fascinating account of his recollections in Frost (1989).

[31] Among others, Professors Louis Pondi (1938–87), Ed Schein, Gareth Morgan, Joanne Martin, Karl Weick.

[32] Frost et al. (ibid.) also cite Ouchi (1981), Pascale & Athos (1981) and Pettigrew (1979) as significant figures within the integrationist perspective.

[33] De Cock & Rickards (1996) summarizes a study of sub-cultures within a programme of culture change.

[34] The software metaphor seems less suited to the integrationist perspective. It may also have some credibility within the fragmentation perspective.

[35] At a popular level there is ironic recognition of the ambiguities of organizational life. 'No one knows what's going on around here, or if they do, they aren't telling . . . this is mushroom management, we are all kept in the dark, and every so often a whole pile of shit is poured over us.'

[36] We could even extend that to innovation, with its largely economic frame, and to creativity, which has been largely rejected as a scientifically observed phenomenon, within orthodox cognitive psychology.

[37] Meyerson (1991: 256). The quote was picked up in Denison (1996), in perhaps the most authoritative recent analysis of the culture–climate debate.

[38] Collins & Porras (1994).

[39] Guido Enthoven has conducted various social innovation experiments, in The Netherlands, which promote the concept of ideology in a positive light, citing J. B. Thompson as an antecedent thinker (Enthoven, 1997).

[40] Collins & Porras (1994: 73ff) suggest that core ideology comprised core values ('essential and enduring tenets') and purpose (fundamental reasons for existence). This differentiation seems less than clear-cut for theoretical modelling purposes, although it may help in an organization's explorations of its core ideology.

[41] Collins & Porras (1994: 55).

[42] Denison (1996) gives a nice summary of the theoretical confusions.

[43] Hofstede (1980).

[44] Nyström (1990) for example.

[45] Denison (1996: 625).

[46] The workers had been associated with the Aston studies, which had pioneered work into relationships between organizational structures and context. See Perry (1992) for a recent evaluation.

[47] Respondents could report on general factors, or on their personal feelings arising from perceiving impact of a factor (such as openness to new ideas, for example). The former leads to organizational climate information, the latter to psychological climate.

[48] Forrester (1961) was cited (Payne & Pugh, 1976: 1168) as support for the pessimistic case that complex systems behaved in ways that were counter-intuitive to results from simple day-to-day experiences and observations.

[49] Payne & Pugh (1976: 1168).

[50] Ekvall (1987).

[51] Professor Harry Nyström and his marketing group at the University of Upsalla acted as independent assessors of the firms' innovative achievements (see Nyström 1990b).

[52] Mohamed & Rickards (1996).

[53] Amabile (1996: 234). See also Amabile et al. (1996).

[54] Denison (1996: 625).

[55] Senge (1990); Ellinor & Gerard (1998).

chapter 7 Leadership and Managerialism

The term 'leadership' means different things to different people. As is often the case when a word from the common vocabulary is incorporated into the technical vocabulary of a scientific discipline, leadership has not been precisely defined and it still carries extraneous connotations that create ambiguity of meaning.

Garry Yukl[1]

Even in the grimmest times in prison, when my comrades and I were pushed to our limits, I would see a glimmer of humanity in one of the guards, perhaps just for a second, but that was enough to reassure me and keep me going. Man's goodness is a flame that can be hidden but never extinguished.

Nelson Mandela[2]

Always, it seems, the concept of leadership eludes us or turns up in another form to taunt us again with its slipperiness and complexity. So we have invented an endless proliferation of terms to deal with it . . . and still the concept is not sufficiently defined.

Warren Bennis[3]

'Do you mean to say, Socrates, that the man who succeeds with a chorus will also succeed with an army?'

'I mean that whatever a man controls, if he knows what he wants and can get it he will be a good controller, whether he control a chorus, an estate, a city or an army.'

'Really, Socrates' cried Nichomachides, 'I should never have thought to hear you say that a good business man would make a good general!'

Plato[4]

Introduction

What they teach you about leadership at business school

Business school courses provide a great deal of material for would-be leaders to study. In particular, the ubiquitous case study often carries in it the context of a business leader's actions and even his or her presumed thought processes. Directly or, more often, indirectly, the study and discussion of cases educates business students as to how leaders behave. The process even helps discriminate between effective and less effective leadership thought and practice. This kind of knowledge may also be augmented with formal courses on leadership theory, a tradition inherited from military academies around the world. Finally, leadership may be introduced as part of the learning from projects and team exercises, some with 'live' projects and business sponsors.

What they don't teach you about leadership at business school

With a few honourable exceptions, business schools teach leadership 'from the outside'. Management students have to address for themselves the questions 'from the inside'. These are what might be called the Field Marshal's baton questions. What sort of leader do I have the potential of becoming? What should I do to fulfil my leadership potential? Will I be able to make a difference when given the chance as a leader? The higher order learning questions might be 'how can I "read" behind leadership actions to understand the processes going on?' 'How can I reach a view on the latest popular theory about getting to the top of organizations?'

These questions will require journeys of personal discovery. A preparatory stage will be illustration of the personal journeys made by others. This chapter offers that preparatory stage through its account of a journey of discovery made into the territories of leadership theory and practice.

In search of leadership's platform of understanding

In this chapter a platform of understanding is established for leadership studies, and a comparison made with the assumptions of the broader organizational behaviour field. The conclusion is reached that the managerial orthodoxy has, once again, tried to restrict leadership to a rational format. Recent studies have taken on a less rational form through transformational leadership ideas. This provides an understanding of the resistances to studying leadership within formal business courses. By giving more voice to humanistic aspects of leadership studies, management studies will be better equipped to deal with the emotional and ethical dimensions of human behaviours in working environments.

Published materials on leadership by the end of the 1980s were estimated to be upward of 10,000 books and articles.[5] I eventually settled for a few handfuls of books, which included some I had retrieved from my own bookshelves.[6] The outline of a platform of understanding eventually emerged, with the major themes indicated in figure 7.1.

Our puzzle-making begins with a summary of key historical eras as these are generally agreed within the paradigm. An earlier strand deals with transactional leadership, and a later one with transformational leadership. Other themes include charismatic and deviant leaders. Overall, these themes suggest that creative leadership may yet be a powerful way of making the subject, at the same time, more action oriented and open to the emerging theories of new leadership.

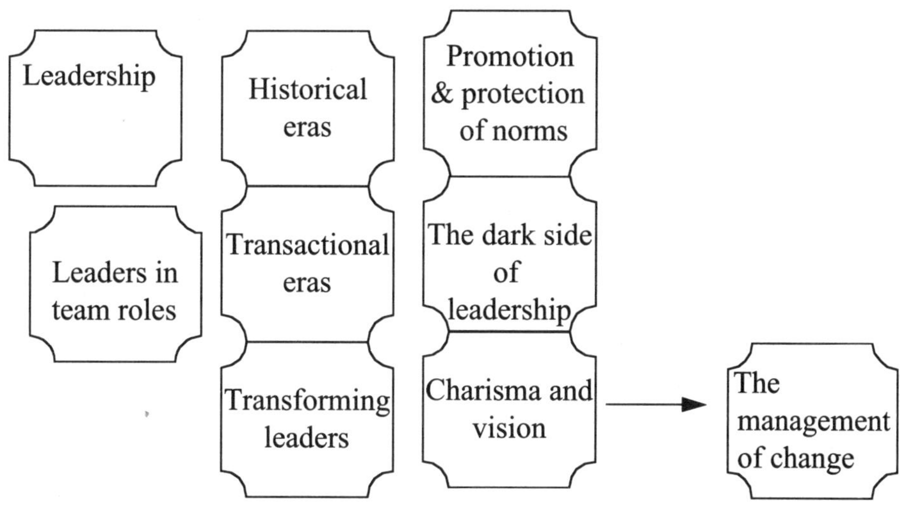

Figure 7.1: Leadership

Historical Eras in Leadership Research

The leadership literature had a rather 'well-shared' platform of understanding. Despite the large number of available sources, there was a good consensus around the key incidents and themes in the field. The following historical sequence of topics is one that is replicated enough to be considered the orthodox view.

Early theories of leadership

It has been said that until quite recently, the whole study of history has concentrated on great leaders, their acts, and the consequences of those acts. To some degree, our everyday ideas of leadership have been influenced by such ancient wisdom. At first in mythology, leaders were god-like, and inspired by the gods, or even gods playing out some earthly drama. For the greater length of recorded civilization, leadership was widely accepted as a God-given gift, elevating the chosen few.[7] These images were eventually replaced with the advance of rationalism, through efforts to understand human behaviour through scientific study and observation.

Modern trait theories

Trait theories were studied with enthusiasm with the rise of psychometric testing measures in the early decades of the century. The search for the attributes of great leaders was on. Early work on leaders had concentrated on the great and famous. Modern organizational studies were as likely to study leadership as one function of organizational life, to be found at various levels in the organization, including supervisory leadership of production line workers. In this section, the term is, unless indicated otherwise, applied in its broader organizational sense.

The American Stodgill, who in 1948 examined the prevailing materials on leaders for a psychological journal, carried out one of the most influential surveys in the field.[8] His evaluation of over 100 studies drew attention to several important points. First, he established that indeed the studies were dominated by efforts at establishing the characteristics as stable traits of leaders of various kinds. Secondly, he pointed out that the work showed severe inconsistencies. Some leaders possessed some traits, others did not. In addition, some traits had quite complex relationships with leadership effectiveness. Dominance and intelligence, for example, were expected to be favourable leadership traits. When these traits were studied experimentally, far too great a variability was found. Furthermore, the appropriate level seemed strongly dependent on specific situational factors.

Stodgill concluded that leadership could never be pinned down through the isolation of a set of traits. The review may well have influenced a shift of attention from traits towards more fluid characteristics of styles or acquirable skills. It also paved the way for the forthcoming interest in contingencies or situational factors contributing to leadership effectiveness. In 1974 his updating of the field indicated that the reaction against trait contributions to leadership effectiveness had probably been excessive, and that a mix of individual relatively fixed personal characteristics as well as stylistic ones was required to explain leadership effectiveness.[9]

He assembled a profile which would be more likely to be found in successful leaders than in the wider population of individuals. The profile reads today rather like the advertisements placed in the situations vacant columns of our newspapers.

> [Wanted, natural leader to head up a division within a major multinational. The successful candidate] is characterized by a strong drive for responsibility and task completion . . . venturesomeness and originality in problem solving, drive to exercise initiative in social situations, self-confidence and sense of personal identity . . . willingness to absorb interpersonal stress . . . ability to influence other persons' behavior, and capacity to structure social interactions to the purpose at hand.[10]

Stodgill helped rescue the field from its earlier search for universal traits for effective leadership. He also contributed to a refocusing away from the differences between leaders and non-leaders, towards the factors resulting in more, or less, effective performance.

Style/skill theories

A series of studies from Stodgill's colleagues at Ohio State University established two dominant dimensions of leader behaviour. Beginning in the 1950s, the studies contributed to the repositioning of leadership studies to emphasize styles and acquirable skills rather than inherited traits which set leaders apart. The categories were given the formal labels of consideration and initiation of structure. The work essentially showed how some leaders were strongly oriented to people around them, while other leaders were more concerned with task-oriented matters. The considerate leaders, as the term implies, have a set of values in which fairness, and awareness of employees' needs are evident. The structure-initiating leaders set about clarifying roles and responsibilities, and what is expected of subordinates.

The early studies suggested that effective leaders are reported as having strengths in both dimensions. The general implications of these studies were that leadership skills were in some way cumulative. The American academics, and highly successful commercial consultants, Robert Blake and Jane Mouton proposed a related theory of leadership.[11] Their managerial grid, first published in 1964, suggested that a leader could become more effective all-round by aspiring to the high–high condition.

To put these empirical style studies in perspective, McGregor published his influential analysis of Theory X and Theory Y management styles in 1960.[12] McGregor, and Blake & Mouton, used the term management style although the style refers to the manager engaged in one aspect of managerial responsibilities, that of leadership. Theory X managers, according to McGregor, had dominated production-oriented manufacturing enterprises in a way that had destroyed commitment and motivation among the work force. He believed that Theory Y management could re-energize the work force thereby producing a more productive as well as a more socially desirable workplace. Unlike the other style researchers, McGregor believed that a humanistic style would be more appropriate to the conditions of the day and was recommended as an improvement over the dominant task-oriented style.[13]

When efforts were made to look more closely at leadership styles, assorted difficulties were encountered. The most general difficulty was the continued failure to find a simple link between leadership style and group performance. As increasing numbers of studies became known, the results were to prove utterly confusing. In some studies, Theory Y styles were found more effective. In others, Theory X styles were more effective. Other studies had no clear pattern of effectiveness by style.[14] Such findings contributed to the decline of leadership models focusing on simple behavioural styles, and ushered in the era of situational or contingency models.

Situational or contingency theories[15]

Trait theories suggested that leadership effectiveness, however that output is measured, could be predicted from a knowledge of the leader's defining traits. A situational theory indicates that effectiveness is not directly associated with a leadership style and will produce different outputs according to circumstances.[16]

Style theories can be extended to take into account additional factors, thereby producing contingency theories. A wide range of combinations of variables has been proposed. These split roughly into situational variables and intervening variables. The broad thrust of this research has been from simpler models, with a few variables, to more complex ones with additional variables, introduced to account for weaknesses in the simpler models.[17]

One of the simple early models examined the impact of leader attitudes towards co-workers.[18] Early results suggested that more supportive attitudes could enhance co-workers' performance if various situational factors were moderately in favour of the leader. If the balance of power in the situation was more strongly in favour or against the leader, supportive attitudes led to less productive leader impacts. This rather tortuous set of outcomes illustrates the complex way contingency theories translate into implications for leaders.

A rather more complex version of contingency theory developed more practical advice for leaders. The original researchers, Hersey and Blanchard, proposed that an effective leader's style takes into account the level of maturity of the subordinates.[19] For low levels of maturity, a directive style is proposed; for intermediate levels of maturity, a high level of supportive and considerate behaviour is effective. For high levels of maturity, a delegative and hands-off style is believed to be better.

Another version of situational leadership proposed a gradient of increasing involvement, beginning with an authoritative style of telling the workers what to do. This moved to a marginally more considerate style in which the leader moved from tell mode to sell mode. The gradient then ascended through consult to involving workers more fully.[20] The approach suggested that treating the workers in an autocratic way was all right if workers did not have the ability or maturity to cope with styles that are more considerate. The model begs the question whether leaders have the abilities to shift gear and respond as required by the specific circumstances of any situation.

Results from empirical tests of situational models were largely inconclusive. In time, the models became even more complex and incorporated intervening variables as well as situational ones. We have seen how climate has been inserted as an intervening variable between organizational structures and effectiveness. Here the principle is retained. The intervening variables help explain weak correlations between leadership inputs and performance outputs. Intervening variables studied included subordinate effort and role clarity, and group cohesiveness. Unsurprisingly, the models were difficult to evaluate in empirical studies, as the situational and intervening variables have to be examined in assorted conditions.

Some of the theories are so complex that they have not been adequately tested; others have been tested with no more conclusive results than the earlier style theories. The following quote reflects a general consensus of researchers by the end of the 1980s: 'The discrepant findings, the problem of causality, and the failure of theory to predict performance in many studies are not encouraging. Further, the plethora of leadership styles and situational factors that the theory and research have put forward do not provide leaders with clear guidance as to how they should behave, even if the findings were less inconsistent.'[21] The difficulties can be traced to the failures of the empirical results to support the theoretical beliefs of the researchers. Leadership research remained under suspicion. As happens under such circumstances, a theory in waiting stepped forward to occupy centre stage.

Transformational and other new-leader theories

The newer studies confronted some of the more mysterious aspects of individual events that had been so much part of the historic accounts of leadership.[22]

Questions were raised about the uniqueness of exceptional leadership from astronauts to quarterbacks; from religious cults to business empires. The vocabulary gave indications of a shift from planned goals to visions; from contingency to charisma; from traits to transforming ideas.

The essential features of this kind of leadership were summed up by one reviewer as a style which involves 'vision, empowers others, inspires, challenges the status quo, and adopts a proactive stance . . . when writing about leaders, or leadership *per* se, or about transformational leadership, or about visionary leadership, and so on, many authors are employing similar themes and motifs to those who write about charismatic leadership in organizations. Together, these approaches have been dubbed "the new Leadership" to reflect the convergence of a number of recent writers on a set of themes on leadership.'[23]

The Voices of Transformation in the 1980s

The pieces of the jigsaw that we consider next introduce us to a changing vocabulary of leadership.

J. M. Burns and transformational leadership

One of the most powerful new leadership ideas was introduced by James MacGregor Burns, a professor of history.[24] Burns observed a fundamental difference between leaders who operated on what might be called the economic model of exchange, whom he called transactional leaders – and those whose behaviours seemed to transcend individual selfishness. These leaders he called transformational leaders. The trait, style, and contingency eras of leadership had become increasingly preoccupied with transactional theories and transactional managers. Burns helped reawaken interest in historical notions of management.

Bernard Bass and leadership styles

Bass is one of the major figures in the field of management. He held positions as Distinguished Professor of Management Emeritus and Director of the Center of Leadership Studies, SUNY, Binghamton, New York. After Stodgill's death, Bass took over his former colleague's comprehensive *Handbook of Management.* His own interests however, were to move him away from the perspective of the earlier studies of leadership, which were mostly transactional in spirit and execution.

According to Bass, leadership styles can be located on a continuum, with transformational management at the most effective and active end, followed by transactional leadership based on positive reinforcement or on management by exception. Beyond the application of transactional leadership behaviours is placed *laissez-faire* leadership.[25]

Inventories have been developed which permit assessment of preferences for the various leadership styles.[26] Bass and co-workers interpret a wide range of studies conducted in the 1980s to indicate that effective leaders show a preference for more of the transformational styles. Leadership programmes have been designed and introduced into various organizations, aimed at enhancing the leadership contributions from transformational styles. The training emphasizes the four Is of transformational leadership, namely idealized influence; inspirational motivation; intellectual stimulation; and individualized consideration.

Bennis and Nanus, and visionary management

The popularity of the term visionary manager can be traced in part to the impact in the 1980s of a book on leadership by Warren Bennis and Burt Nanus.[27] A study of ninety exceptional organizational leaders found four components of visionary leadership. Each leader interviewed revealed a compelling vision of the future for the company, which linked past experience, an appraisal of the present circumstances, and '. . . a view of a realistic, credible, attractive future for the organization that is better in some important ways than what now exists'.[28] This captures the visionary product created by the leaders. The three other factors were described as communicating the vision, building trust, and effective self-awareness and presentation. Such terms are now part of the vocabulary of management.

Peters and Waterman's excellent leader

In assessing new leadership concepts in popular literature in the 1980s, it makes sense to ask 'what did Peters and Waterman have to say?' In a key passage on leadership, in *In Search of Excellence*, we find a recognition that corporate excellence requires repeated dedication to the multiple and minute requirements of the workplace: 'the subtle accumulation of nuances, a hundred things done a little better'.[29] Then there follows a brief encapsulation of transformational management, with acknowledgement to the work of MacGregor, Burns, and Warren Bennis. Although Peters was to become more radical in his later books, here the emphasis is on the sheer hard work of leadership. Even the transforming leader 'is concerned with minutiae . . . with the tricks of the pedagogue, the mentor, the linguist'.[30] The emphasis is on the leader as the shaper of values, quoting a much earlier authority from the 1950s : 'The institutional leader is primarily regarded as an expert in the promotion and protection of values'.[31]

Nadler & Tushman's touch of magic

There is an implicit theme within much of the new leadership ideas that leadership studies had been overly concerned with the rational. The clearest return to the pre-scientific vocabulary comes from the work of Nadler and Tushman, who consider that exceptional management involves what they term magic leadership.[32]

Their work leads them to study charismatic leadership. In particular they confront the issue of the morality of leadership. Are the manifestations of evil leadership distorted examples of transformational leadership? This was a question we also posed in terms of the products of creativity. We will consider the question a little later on, after taking a closer look at the charismatic theories of leadership.

Charisma and Vision in Transformational Leadership

The earliest views of charisma

The theological status of charisma, based on the original Greek term, can be traced back to a God-given gift of grace.[33] Charismatics, blessed with grace, are able to influence and convert others to a more spiritual orientation. There is an interesting similarity here with the concept of inspiration, a theological approach to the God-given gift received through the breath of God. This gives charisma and creativity a strong historical connection.

Weber's view

The ancient views were reworked by Weber. He considered modern organizations to have evolved from more primitive social systems in which authority arose from traditional or charismatic forces. In general, the charismatic emerged through special personal characteristics, often constituting a break in the traditional order. A charismatic leader who attracts a following will inevitably lead to a succession problem. The process leads to a routinization, with authority vested in secondary leaders within a more routinized social arrangement. Weber considered the arrival of the modern bureaucratic organizational form as evidence of the weakening of the charismatic upsurges of historic times. However, he also considered that the charismatic tendency could re-emerge in modern times of distress 'whether psychic, physical, economic, ethical, religious, or political'.[34] Weber's own influence on organizational theory can hardly be over-estimated, and it runs through the new leadership ideas, although generally unacknowledged.

Modern views of charisma

Various descriptions of charisma can be found in the recent leadership literature.[35] Weber's ideas have been carried forward by those who argue that the non-rational exercise of power operates routinely in everyday social settings including business organizations. This suggests that most examples of power and dominance over others represent aspects of charismatic leadership.[36] One researcher who has specialized in the phenomenon of charisma offers a working definition. He suggests that, in new-leadership terms, charismatic leadership deals with:

> relationships between leaders and followers in which, by virtue of both the extraordinary qualities that followers attribute to the leader and the latter's mission, the charismatic leader is regarded by his or her followers with a mix of reverence, unflinching dedication and awe. This devotion is due to the charismatic leader *qua individual* and not by occupancy of a status or position that is legitimated by traditional or legal-rational criteria.[37]

Charisma and visioning

The new leadership literature tends to be accompanied with many references to the visionary characteristics of charismatic leaders.[38] Texts that have been less enthusiastic about the concept of charisma also emphasize the visioning component within effective leadership. We have already seen the influence of Tom Peters in that respect. In general, the nature of a vision, and its symbolic impact on others, is well worked out. Often, though, the process is described with few details of how the desired visions are produced.[39]

Charisma, power and transformation

One associated feature of all charismatic leaders is the wielding of considerable personal power. Frequently the followers express their own sense of being energized through the experience of involvement with the charismatic leader. It has been suggested that the personalized power of the leader may produce obedient and submissive followers or 'conversely' the power may contribute to the empowerment of the followers.[40] Furthermore, for better or for worse, the exercise of power seems intimately connected with revolutionary changes or transformation. Charismatic leadership and transformational leadership are intimately allied.

Charisma's dark side

The mysterious side of charisma and creativity has also been associated with dangerousness and even madness. Byron was only one extreme example of the charismatic poet famed for being mad, bad and dangerous.[41] Charismatic leadership, for these reasons, has tended to be regarded with suspicion within the new leadership literature. However, leadership ancient and modern does have a dark side, also rarely commented upon.

Leadership studies offer in general a rather idealistic perspective of the phenomenon. James MacGregor Burns wanted to exclude dictators from his elite group of transforming leaders. Another distinguished academic, Abraham Zaleznik of Harvard Business School, regarded leaders as having a strong moral authority in their influence on their followers, and possibly unusual personality characteristics.[42]

Manfred Kets de Vries, a student of Zaleznik, was sufficiently intrigued by these psychoanalytic suggestions to turn the subject on its head and examine the dark side of leadership. He wanted to know what characteristics might produce psychoses in leaders. He analysed examples of processes that might select-in psychotic leaders whose behaviours deal with suppressed needs within the culture. A culture with high regard for self-interested individualist behaviour will support the rise of the narcissistic leader. The developing pathology may reveal itself in ruthless and grandiose behaviour, and either discreet or blatantly manipulative approaches.[43] Petty tyrants are particularly common, as accounts of work-place bullying attest.

Emergent Leadership

One additional perspective on leadership deserves mention. The concept is that of emergent leadership. It can be traced to early work in Harvard Business School's Department of Industrial Relations, and particularly to its founder, Elton Mayo, and the sociologist George Homans.[44] Homans' rather complex analysis of human groups is less important than the basic principle – that the individuals interact under environmental influences with emergent consequences for the social structure and external (organizational and environmental) factors. The term informal structure is sometimes used to indicate Homans' emergent structure.

Later the idea of emergent leadership was developed as part of theories of group development and dynamics. David Cartwright and Alvin Zander typified the approach with their definition of group leadership as 'the performance of those acts which help the group achieve its preferred outcomes'.[45] This approach has the merit of connecting up leadership to observable actions and actors. It opens the way to a subtle view of groups having interchangeable leaders. Acts of team building and maintenance, for example, now come under the category of leadership. Furthermore, it clarifies the confusion regarding leaderless teams. By definition a team will from time to time have individuals acting to further its collective aims. At any given time the team leader may or may not have formal status in such a role. Evidence suggests that leaders will always emerge within any social group, and that power and influence is generally skewed towards emergent leaders.[46]

Making Sense of the Leadership Platform of Understanding

The bits of the jigsaw of leadership have now been collected, and partially assembled in the previous sections. To go beyond the views expressed, we will look for explanations based on different perspectives or paradigms. This analysis will help us understand how the perspectives might fit into a managerial orthodoxy, or perhaps be effectively silenced from within that orthodoxy. These considerations lead us to the more personal questions raised on behalf of business students at the start of the chapter: 'What can I learn of leadership and management through practical involvement and activity?' Finally a case is made for re-applying creative leadership approaches as a means of developing new leadership skills and understanding.

Taking a paradigmatic view

From a rational perspective, leadership is a field full of unexplained uncertainties. The multiple studies failed to give any adequate set of characteristics. Definitions abound.

Our paradigmatic analysis would start from the assumption that studies would be aligned with the dominant view. The early studies were mostly quantitative

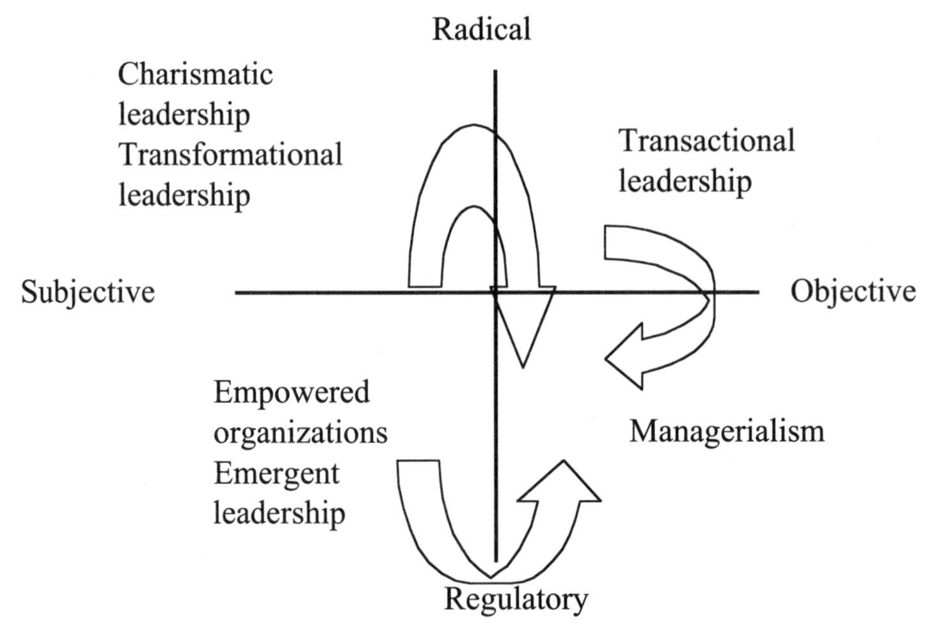

Figure 7.2: Can leadership contribute to business studies?

studies of leadership behaviours and outcomes. If only these studies had yielded reliable and replicable results, leadership might have been plugged into 'what they teach you at business school', perhaps within the more general organizational behaviour courses. As we discovered from our pieces of the leadership jigsaw, the early studies did not give any such clarity to the field. Quantitative studies of leadership factors therefore remained a minority pursuit.

New ideas came along in the 1980s, associated with visions, charisma, transformational capabilities and empowerment. The ideas were supported by the popular interest in outstanding organizations and outstanding leadership. From the point of view of the orthodox business worldview, with its emphasis on what can be measured and codified, these were tricky concepts to accept. Some efforts have been made to capture them using the same sort of measuring approaches as had been applied in earlier studies.[47] In general, however, the constructs derive different perspectives. Our representation of these possibilities, now familiar to those provided in earlier chapters, is shown in figure 7.2.

To understand charismatic leadership we consider that we are dealing in what the orthodox managerial rationality would describe as irrational, perhaps subjective and radical.[48] There is substantial evidence that charismatic leaders can have a dark side, and can achieve spectacularly disastrous changes. Little wonder that the subject is not welcomed within the usual business school curriculum.

Transformational management has been somewhat sanitized. The leaders studied, and transformations achieved, are generally wholesome and desirable. The recent efforts to quantify transformational leadership might be taken as an expected attempt to 'tame it' to make the results more acceptable to the orthodoxy (as shown in figure 7.2).

Transactional leadership approaches are essentially rational. They will be in essence versions of the transactions at the heart of the rational economic model of chapter 10. In principle, we might conceive of such an approach permitting a leader to achieve radical and unexpected or creative change. However, a strictly rational analysis would anticipate leadership to do no more than execute what is rationally correct. The expectations for transactional leadership are likely to be more regulatory than radical (figure 7.2 again).

Empowerment processes and emergent leadership may derive from yet another perspective. There is potential for radical change through the empowering of workers and permitting self-structuring groups to emerge. These are practical concerns for organizations still operating in traditional controlling mode. Giving power to the workers sounds more revolutionary than developmental. In practice, however, the rhetoric of empowerment seems most frequently to describe individuals and teams that discover new ways of achieving the goals of the prevailing management system. Emergent teams tend to emerge as means of achieving corporate goals, rather than as means of disrupting them.

In other words, empowerment and emergent leadership might be explained as activities of meaning creation not revolution creation.[49] If the meanings are those provided by the managerial orthodoxy, the processes will rediscover the purposes and rational logic of that orthodoxy. The prevailing rational view has again tamed the processes of new leadership (figure 7.2 again). A practical example might be found in the structures 'designed in' to permit empowerment and emergent leadership within a top-down and imposed corporate change effort. For all the vocabulary, it is clear that the intention is not to ferment radical ideas, but to encourage a wider sharing of acceptable views (visions?). In short, we will gain a better understanding of empowerment and emergent leadership principles if we seek the explanation in terms of orthodox views, heresies, and suppressed voices.

What you can learn for yourself about leadership

Following the general approach you will be able to construct your platform of understanding based on personal experience. The pieces of the jigsaw will be those you collect and examine for yourself. The analysis will be able to deploy the tools we used here for revealing assumptions behind ideas and plans for leadership changes.

So, for example, if your company plans to introduce a process of transformation (the subject of our next chapter), you will be more sensitized to spotting the assumptions behind the process. Does the process assume shared values (integrationist view) and yet talk of encouraging entrepreneurial attitudes?

Furthermore, you may be able to understand better the behaviours of your organizational leaders. You should be in a better position to understand effective and ineffective behaviours by connecting them with the models of leadership discussed. In particular you may be more tuned to the 'new leadership' approaches, and less satisfied with conclusions of superior rationality or innate characteristics.

Among the new leadership approaches, the notion of leaders as carriers of culture and of meaning provides particularly powerful ways of seeing what is going on.

Creative leadership as a proposal for 'new leadership' action

One promising proposal for developing understanding and leadership skills is through an examination and application of the systems for stimulating creativity (described in chapter 2). The leadership role within a creative problem-solving group is essentially that of empowering others, who discover they are capable of greater achievements. This approach converts the use of creative problem-solving systems into a system for self-development and learning. These systems emphasize the importance of a leader releasing creativity from the team, rather than producing creative solutions for him or herself.

This helps shift emphasis away from what is now considered an unhealthy attention on heroic leadership[50] towards the spirit of transactional leadership, namely encouraging others to greater leadership aspirations and performance.

Notes

1 Yukl (1981: 2).
2 Mandela (1994: 749).
3 Bennis (1959).
4 Adair (1989: 30).
5 By 1990, the third edition of Bass and Stodgill's *Handbook of Leadership* included 7,500 bibliographic references. Yukl (1989) offered an estimate for the total field of 10,000 reported documents.
6 In historical sequence, the books were: Yukl (1981); Hersey & Blanchard (1988): Adair (1989); Kets de Vries (1989); Lord & Maher (1993); Hunt (1991); Bryman (1992); Gryskiewicz (1993); Starratt (1993); Bass & Avolio (1994); and Bennis, Parikh & Lessem (1994).
7 Adair (1989) points out that even today the Greeks, who were among the first to philosophize about leadership, do not use the term leader to refer to industrial pioneers. In Germany, since Hitler's association with the term *Führer*, synonyms for leader are widely preferred.
8 Stodgill (1948). See Bryman (1992) and Yukl (1981) for an appreciation of the impact of Stodgill's work.
9 Bryman (1992), Yukl (1981) and Hunt (1991) reach similar conclusions regarding Stodgill's views and their impact in shifting the emphasis, perhaps too much, away from trait research.
10 The text is essentially from Stodgill (1974: 81).
11 Blake and Mouton's work (for instance, 1964) is highlighted in basic organizational texts. However, the more specialized texts on leadership rather pointedly ignored it, possibly regarding it as derivative of the more academically acclaimed Ohio studies, or those of Kahn & Katz (1953) and Bowers and Seashore (1966).
12 McGregor (1960).
13 Later, long after the first wave of enthusiasm for style theories of leadership had waned, it was proposed that McGregor's work should be modified to go beyond Theory Y to Theory Z, in effect a Theory X plus Y leader.

[14] For example, an emphasis on initiating structure was shown to be more effective under certain stressful conditions, less effective under conditions of lower stress (Kerr et al., 1974).
[15] Yukl (1981) presents contingency approaches as a subset of situational models.
[16] Or, more generally, we may regard a situational or contingency theory as suggesting that for a given set of inputs into a system the outputs are contingent on specific situational factors.
[17] This is often a warning signal of research that is *degenerating* (Lakatos, 1970).
[18] Fiedler's least preferred co-worker work (Fiedler, 1967), which requires considerable leaps of imagination to connect the measurement applied to the postulated characteristics of the leaders studied. The work has been extensively studied and debated, somewhat inconclusively.
[19] Hersey & Blanchard (1977). The behavioural ideas contributed to the widely utilized series of books of which *The One Minute Manager* (Blanchard & Johnson, 1982) had particular appeal to practitioners.
[20] Tannenbaum & Schmidt (1973). House & Mitchell (1974) gives a comprehensive evaluation of empirical work on contingency theories.
[21] Bryman (1992: 20). See also Hunt (1991); Day & Lord (1988).
[22] Starratt (1993).
[23] Bryman (1992: 113).
[24] Burns (1978).
[25] Bass & Avolio (1990, 1994).
[26] For evidence see the various articles in Bass & Avolio (1994). The measures can produce self-reports or assessments of leaders after direct observation or from documentary information. The technical criticisms directed at the earlier trait/style studies can be applied to these studies (Bryman, 1992).
[27] Bennis & Nanus (1985).
[28] Bennis & Nanus (1985: 89), quoted in Bryman (1992: 136) and Bennis et al. (1994).
[29] Peters & Waterman (1982: 82) quoting Henry Kissinger.
[30] (Ibid.: 82).
[31] Selznick's quote also includes the observation that: 'The inbuilding of purpose is a challenge to creativity' (Peters & Waterman 1982: 85).
[32] Nadler & Tushman (1989). Tushman also developed a case that change requires discontinuous jolts, not easily studied within traditional assumptions of organizations as systems in some kind of equilibrium with their environments (Tushman & Romanelli, 1985).
[33] The Three Graces, (the charities) imparted graciousness to human life. Hence charismatic, pertaining to charism. Weber uses the term to illustrate the power of the temple priests, and how the power loses its 'magic' through ritualization.
[34] Bryman (1992: 24) citing Weber.
[35] Bryman (1992); Hunt (1991); Starratt (1993).
[36] This has been challenged by Shils (1968) as extending the concept so as to lose much of its focus and conceptual power.
[37] Bryman (1992: 41–2).
[38] Bryman (1992) numbered thirty different indexed references to visions, Starratt (1993) twenty, Hunt (1991) seven.
[39] For example, Hunt (1991) cites Conger (1989); and various Sashkin (1988) and co-worker studies. In contrast, there have been far more proposals on how to develop skills at visioning from researchers interested in techniques for stimulating creativity. See, for example, the proceedings of the conferences of the European Association for Creativity and Innovation, at Noordwijk and Darmstadt, and the Prism conferences at Greensboro,

NC, Buffalo, NY and Quebec City, Canada. (Colemont et al., 1988; Rickards, Moger et al. 1992, Gryskiewicz 1993; Isaksen et al. 1993a, 1993b; Bédard 1994; Geschka et al. 1995). See also Parnes (1988, 1992). Parker (1990) gives an excellent case example of organizational transformation involving extensive facilitated visioning.

[40] See Bryman (1992) for a discussion of this point.

[41] Hofstede (1991) made a similar point about cultural differences. What's different is dangerous.

[42] Zaleznik, A. (1977).

[43] Robert Maxwell is now the almost obligatory British example.

[44] I am following the account in Huczynski & Buchanan (1997).

[45] Cartwright & Zander (1968: 304).

[46] See Yukl (1989) for an account of emergent leadership in groups.

[47] Bass and Avolio's work (1990, 1994) is possibly the most widely studied and validated example of classical quantitative methods directed to studying new management concepts.

[48] As elsewhere, this description has to be studied carefully. The terms subjective and radical have been retained and carried over from the earlier studies, particularly from Burrell & Morgan (1979). They may be seen as dangerously 'contaminated' terms, having existence only as oppositions to the values and terminology of the 'objective' orthodoxy.

[49] The 'heresy' of interpretivism or meaning creation, as indicated in chapter 1. If the heresy is distorted as described it may be seen as 'tamed' by the dominant rational worldview of the organization.

[50] Bryman (1992).

chapter 8 The Management of Change

Why do some men hunger, even rage for change, doing all in their power to create it, while others flee from it? I not only found no ready answers to such questions but found that we lack even an adequate theory of adaptation, without which it is extremely unlikely that we will ever find the answers.

***Alvin Toffler*[1]**

Liberation Management appears ten years, almost to the day, after the publication of *In Search of Excellence* . . . While *Search* condemned the excesses of dispassionate 'modern management practice', it nonetheless celebrated big manufacturing businesses . . . Five years later I declared that 'there are no excellent companies' (*Thriving on Chaos*) . . . in retrospect I don't think it was a revolutionary book . . . I hope *Liberation Management* is revolutionary.

***Tom Peters*[2]**

It is time to obliterate the cow paths . . . We should 'reengineer' our businesses: use the power of modern information technology to radically redesign our business processes in order to achieve dramatic improvements in their performance.

***Mike Hammer*[3]**

Reengineering is in trouble. It's not easy for me to make this admission. I was one of the two people who introduced the concept.

***James Champy*[4]**

Introduction

This chapter will follow the procedures established in earlier chapters for puzzling out a topic of interest. Before moving into the more unmapped territories of change, we will look briefly at a much better charted territory covered in business school courses. By identifying what is legitimized and taught we will have some indication of what is left – the less orthodox views. It might be imagined that change would be at the centre of business studies. What seems to be the case is that the schools teach a wide range of topics, most of which have some value within processes of managing and introducing change. If we use our jigsaw metaphor, the process supplies lots of pieces of a jigsaw, in the hope that the recipients will eventually benefit by putting the pieces together in their subsequent careers.

The orthodox bits of the change jigsaw

There is a specific aspect of business school orthodoxy that deals with the nature of organizational structures, how they function and how they are designed. This falls within a teaching classification with course labels such as OB/OD (organizational behaviour and organizational design). A historically thorough review of organizational theories is provided on these courses. By custom and practice the key names are taught as a litany, starting with the father of organizational theorizing, Max Weber. A (simplified) version is provided of his theory of the modern hierarchical organizational structure with its associated bureaucratic characteristics. Students then learn of the design school of thought, which proposed that organizations had differing forms that were influenced, perhaps determined, by their environments. The school offers a view of an organizational world that has definable structures that can be designed for efficiency. It is a world of causal links between the identified design and the subsequent performance of the organizations.

Technology has been singled out as a major influence on organizational structure and performance. This is sometimes called technological determinism and is traced to the work of the English academic Joan Woodward and American researchers Thompson and Perrow.[5]

Contingency theory

The design school of organizational theorists was strongly influenced by the contingencies or possibilities determined by circumstances in a given situation. Among the most influential contingency theorists were the Harvard-based team of Lawrence and Lorsch, who proposed further refinements to the environmental factors (including technological complexity) influencing organizational design.[6]

A leading theorist, Lex Donaldson, is Professor of Organizational Design at the Australian Graduate School of Management, University of New South Wales. He recently summarized the achievement of the contingency school as providing a comprehensive theory of structural adaptation. Donaldson is one of the most committed of researchers to what we have labelled the rational orthodoxy. He calls his theoretical perspective by the older name positivist theory, a term we will come across in mainline economic theory in chapter 10. Donaldson is engaged in academic dispute with those who see the approach as indefensibly deterministic. His critics include others of the modern Australian school of organizational theorists, such as Stewart Clegg, concerned with the human aspects of organizational systems, including political power struggles.[7] Another line of opposition comes from Donaldson's former supervisor, John Child, who considers that managers have a degree of free will in the strategic decisions they take. The debate is described as the technological determinism versus strategic choice debate.

Summarizing the change orthodoxy

'What they teach in business school' about organizations and change is broadly sympathetic to the design school, contingency theory, and the openly positivist view represented by Donaldson. Theories based on power struggles, for example, remain less acceptable. We need not be surprised that the managerialist orthodoxy in most business schools regards them as distinctly heretical! However, the orthodox approach does not just exclude theories based on power struggles. As we are about to see, there are a number of approaches to change that have attracted a great deal of attention outside business schools. They will be revealed as we look more carefully at the bits of the jigsaw of change management.

Puzzling out change processes: The very complex puzzle of change processes:[8]

There is no contemporary text that has authoritatively puzzled out the territory of change management. As a result, the 'handfuls of books' had to be scanned for shared beliefs about influential figures and themes. This process eventually suggested a set of jigsaw pieces as indicated in figure 8.1.

The jigsaw pieces will help us explore way beyond what I have called managerial orthodoxy. They also help to reveal the coherent nature of beliefs within that orthodoxy. Shifting metaphor, we might see the orthodoxy as the roots of a kind of Darwinian tree with a range of branches spreading out from its origins, as shown in figure 8.2.

The path through the change literature begins with the efforts of Kurt Lewin, without doubt a pioneering figure in any platform of understanding of organizational change. Lewin's work represented one of two kinds of systems approach, each of which we consider here. Lewin belonged to the tradition of so-called soft

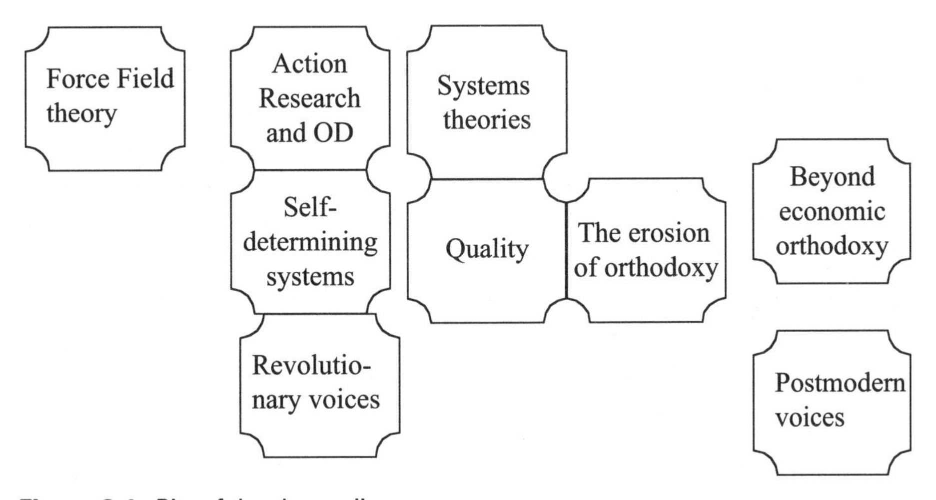

Figure 8.1: Bits of the change jigsaw

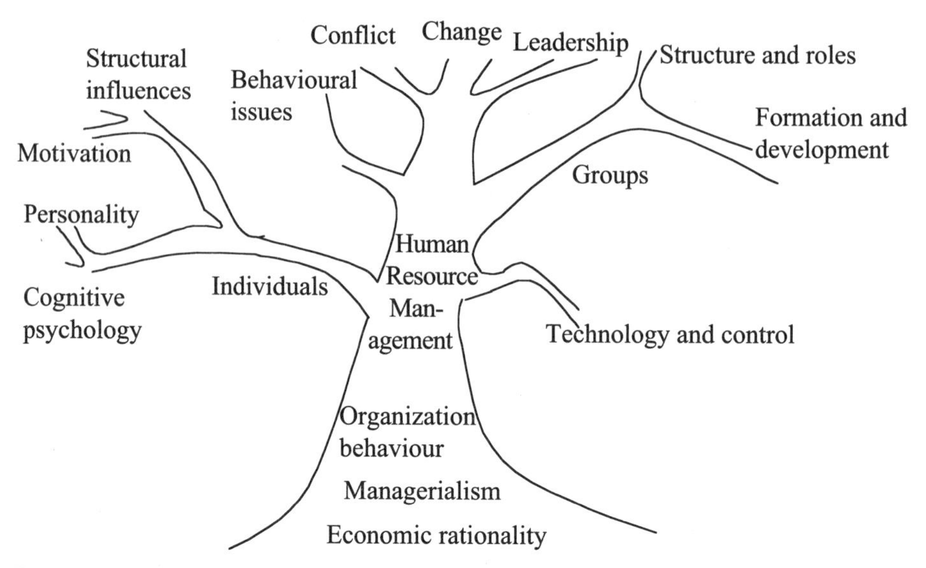

Figure 8.2: The Darwinian tree of managerialism

systems, in which attention is paid to the human and social factors. The second tradition is that of hard systems approaches, which have a more deterministic form.[9] Each tradition developed its own model of systemic learning as a change process. Proposals of a more radical nature are then considered, again roughly divisible into the more humanistic developments and the more structural ones. One recent revolutionary tendency is set aside for the next chapter, namely the so-called postmodern turn in thinking that makes claims to replace all previous orthodoxies.

Lewin and the Development of Action-centred Change Theories

Kurt Lewin has been widely regarded as a pioneer and a major influence in the field of social psychology.[10] Lewin has as much right as anyone to be hailed a hero of the revolution in thinking about change that has competed with the orthodoxy we have encountered in previous chapters. However, we will see that, from the perspective of today's platform of understanding, the impact of his ideas has been distorted and diminished, often 'tamed' to reappear as rather innocuous variations of the prevailing orthodoxy.

Lewin's early ideas were influenced by the Gestalt school of psychologists.[11] An essential aspect of Gestalt psychology was the notion of individual perception as a coherent structure or form. Gestalt researchers developed 'laws of closure' through which an individual arrives at understanding of a whole when examining incomplete data. Lewin extended these ideas from individual experimental psychology. He proposed that a social group would develop a unified Gestalt. Thus to study individuals it was necessary to study the nature of their perceptions of the social group in which they operated.

Lewin was not interested in studying individuals as unchanging subjects of investigation. He reasoned that the purpose of such work was directly to influence change, particularly through enhancing the learning processes. Earlier ideas of psychological research involved objective and detached researchers. Lewin's researchers were involved in the action. Lewin's early contributions to social science concerned themselves with the social and ethical nature of totalitarianism. He applied his analysis of the forces at work, and suggested ways of intervening so as to induce or restore more psychologically healthy social systems. He introduced the term action research in a theoretical paper in 1946 as a theory of informed practice for dealing with the critical issues of the day such as fascism, racialism and economic inequalities.[12]

Lewin is still remembered for his Force Field theory. It represented individuals in organizations as operating in a state of dynamic equilibrium, established by a series of forces which effectively act as a coherent force field.[13] We will look at some of its practical implications in a later section. The conceptual power of his Force Field theory lies in treating individual behaviours as intimately influenced by a totality or Gestalt. According to Lewin, change is regarded as a process in which the psychological forces are in some way relaxed, for example, in a specially designed learning environment. The unfreezing permits a reshaping of beliefs, and the possibility of a group establishing a new set of social dynamics. The three stages of change therefore are summed up as unfreezing, changing and refreezing. The theory has underpinned organizational change efforts ever since.

Lewin was not to live to see the fruits of his work. He died in 1947 shortly after helping to found the National Training Laboratory (NTL) in Group Development, at Bethel, Maine. The NTL movement has had enormous impact on group dynamics theory and practice world-wide. One of its most enduring contributions has been the laboratory method of learning through the T-group or training group approach.[14]

OD, Action Research and sociotechnical systems theory

The NTL was also to pioneer the rise of organizational development, or OD, as a professional body. The movement retained the principles of Action Research as one of its characteristic methods of introducing change into organizational and social groups. Roughly contemporaneously, the Tavistock approach developed in Europe. Again, the emphasis has been on the integrity of groups, and the procedures required to influence and change them. Within the Tavistock approach, much work has been done on the relationship between the technological infrastructure of a group, and its social psychology. There are considerable overlaps, at the levels of basic values of participation and learning methods, between the European and North American movements. However, as we will see, the European movement has tended to adhere rather closely to the core of Lewin's ideas, whereas the American approach has arguably become 'tamed' to a more rationalistic form.

The Sociotechnical and Psychodynamic Schools

The European version of Action Research has been most coherently expressed through the work of the Tavistock Institute.[15] The 'Tavi' has over the years attracted high calibre social scientists who have contributed in the spirit of Lewin's call for socially directed research programmes. The ethos of the institute was to develop a new approach to social change through direct involvement in social issues.

One of the early studies of the institute came to symbolize its sociotechnical approach. Tavistock workers Bamforth and Trist were involved in a change process through which the miners at a colliery in Bolsover, Derbyshire, changed their working procedures. Following the principles of action research, the miners and change agents co-designed a new method of coal-mining based on the concept of autonomous teams. Work requirements were no longer imposed by the external system, but were created, and modified in light of experience, by those directly involved in the production of the coal.

Productivity gains were substantial and sustained. The system was to become an organizational innovation in the mining industry which totally replaced the earlier working methods. Furthermore, the change was achieved with great gains in personal satisfaction for team members. The coal-mining environment was to remain dangerous and physically unpleasant throughout the twentieth century. That such an unlikely environment could be the host for changes in morale and productivity added to the reputation of the study and of its theoretical framework.

The Tavistock has retained its commitment to research in action mode to present times. The sociotechnical tradition has been developed and widely extended to include approaches for participative design of information systems, and larger-scale organizational restructuring.[16] The training to become a Tavistock change-agent retains the psychodynamic traditions of its earlier years.[17]

Soft systems methodology (SSM)

An example of a coherent soft-systems approach to change has been pioneered by Peter Checkland, originally in ICI, and developed by co-workers at Lancaster University, in England.[18] The approach seeks to help an organization, or other social group, to understand its own sets of beliefs, and to construct coherent paths for changing them. In essence the soft-systems approach seeks to encourage self-initiated learning by those involved in the system. It is essentially a special kind of learning about the nature of one's own beliefs.

In Checkland's approach, the search, supported by a skilled facilitator, aims to identify a powerful description that captures many of the beliefs and practices of the system. Checkland refers to this as the system's root definition. Another important practical component is that of building a rich visual picture of the situation. In principle, the individual or team building the rich picture is searching for a holistic overview of the system. As with Lewin, the search is directed towards discovering a Gestalt that provides meaning for those interested in understanding or seeking to change the system.

The 'Taming' of Lewin's Legacy

Lewin often expressed his ideas in the classical scientific format of clinical and objective analysis.[19] This was necessary to communicate with professional psychologists of the day. Perhaps as consequence, Lewin is regarded as supporting a rather traditional approach to diagnosing change, rather than introducing a revolutionary, action-based approach.[20] Subsequent developments were to be even more towards a less revolutionary treatment of his work.

By the 1970s, the dynamics of Lewin's Force Field were widely taught as a kind of analytic technique. One visually graphic approach represented the organizational system undergoing change by a wavy horizontal line on a flip chart. The restraining forces were drawn in as weighted bags pulling the system to earth; the change forces as gas-filled balloons pulling the system up to the heavens. Participants had to agree which were the heaviest bags, and brainstorm ways of lightening the weight of ballast restricting the take-off of the idea being proposed.[21]

The analysis has some merit in sensitizing problem-solvers to a wider range of influences than might otherwise be addressed. At the same time it risks losing Lewin's inherent Gestaltist beliefs. We might see the shifts as presenting the approach in a way more acceptable to the dominant orthodoxy. Similar shifts occurred in practices within the Organizational Development and Action Research movements, as we will now see.

Organizational development (OD)

One of the most widely quoted definitions of OD and its relationship to Action Research can be found in a textbook by French and Bell, two American pioneers, who could claim direct involvement with Lewin. They define OD as: 'a long-term effort to improve an organization's problem-solving and renewal processes, particularly through a more effective and collaborative management of organization culture – with emphasis on the culture of internal work teams – with the assistance of a change agent, or catalyst, and the use of theory and technology of behavioral science including action research.'[22]

The researchers define action research as 'a data-based problem-solving model that replicates the steps involved in the scientific method of enquiry. Three processes are involved in action research: data collection, feedback of data to the clients, and action planning based on the data.'[23]

The vocabulary of OD is clearly that of the orthodoxy of management science. Little remains of Lewin's original beliefs of discovery learning. Indeed, one recent study considered that Lewin's three-stage model of change and OD stand in opposition.[24] One recent review described it thus: 'Action research can . . . be viewed as a cyclical process with five phases: diagnosing, action planning, action taking, evaluating, and specifying learning . . . We consider all five phases to be necessary for a comprehensive definition of action research.'[25]

Schein & Beckhard as exemplars of OD change practitioners

Ed Schein has already appeared in chapter 6, where we encountered his contributions to our understanding and changing corporate culture. His book on process consultancy includes a range of practical concepts for the change agent.[26] Schein writes with great clarity about establishing a psychological contract as a preliminary step to gaining trust. In essence, the group can be seen as operating in Lewin's Force Field. The process has to be moved on to the unfrozen stage by working at developing openness and agreement. Only then can new structures be proposed. The effective process consultant recognizes the perceptual and psychological nature of this process.[27]

Richard Beckhard is another action researcher with an acknowledged lineage to Lewin.[28] His change inequality states that the dynamic equilibrium in a force field can be disrupted and swung towards a new equilibrium state if the costs of change are weaker than enablers of change. The three enablers are dissatisfaction with the status quo, clear or understood and desired future state, and practical first steps. The costs have to include considerations of the psychological costs of change. The formal application of the model permits a rapid sharing of ideas, and consideration of fresh ideas, for example, if the participants have met together to share their differing change responsibilities.

Schein and Beckhard have become prominent figures for their consultancy work and their writings about change. They are likely to represent its orthodoxy in important ways. Thus, the values implicit in their ideas are the values of the psychodynamic school, with its connotations of participation, shared and coherent visions. However, the enactment of the ideas are through simply expressed, rationalistic structures and interventions. The techniques seek to elicit goals or objectives of a meeting, in rational discourse. Furthermore, the interventions seem in practice to reinforce existing dominant forces in the Force Field. Support from the top or senior people involved seemed a necessary requirement for change.[29]

Such applications may contribute focus and energy within change programmes. However, the methodology generally seeks the approval of the prevailing power structures. These features reduce the likelihood that OD under such constraints can secure radical changes in an organization.[30]

Lewin's innovative vision was of a new kind of science of participative discovery. This vision seems to have become entangled with this shift in beliefs within the OD movement, which threatens to reclaim it as an orthodox rationalistic approach for managing change.

The Hard-systems Tradition

Lewin pioneered interest in what was later to be considered soft-systems approaches.[31] There is a contrasting hard-systems tradition which turns out to be more easily aligned with the managerial orthodoxy. The historical accounts suggest that hard-systems theory can be traced to the writings of Ludvig von Bertalanffy.[32] Bertalanffy developed his ideas in highly mathematical format, although subsequently their conceptual implications were taken and used in less formal ways.

Cybernetics, or the science of control systems, has developed its hard-systems models to great effect for understanding engineering and communication systems. It was originally named and developed by the mathematical genius Norbert Wiener (1894–1964) in the 1940s.[33] Influenced by Wiener, MIT subsequently became an internationally recognized centre for systems dynamics, under Jay Forrester.[34] The hard-systems view is that organizations have been designed in certain ways, which reveal their interrelationships through analysis. These, especially interrelationships influencing information flows, communication and control, may require design changes, indicated by systems principles.[35]

A sophisticated hard-systems approach can be found in the prolific and conceptually challenging writings of the English polymath Stafford Beer.[36] He is now considered to have pioneered managerial cybernetics, and his most famous model was inspired by his knowledge of the control processes involving the human brain and nervous system. The model incorporates multiple feedback mechanisms and levels within the system, which has five layers, each interacting with its partners and environment.[37] The system has been applied to a wide range of organizational systems, and even to a famous project in which the Chilean economy was modelled and demonstrated to a receptive President Allende.[38]

The philosophic gulf between hard and soft systems is not easily bridged.[39] As a simplifying device, however, it is relatively easy to see the systems schools aligning themselves on one side or the other of the hard–soft divide. Hard systems are more concerned with issues of control and prediction of systems performance. Soft systems have been more concerned with the capacity of human actions in systems to adapt and modify the system's characteristics. These ideas of self-development and learning have made a particular contribution to the literature of organizational change.

The Learning Systems Schools

Large numbers of popular books on learning organizations and learning companies were written, with a peak somewhere in the late 1980s.

Argyris, espoused theory and double loop learning

Chris Argyris of Harvard University has, over the years, accumulated an impressive body of writings examining the more complex and conflicting sides of change. He argued powerfully that organizational systems present one view of the world to themselves and others, an espoused theory of how businesses are supposed to run. The espoused theory will carry in it the prevailing orthodoxy about rationality, scientific management, control, and prevailing beliefs about how people behave and can be influenced. Espoused theories can change, but only slowly. The espoused theory survives and persists if the organizational members can repeatedly reinforce it through their discourse, that is to say through their explanations of what is happening.

A well-known story illustrates espoused theories. This is the folk tale of the Emperor's new clothes.[40] Here, the espoused theory of the Emperor and his subjects is that the Emperor knows best. If the organization is to break this Gestalt there may well be need for a jolt and a moment of insight. The espoused theory no longer seems to make sense. Argyris points out that the process of denial can involve several layers of defence. The theories in use are denied, and on being challenged, the denial is itself denied. 'What do you mean deceived? I'm the emperor. Emperors don't get deceived by common tailors.'

In our story the onlookers break out of their learning loop into a new kind of consciousness of the emperor and his lack of clothes. The double loop might involve them realizing that emperors can be deceived. Argyris, like Lewin, reminds us that beliefs may take a lot of breaking. As one of our powerful organizational beliefs is about the rationality of its actors, it follows that rational thinking may not be the best way for us to challenge beliefs about our rationality. For better practical outcomes, we need better awareness of the nature of theory.[41]

Peter Senge and the fifth discipline

Peter Senge is another writer who offers a learning perspective within a systems framework. His influential book, *The Fifth Discipline*, is subtitled *The Art and Practice of the Learning Organization*.[42] He argues that only through what amounts to a shift to a systems paradigm can organizations shed the load of assumptions and beliefs inherited from the production systems of the industrial era.

The fifth discipline is no less than systems thinking, which permits the harmonious development of the other four. These are the disciplines of personal growth; working out the significance of mental models; building a shared vision; and achieving team learning.[43] Senge presents production and managerial systems as self-reinforcing single loops. He shows that many efforts to disrupt a routine cycle of activities, far from making things better, actually set up a second, opposing cycle of activities which accentuate 'negative feedback' into the first loop. By more careful analysis and intervention, benign cycles of actions can be set up.

Senge has found a way of extending Lewin's Force Field analysis, and Argyris's double-loop learning, to today's fast-changing operational systems. Senge's vicious circles may be seen as Force Fields in which the actions are drifting the system away from the desired direction of change; his benign circles as systems in which the forces have been unfrozen and reset to support the desired changes. Senge illustrates aspects of systems as a dynamic life cycle reacting sometimes inappropriately to external stimuli. He shows the significance of goal-oriented or purposive behaviours, and the benefits from finding ways of understanding and seeking to change insider perceptions of the rationale of the organizational system. He also indicates the potentially damaging impacts of misunderstandings through different needs of individuals within the system.

Senge's particular brand of systems thinking helps individuals and corporate planning groups become more sophisticated in their judgements of production and control decisions, for example.[44] The approach does claim to enhance reflection and learning so as to open the way to more radical insights for change. In practice, however, the methodology risks being simplified and 'tamed' into yet another way of achieving incremental systemic change, while preserving the deeper structural and cultural characteristics of a company, while providing means of efficiency in terms of systemic alignment.

The Transformationists: Kanter, Handy, Peters

In the decade after the mid-1980s a range of proposals emerged that appeared to offer prospects of transforming the essential nature of organizations.[45] We will look at the contributions made by Rosebeth Kanter, Tom Peters and Charles Handy.

Rosebeth Moss Kanter

Kanter acquired a high public profile after her book *The Change Masters.*[46] She based her arguments on careful research that had shown significant differences between firms that successfully mastered change, and those that had not. Her conclusion was that change mastery required innovative methods of releasing the potentials of all employees, through educational programmes, and appropriate local organizational structures. She suggested that the efforts required changes in beliefs and practice. These changes required deliberate efforts by skilled and trained agents of change.

The final chapter of *The Change Masters* suggests that American business requires a Renaissance that can be achieved by encouraging multiple innovative contributions from employees who have the power to influence their own work. In spirit, Kanter follows the traditions of humanistic writers on management. Her Renaissance is a gentle revolution in which enlightened managers support progress 'because of its humanistic as well as its economic benefits'.[47] 'You can do it,' she tells Corporate America, 'and the revolution does not have to be a bloody one.'

Tom Peters

Kanter's book appeared at roughly the same time as the best-selling text *In Search of Excellence* by Tom Peters and Robert Waterman.[48] Like Kanter, the authors presented examples of successful companies, and extracted messages for other companies to become more like those successes. Peters and Waterman were not so much pioneers and innovators, but catalysts of change, and carriers of ideas that had been around for a long time.[49] Their operational message was that successful large companies had overcome the constraints imposed by classical organizational structures and cultures. Peters and Waterman were never to write a further substantial book together. Waterman has produced work that can be seen as an extension of the messages of the earlier success. Peters has followed a more revolutionary path. In some ways, he resembles a fundamentalist preacher, increasingly driven to secure followers and rescue them from the punishment inevitably to be visited on doomed unbelievers.

This approach has attracted the critical attention of academic researchers who have been less than generous in their evaluation of the Peters and Waterman book, and subsequently of the Peters phenomenon.[50] For Peters, we have only overcome the straitjackets of rationality by a kind of purifying madness. He describes the manifestations of madness required – the obsessiveness, or passion for excellence in serving the customer. He implies that the description madness is to misunderstand the outpouring of energies that can be directed to transform bureaucratic organizations, that have permitted Lilliputians to bind Gullivers all over the organizational world.

Charles Handy

Peters recognized the importance of challenging orthodoxy. In this he resembles the third of our modern revolutionaries, Charles Handy. Handy, a former Shell executive, wrote a thought-provoking book that catapulted Handy to international status as organizational prophet. Handy proposed, in *The Age of Unreason,* that we were living in unreasonable if not crazy times.[51] He wanted each individual to seek those creative and unexpected alternatives that went against conventional wisdom. This offers people better chances of surviving and perhaps changing the larger social systems of which they are part. He went on to anticipate a shift in work patterns requiring a portfolio of contractual activities as organizations shift to a core of full-time employees, and other arrangements with 'flexible workers and flexible supply structures'[52] on the outside.

In their different ways, Kanter, Peters and Handy have served as gadflies encouraging revolution. Peters has become increasingly violent in his advocacy of revolutionary methods. Kanter and Handy stand for a gentler kind of change process. Kanter is the most sociological, and the writer who puts the most emphasis on benefits from participative methods. Handy has offered the most incisive prediction of the ways in which organizational life seems to be fragmenting.

The Total Quality Revolution

The hard-systems tradition was to provide even more widespread impact on organizational change approaches. A major revolution in production methods sprang up under the rubric of Total Quality.

Deming and the origins of the Total Quality story

The often repeated story of Total Quality Management is now told in the textbooks in a standard way. In the pre-quality era, organizations had ignored the quality of their practices and products.[53] Work was characterized by making and selling. An American visionary by the name of William Edwards Deming pioneered the quality movement.[54] Deming, with a Yale doctorate in physics, developed ideas of statistical quality control during the Second World War. In the early post-war years there was initial interest in upgrading the production through statistical monitoring. This interest declined, and Deming through assignment to Japan found a far more receptive culture. There, the ideas of quality, originally developed in the Bell telephone laboratories of America, were embraced through the efforts of pioneers who were to be later hailed as the Japanese quality gurus, including Deming himself, Joseph Juran and Arman Feigenbaum.

The diffusion of Total Quality ideas

Articles began to appear in Western publications, linking Japan's economic success to their espousal of Total Quality ideas, and statistical control procedures. In 1980 Deming explained his ideas on an American TV programme, and an explosive growth in interest in quality followed. The timing coincided with increasing efforts in the West to understand and learn from Japan's success. Perhaps the account of American ideas ignored and then exported to Japan gave added impact to Deming's story.[55] By the 1980s a resurgence of the ideas in the West was supported by a newer generation of workers, of whom Philip Crosby is particularly well-known.

The basic principles

Total Quality commits organizations to the search and implementation of changes that enhance quality through manufacturing and production. An attempt to capture the main principles of Total Quality recently produced the following definition: 'TQM . . . refers to a management process directed at establishing organized continuous improvement activities, involving everyone in an organization in a totally integrated effort towards improving performance at every level.'[56]

Three components of the definition are worth expanding, as they capture some of the potential difficulties as experienced by organizations encountering the total quality movement. The first is the aspiration of getting work done with minimum unplanned errors or defects in outputs. This is the famed principle of being right first time. In production units the statistical control measures can be targeted to achieve fewer and fewer defects, in a drive to zero defects. The drive towards output perfection is the motivation behind continuous improvement efforts, which is the second of the principles. Finally, the process recognizes the interconnectedness of organizational activities, and aspires to taking a systems view of planned change.

The paradoxes of TQM

TQM presents contemporary businesses with puzzling contradictions. For example, the involvement of all workers seems to encourage the participation required for corporate innovation. Yet, the universal prescriptions of the approaches can appear no less mechanistic than the classical bureaucratic control from the top through the tiers of a pyramidal structure. A further paradox lies in the emphasis on a total systems approach, while too often the changes are introduced in a piecemeal fashion.[57]

The paradoxes become more acute as evidence emerges that, by the late 1980s, a minority of organizations reported significant successes through TQM, whereas a majority had become disillusioned. Between sixty and eighty per cent of firms have reported unsuccessful programmes.[58] Regardless of collection errors the figures point to a substantial level of disillusionment among firms that have attempted to introduce total quality methods.

The quality standards movement

In the 1980s, the quality movement developed its own self-sustaining support networks. For example, pressure groups and government-supported initiatives emerged to promote the activities of total quality. There have been various widespread award schemes nationally and internationally. The Deming quality award has become much sought after as evidence of manufacturing excellence. For smaller firms, certification became a doorway to admittance as a preferred supplier to larger firms and government contracts. In search of quality became for some in search of quality certification. The UK BS7550 quality award and the related European ISO 9001 played their parts in diffusing the concepts of quality to wider sectors in industry.

Quality at the crossroads

What can we make of the quality movement as a vehicle for organizational change? By the 1990s, the voices criticizing the broader quality movement could argue that the results remained less than convincing as means towards organizational transformation. Even where the programmes achieved successes, the approaches inevitably led to diminished returns on effort and greater competition in the marketplace. The appeal of the more quantitative aspects needs little explanation. The dominant management orthodoxy favours that which can be measured and controlled. At one level, the quality approach was aligned with that orthodoxy. Its vocabulary was challenging, and promising, without being threatening to the deeper beliefs about management and control.

Professor John Bessant of Brighton University's Centre for Research in Innovation Management captures the more humanistic and visionary aspects of the movement in his writings. He considers the likely consequences of the classical production processes as treating people as cogs in a machine, and contrasts TQM, which 'seeks instead to build on worker involvement, creating mechanisms for increasing their ownership and responsibility for quality and providing the training, tools, and top management commitment to support it . . . [T]he underlying philosophy is one of continuous improvement. This is achieved by systematically searching out and revealing problems, followed by equally systematic solutions using the creativity and experience of all involved.'[59]

As Bessant also observed, the processes of quality operate in a developmental and incremental way.[60] For more significant change, the organization has to find ways of achieving more structural and deep-rooted transformations. The quiet revolution of quality was to pave the way for far more radical change proposals.

Business Process Reengineering

In the late 1980s, a wave of self-criticism hit Corporate America regarding its decline in manufacturing competitiveness compared with Japan and the Asian 'Little Tiger' economies. A business idea appeared that offered prospects of planned change that was of a more revolutionary nature than the recipes of the quality movement. This was Business Process Reengineering, or BPR. We can immediately see some pointers to its likely appeal within organizations. Business, Process and Reengineering, three words each likely to be non-threatening to a rational manager paradigm, yet collectively offering a promise of transformation and competitive success.

Hammer Michael

The contagious impact of the idea can be traced to a *Harvard Business Review* article by Michael Hammer under the inspiring title *Reengineering work: Don't automate. Obliterate.*[61] At that time, the technological advances in electronic data processing were developing at accelerating speed of time to market. Hammer offered an explanation why computerized information systems were rarely delivering the hoped-for organizational gains. Hammer concurred with the view that industry had moved into a time in which information management was the key to organizational change. Information could be speeded up to achieve revolutionary increases in operations and competitiveness.[62] His explanation was that the new opportunities were being lost because the business structures and processes in organizations had been designed in a previous non-electronic era. To achieve the benefits of computerization the old pathways have to be replaced by 'super-highways'.

The diffusion of the BPR vision

Its prescriptions synthesized and articulated the dreams of many information technologists who had struggled to introduce new systems under conditions of limited cross-functional co-operation. The notion also found great support from those with electronic solutions to organizational problems, especially in computer hardware, software and consultancy sectors. The idea was then extensively popularized, not least by a best-selling book co-authored by James Champy, *Reengineering the Corporation.*[63]

Reengineering provided organizations with a rationale for shifting towards more skilled and appropriate jobs. In practice, this requires a re-evaluation of tasks and creation of more efficient business flows. Corporate enthusiasm quickly extended the implications of the basic idea until it became advocated as a universal recipe for organizational transformation. Its most obvious distinction from the many versions of planned changes of the quality programmes was its acknowledged radical rather than incremental nature.

Hammer's call for obliteration of obsolete practices was widely taken as an invitation to obliterate jobs. Reengineering has often been marked by rapidly executed programmes of redundancies. The redundancies acquired a new label of downsizing or rightsizing, and had the relatively novel aspect of targeting the middle ranks of administrators. By the mid-1990s there were many claimed examples of corporate use of BPR. Academics were beginning to recognize the impact of the phenomenon on change practitioners and consultants.

Criticisms of BPR

Academics tend to be suspicious of revolutionary movements promising a Utopian future. It was not clear that the approach offered anything that would deal with the behavioural difficulties widely experienced in earlier planned change programmes. In practice, the approach was considered to have disregarded these difficulties, concentrating on goals and targets derived from estimates of theoretical efficiency gains. Furthermore, there was suspicion that the rhetoric of empowerment might be concealing what amounted to a more sophisticated form of scientific management. It threatened to result in a residual core of workers valued mainly for their delivery of productivity targets in complex environments dominated by new technologies.[64]

Perhaps the most balanced evaluation of the impact of BPR in practice came from its co-founder, James Champy. 'Many companies reported big changes and reaped big rewards. An American mining company . . . saw its revenues increase by 30 per cent and its market share by 20 per cent, while its costs went down 12 per cent . . . A North American chemical company cut its order-delivery time by more than 50 per cent and its costs by more than $300 million. There have been many equally dramatic success stories. On the whole however, even substantial reengineering payoffs appear to have fallen well short of their potential . . . This partial revolution is not the one I intended . . . I have also learned that half a revolution is not better than none. It may in fact be worse.'[65]

BPR is in essence a justification for empowerment, rather than a means of achieving it. And without unified collaboration towards corporate goals, an organization is unlikely to achieve the economic and production gains estimated.

Making Sense of the Jigsaw Pieces of Change

How might we make more sense of the multiplicity of ideas in the writings on change? Once again, we apply the critical approach of identifying those components that are consistent with a dominant view. We also expect to find opposing views or heresies that have been distorted by the dominant view. Our customary mapping is shown in figure 8.3.

The business orthodoxy is objective and functional: 'What they teach you at business school' is that change theories are based on identifying key features

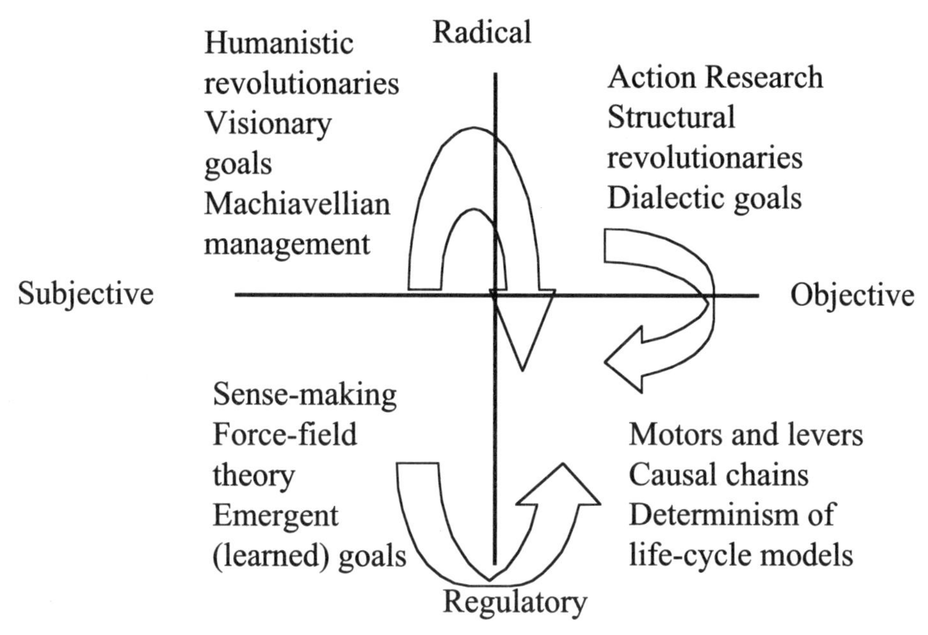

Figure 8.3: Change

within an organization and its environment, and then on designing appropriate structures to fit the requirements. This is precisely the orthodoxy we repeatedly encountered in other chapters, and as such fits into the so-called functionalist box, with the usual sets of beliefs about plannable and regulatory change processes.

Lewin's humanistic innovation 'tamed' and objectified

Lewin began from a non-orthodox theoretical position of a Gestalt psychologist. His innovative and revolutionary proposals for participatory discovery fit nicely into a radical and humanistic perspective. As such, they would be open to rejection as contrary to the accepted ways of conducting 'scientific' research. That is what has happened. We recall, however, that even Lewin used the vocabulary of the orthodoxy in his 'scientific' papers. Furthermore, the emerging schools of action research and organizational development largely followed the route of presenting their work as close to the dominant tradition.

Soft-systems approaches regarded as too subjective

The soft-systems approaches became associated with organizational learning, with an inclination towards self-discovery and meaning management. Again, we have an approach that fits poorly with the more rigid treatments of organizational design theorists. It is too 'subjective' in nature. This offers an explanation why change processes involving self-learning systems have been largely kept out of the business studies curriculum.

Hard-systems approaches are not adequately predictable

What then of the Quality Movement, and Business Process Reengineering? Both align themselves with the hard-systems school of objective modelling and prediction. Yet the movements are treated with considerable suspicion, not just among the advocates of more behavioural and humanistic approaches. It seems a little strange that they are not more welcomed into the business studies curriculum as empirical investigations that might shed light on the orthodox contingency view of planned change. The objections seem to indicate a concern that the approaches may claim to be scientifically grounded, yet they offer no coherent theory open to rigorous empirical testing.[66] More simply, perhaps, the empirical evidence is still not satisfactory as far as outside observers are concerned.

The way forward for organizational change programmes

The last years of the twentieth century remained a time of considerable organizational uncertainties. One certainty was that organizational decision-makers continued to finance approaches based on hard-systems logic. Quality Programmes had been replaced by BPR. BPR was under threat by the next wave of programmes urging highly sophisticated knowledge engineering programmes. The decision makers were still listening to the dominant voices advocating improved rational behaviours through improved technology. Some of the vocabulary associated with the hard systems was that of the soft-systems tradition: empowerment, participation, self-directing teams, became common within such change programmes. Those involved, along with the supporters of more integrative approaches, warn of the cynicism such vocabulary generates, which was out of alignment with managerial behaviours that had not changed.

The resistance of the managerial orthodoxy to soft-systems ideas points to the advantages of integrated systems approaches. This may be the way forward for change programmes. We may have to find ways of developing and extending the ideas of Senge, and his admirers. This will involve the development of 'learning to learn' skills. Senge showed how to combine soft-systems learning principles, with some of the hard systems analyses of production and information flows. The various metaphors of discovery in this book constitute another contribution that encourages managers to become action researchers, and to combine learning with informed and innovative actions.

Notes

1 Toffler (1972).
2 Peters (1992: xxxi).
3 Hammer (1990: 104).

[4] Champy (1995: 1).

[5] Buchanan & Huczynski (1997, 3rd edn) gives a concise account of historical influences.

[6] Lawrence & Lorsch (1968) was an influential early text for management researchers.

[7] Lex Donaldson (1996) provides his most recent case for positivist organizational theory. For more on the debate, see also Child (1977); Donaldson (1988).

[8] I eventually chose Buchanan & Huczynski (1997, 3rd edn); Burnes (1992); Dawson (1994); Kolb, Rubin & Osland (1991) for surveys of the organizational change literature; and Benne et al. (1975); Child (1977); and Mervis & Berg (1977) for earlier material. Ketchum and Trist (1992) outlined recent and historical thinking on sociotechnical theory. Argyris (1990); Bateson (1979); Rickards (1985); Senge (1990); and Tomlinson & Kiss (1984) stood for learning and systems theory work. Peters (1992) and Kanter (1985) provided insights into organizational transformational ideas of the 1980s and 1990s; Walton (1989) gave a convincing introduction to Deming and the quality movement; Hammer & Champy (1993) introduced Business Process Reengineering. De Cock (1996) directed me to a range of secondary references especially Giddens (1990). Clegg et al. (1996) was a welcome late addition to the study. Van de Ven & Poole (1995) may well prove a major contribution to the field.

[9] The two approaches are sometimes addressed as opposing one another (e.g. Tomlinson & Kiss, 1984); sometimes as intimately connected, as in sociotechnical theories (e.g. Miller & Rice, 1967).

[10] He receives similar accolades in Burnes (1992), Dawson (1994), Mervis & Berg (1977), Susman & Evered (1978) as well as in earlier documents such as Benne et al. (1975), Miller & Rice (1967).

[11] Lewin's grounding in Gestalt is becoming forgotten. We may expect this as Gestalt remains a relatively silenced voice, even among psychologists. See, however contributions by Mayer (1995) and Gruber (1995) in Sternberg & Davidson (1995), reclaiming Lewin to the Gestaltist fold.

[12] As often happens, there are other claimants. His colleague Benne subsequently acknowledged Lewin's efforts, while noting the alternative claims that might be made for 'John Collier of the US Bureau of Indian Affairs' (Benne et al., 1975: 31).

[13] These forces represent external psychological pressures and internal felt needs operating on an individual. The field can be seen as analogous to the creative press; and at a group level as analogous to the environmental climate.

[14] Benne et al. (1975) contains excellent accounts of the origins and workings of the NTL.

[15] Not to be confused with the Tavistock clinic, another prestigious institution, which imported Jung's psychoanalytical methods to the UK. The institute and clinic operated in close proximity, on Tavistock Square, for many years.

[16] See the ETHICS system (Mumford, 1981); and Ketchum & Trist (1992).

[17] Melanie Klein and W. W. Bion are regarded as formative influences. See Astrachan (1975) for an account of early practices.

[18] Checkland & Scholes (1990).

[19] An example of ***abstracted empiricism.***

[20] See Eden & Huxham (1996) for a recent review.

[21] Charles Clarke popularized this visual metaphor, which he developed within the Goodyear Corporation, probably in the late 1960s.

[22] French & Bell (1978: 15).

[23] French & Bell (ibid.).

[24] Dawson (1994: 14).

[25] Susman & Evered (1978: 588).

[26] Schein (1969). Readers may find similarities with the work of Blake and colleagues (for instance, Blake & Mouton, 1964; Blake et al. 1989).

[27] Experienced facilitators of ideas sessions include a *warm-up session* before inviting the group to tackle the key issue to hand. Inexperienced facilitators rush in or, if they do plan a warm-up, are still prone to handle it as a ritual whose significance is not appreciated. I suspect much the same applies for a wider range of group interventions.

[28] Beckhard co-edited a series of books on OD with Ed Schein. By 1981 the series had reached nineteen titles with a distinguished list of authors incorporating Beckhard and Schein themselves. The list also includes Lawrence and Lorsch, who helped pioneer the contingency approach to management thinking; Jay Galbraith; David Nadler; John Cotter; Richard Hackman & Greg Oldham; Edward Lawler; Susan Mohrman & Thomas Cummings; Robert Blake, Jane Mouton & Anne McCanse; Larry Greiner & Virginia Schein. By 1989 the series had reached twenty-three titles (Schein & Beckhard, 1989). As a training and OD intervention technique his approach was being taught internationally by the 1970s. For example, in the UK considerable activity occurred in the National Health Service, ICI, and in the Shell Organization.

[29] In the words of a graffito: the meek shall inherit the Earth – if that's all right with the rest of you. If a group has to work out a creative way of selling its ideas, it is operating against the values of involvement of all key participants in the change.

[30] A sensitive analysis reaching a similar conclusion was made by two major OD practitioners (Mervis & Berg, 1977).

[31] Tomlinson & Kiss (1984).

[32] Bertalannfy, L. von (1968), decreasingly cited now as the field formed its specialized sub-groupings. He is credited with the formal proof 'that closed systems can not behave equifinally. Therefore viable systems are not closed.' (Beer, 1966: 288).

[33] Wiener (1948). He studied mathematics (with Bertrand Russell) at Cambridge, zoology at Harvard, and philosophy at Cornell. He remained a professor of mathematics at MIT for nearly thirty years.

[34] For instance, Forrester (1961). Forrester's work also influences Senge (1990).

[35] See the contingency-based theories in chapters 6 and 10.

[36] Beer, a humanist before anything else (see, for example, Beer, 1979), would not, I hope, object to my allocating him to the ranks of the hard-systems thinkers by virtue of his influential 'base' models of the firm.

[37] A colleague of Beer's provides a lucid lay account (Leonard, 1994).

[38] Beer (1981).

[39] See Churchman et al. (1957); Kindler & Kiss (1984: 1).

[40] Folklore provides us with ways of retelling in a less threatening form aspects of espoused theories and theories in use, that is to say of permitted and unthinkable behaviours.

[41] Bateson (1979) is not easy to read, but writes with insight on these matters.

[42] Senge (1990). The distinguished information theorist George Huber has also begun developing important ideas linking organizational learning, creativity and innovation (for instance, Huber, 1998).

[43] The disciplines seem widely interpenetrable. Their heritage from Lewin, Beckhard, Schein seems clear, although unacknowledged in the book.

[44] *The Goal* (Goldratt & Cox, 1989) presented many similar principles in the form of a novel.

[45] Here I have been guided by the mass appeal of the writers.

[46] Kanter (1985).

[47] Kanter (ibid: 365).

[48] Peters & Waterman (1982).

[49] The book appears to claim that the model emerged from their researches reported in it. I still have a version of their 8S model in a document written some years earlier by workers in their old consulting firm McKinsey.

[50] Carroll (1983) was an early critic. See also Thomas (1993).

[51] Handy (1988), taking his title from a quip by his fellow Irishman George Bernard Shaw.

[52] Handy (1994: 66).

[53] In the marketing literature a similar story is told of production orientation replaced by a marketing orientation. Both stories have a tendency to represent the changes as progressive stages in economic development, and provide us with examples of evolutionary motors.

[54] Walton (1989) gives a good biographic note and general account of Deming's work. Deming consistently acknowledged the earlier work of statistician Walter Shewhart of Bell Labs (Shewhart, 1931), for example in the now-famed Deming wheel (Plan, do, check, act . . .). Walton omits to mention the connection between Shewhart and other Quality Gurus, especially Juran, Feigenbaum and Ishikawa (Bessant, 1991).

[55] Boje & Winsor (1993).

[56] Almaraz (1994: 9).

[57] Tuckman (1994). A confusion arises also for workers who feel they have to avoid errors, while at the same time be engaged in seeking continuous improvements.

[58] The studies were of UK and American firms, reported in Fisher (1994).

[59] Bessant (1991: 25).

[60] Bessant (ibid: 265).

[61] Hammer (1990).

[62] This is my gloss on the still-emerging story of the information revolution. See Grint (1994), Conti & Warner (1994) for deeper analytic examinations of Hammer's ideas.

[63] Hammer & Champy (1993).

[64] Grint (1994).

[65] Champy (1995: 2–3).

[66] It is a matter of speculation whether the waves of Total Quality and Business Process Reengineering will become 'respectable' components within business studies. The claimed achievements seem to depend on participation, learning, and emergent behaviours, all of which cut across the dominant managerialist perspective.

chapter 9
Postmodernism: A Jolt to the System?

Post-modern social science focuses on alternative discourses and meanings rather than on goals, choices, behavior, attitudes . . . Post-modern social scientists support a refocusing on what has been taken for granted . . . the insignificant, the sacred, the eccentric, the disqualified . . . Post-modernists, defining everything as a text seek to 'locate' meaning rather than to 'discover' it. They avoid judgement . . . rearrange the whole social science enterprise . . . offer indeterminacy rather than determinism, diversity rather than unity, difference rather than synthesis, complexity rather than simplification . . . truth gives way to tentativeness . . . relativism is preferred to objectivity, fragmentation to totalization . . .

Pauline Rosenau.[1]

The literature on postmodernism is so vast, diverse, and unwieldy that even the initiated cannot keep up with it, let alone make coherent sense of it all. Moreover, the literature encompasses philosophy, literary criticism, culture studies, economics, sociology, cultural anthropology, history, psychology, and various combinations of these, and is written in a variety of styles and perspectives.

Robert Hollinger[2]

The violence and the obsession with sex that increasingly dominate society's popular culture are at least in part . . . a cry for something more 'raw', something closer to our creative potential. The whole of postmodern society is struggling to reinvent itself.

Danah Zohar and Ian Marshall[3]

Introduction

Some years ago Gibson Burrell and colleagues at Lancaster were exploring the implications of Foucault's work on postmodernism on organizational thought. A paper submitted to the prestigious management journal *Administrative Science Quarterly* was questioned by the reviewers. 'All three [reviewers] questioned the relevance of an "unknown French philosopher" and asked "what could an American audience learn from such thought".'[4]

A few years later, an expert in Operations Research went to a conference on new thinking in management. Afterwards he was in a mood of consternation that he might have missed meeting the most mentioned person in the conference. 'Everyone kept talking about this bloke,' he told me. 'I kept waiting for Foucault to turn up, but I never met him. They say he's revolutionizing management thinking, but I've never heard of him. I've not seen any mention of him in the journals. It doesn't make any sense.'

What Foucault's converts were talking about at the management conference (that was held some years after his death) was probably what Burrell wanted to write about in the ASQ. These researchers were interested in an approach to discovering insights known as postmodernism. This chapter is one more attempt to introduce the ideas of Foucault and other postmodernists to a wider audience.

The journeys of exploration to study postmodernism

In this chapter we encounter the cultural and philosophic movement known as postmodernism. We will see that, among other things, it claims to replace old ways of thinking with new ones. We will approach 'from the outside' following the now familiar way of puzzling out bits of the jigsaw towards a platform of understanding of the subject. We will also resort to experimental methods more aligned with the postmodern approaches. The first part of our journey begins with an exercise that introduces some of the postmodern themes of reality, authority and trust.

We will start with a little thought exercise. You will have to trust me that the exercise is worth playing. I make no promises of what you will learn. The exercise is about to start. Are you ready for the exercise? If not, please feel free to skip the following section.

The start of the exercise

Try to imagine you have woken up in a strange world. It's a bit like Alice stepping through the looking glass, or disappearing down a rabbit hole. In this world there are no experts. It no longer has need of them. OK so far? Good. Can you imagine how different it is here to the world you used to live in? Think about that.

Perhaps you are wondering what this place is? I think it's a region of the postmodern world, but that's not for me to say, is it? There are no experts around here. Maybe there is no sense to anything any more.

Are you wondering about who I am, and my part in this world? Are you part of a world that I have created, or am I part of a world that you have created? Whatever you think, it's no good relying on me, in this place. You might have trusted me to get you here, but my advice can't be trusted now. Remember, we have no experts here. Do you suppose that's a puzzle you have to puzzle out?[5] Don't let me stop you.

Perhaps you are wondering how you get out of this world. If and when you do, maybe we will meet again. Or maybe we won't. Anyway, please excuse me, I'm getting out now. I have other things to do away from this place. It was fun visiting with you. Goodbye.

Meanwhile, back in the 'real' world

If you engaged in the exercise above, it may have given you cause to stop and reflect on some aspects of 'reality' that are generally taken for granted. You may have wondered more about the 'I' in the piece of text. You may have wondered about the nature of authority. In a special sense authority means what an author does, and the legitimacy with which the author is somehow invested. The legitimacy of authority is one very importance concern for postmodern thinkers. Postmodernists have developed their own approaches to help reveal the ways in which authority preserves its dominant position. In the illustration, the authorial 'I' deliberately 'spoke' in a different way to that presented in typical texts. I tried to make the writing less formal and more personal. Such devices are favoured in postmodernist writings to bring the hidden aspects in modern writings more into focus. It represented one way of 'reading between the lines'. The exercise also hints at the importance placed on how meaning is constructed. As we will see, postmodernism pays attention to 'the meaning of reality, and the reality of meaning'.[6]

Why might postmodernism be significant in business studies?

There are various reasons why managers and management theorists might be advised to examine the basic ideas of postmodern thinking.[7] One reason might be to develop another skill at discovering some of those suppressed voices we have been encountering in our earlier chapters. The skill will be one that adds to the approaches already suggested for puzzling out hidden meanings concealed behind a dominant way of seeing things. At the very least, it offers a possible jolt to conventional ('modern' and 'managerial') ways of seeing things.

An Exploratory Journey Towards Postmodern Territories

To approach the postmodern territories I collected a handful of books from the social science shelves of a general bookshop.[8] From them, the map for the journey was assembled, as shown in figure 9.1.

Premodern, modern, postmodern

The jigsaw puzzling revealed considerable usage of the terms premodern, modern and postmodern. The terms refer both to chronological eras and to modes of thinking. For most purposes, the eras are roughly classified according to their dominant mode of thought.

The earliest era, the premodern, refers to the beliefs that made up the entire period of history before the advent of a particular kind of scientific approach. The premoderns believed in supernatural forces that had created the natural world.[9]

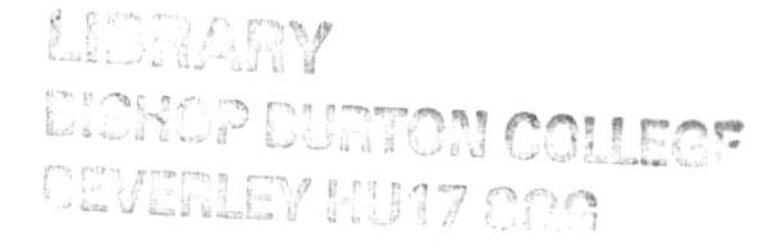

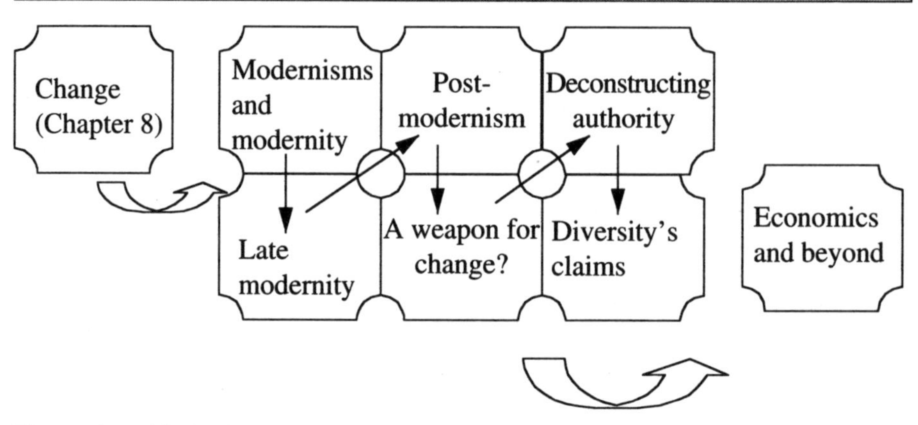

Figure 9.1: Modernism and its trials

This implied that the consequences of human actions were outside human control. This generated a fatalistic view still encountered among fundamentalist sects of various kinds.

These views were challenged by the influence of a movement that claimed for itself the term 'modern'.[10] In the eighteenth century the Western world was engaged with the consequences of scientific enquiry, which was increasingly regarded as a way whereby mankind could take control of its own destiny. Science was the instrument through which progress could be achieved. The period was one of great optimism for the social benefits of science, and became known as the Age of Enlightenment.

> The European Enlightenment of the eighteenth century marks a high point in Western history. Although its roots go much farther back in Western history and it continued to develop long after the eighteenth century, a program for improving human life was worked out. The enlightenment project, as it has been recently called, is based on the assumption that ignorance is the basic source of all human misery and that elimination of ignorance and its replacement with scientific knowledge, would pave the way for endless human progress.[11]

It was the great moral aspirations of the Enlightenment, and the increasing evidence of the power of science to explain the natural world that sustained the Enlightenment views almost to the present day. It became the orthodoxy behind the newer fields of knowledge. The term modern began to be used as an indication of 'enlightened' advances over more primitive ones. Modern medicine replaced primitive or folk remedies; modern cosmological principles replaced geocentric views of the universe; and everywhere logic, rationality and truth replaced ignorance and misplaced primitive beliefs.

There have always been critics of the overall package of beliefs associated with modernism. Some views were attempts to hold on to the traditions and values of a bygone age. Others were more concerned to transcend or go beyond modernism. Over the last few decades, the broad wave of non-traditionalist opposition to modernist beliefs has become known as postmodernism. The multiplicity of views have in common a deep distrust of the modernist beliefs.

To summarize, modernists labelled their own mode of thinking enlightened and, by implication, all previous modes primitive and unenlightened. The Western Enlightenment lasted roughly two centuries before it was itself challenged as being dangerously ill-conceived. The challenge came from a postmodern movement which rejected the modernist way of thinking as based on weak assumptions about the nature of truth, reality and social progress. Furthermore, the modernists stood accused of effectively suppressing all opposition to its own assumptions.

A 'Bluffer's Guide' to Postmodern Terms

A 'Bluffer's Guide' to postmodernism is a rather nice idea. There is something postmodern about a text that offers a way of appearing to be authentic to someone who otherwise would not be able to make that claim convincingly. When the topic itself is about the nature of authenticity, there is additional irony around, which, as we have seen above, is a characteristic of postmodern attitudes to modern conditions.[12] Here, then, is a vocabulary of postmodern terms.[13] It may be accepted unreflectively 'from the outside' by anyone wishing to present the appearance of being a postmodern thinker. It may serve as a focus for reflection into 'Bluffer's Guides'. Such modes of thought are more in the spirit of postmodernism, and may open the way to exploring postmodernism 'from the inside'.

Affirmative and sceptical groupings of postmodernists

Postmodernists reject modernist approaches to understanding in two ways. Affirmative postmodernists conceive of possible replacements to modernism; sceptical postmodernists, as their label implies, have nothing to put in its place. The affirmative view is hopeful but at the risk of internal contradictions such as opposing authoritative views and seeking to replace one orthodoxy with another. The affirmative voices tend to be American and Anglo-Saxon; the sceptical ones more influenced by the Francophone pioneers.

Authority and authorship

The power of an authority or author in a modernist text is taken for granted. The role of authorities is one that is challenged by postmodernism. The way in which authority is wielded in modern texts is demonstrated by postmodern writers who deliberately intrude into the flow of their texts. (Like I did, in the exercise above, and have tended to do elsewhere in the text.)

Decentring

Totalizing processes lead to a centrality of some issues and a marginalization of others. Postmodern examinations seek the hidden and the marginalized so that a process of decentring occurs.

Deconstruction

Deconstruction, popularized by Derrida, brings a range of postmodern techniques which reveal hidden possibilities within a text that have been concealed if a modern totalizing position is accepted. Thus any claim in the text to an absolute truth cannot be sustained. Specific words, metaphors, overall style can indicate new possibilities. Deconstruction has been widely used to reveal hidden attitudes about gender, race, sexuality and social status.

Difference, differend and differance

Postmodern analysis is sensitive to the way in which a term implies some unstated contrary. Creativity can have no isolated meaning without connection with the notion of that which is uncreative. Innovation is partially defined by what is considered not innovative. The concept of an innovative organization loses all meaning if there is no understanding of the nature and existence of not-innovative organizations. Efforts to eliminate the hidden differences throw up paradoxes.

Modernism

The dominant approach to studying and understanding is based on the methods of scientific enquiry, and the presumptions that rational application of the methods will yield truth and reveal false beliefs. Modernism is generally considered to have flowered during the Enlightenment period of the eighteenth century.

Postmodernism

A term popularized in the late 1980s, referring to a style of thought which opposed the contemporary modern approach in a range of intellectual efforts, especially in the fields of literary criticism, cultural and historic studies. The term also applies to an era that replaces the previous, modern or scientific era. Modernism assumes the existence of a truth that can be uncovered from facts. Postmodernism rejects the possibility that a unique and true explanation can be derived so as to relegate any alternative to the category of a falsehood. This view has been (simplistically) attacked as one that implies hopeless multiplicity of possibilities under any set of conditions.

Representationalism

Accepted facts are considered to reflect beliefs of figures of authority Plans, mission statements, employees' handbooks are representations of a privileged top management view. The process of representationalism is the manner in which a dominant view persists and replicates itself, thereby excluding other possibilities. The process is believed to be one of justification of a view, and cannot make scientific claims of rationality or logic.

Reflexivity

The thinking-about-thinking processes which help discover the theories behind theories. Strictly speaking, reflexive thinking has been important as a form of learning theory that need not be the exclusive province of postmodernism. Postmodern considerations induce reflexivity about modernist taken-for-granted assumptions of reality and of alternative possible realities.

Simulacrum

A representation based on a copy of an original that never existed. A simulacrum derives from the process of simulation. Baudrillard developed a rich vein of theorizing that regards science as a method of production of simulacra, which are then treated as real (how 'real' is a gene, anyway?).

Texts and textuality

Anything that attracts human scrutiny can be regarded as a text. A postmodern reading seeks to avoid the errors of totalizing the text, which requires the authority of the critic or the evidence of a creator and author of the text.

Totalism

The modern text expresses a position or belief in a total unambiguous state of affairs. Totalization is a postmodern term for the dominant belief stated or implied in a text. A totalistic acceptance of a belief is unacceptable according to postmodern notions. The belief might be scientific or religious, or personal. Totalism is also rejected in criticism of evaluations of works of art or scientific hypotheses as true or false.

Voice

The voice is a term used to indicate a perspective within a text. The author's voice expresses a set of beliefs which can be understood through postmodern analysis, especially deconstruction, when previously concealed, alternative perspectives or voices may be heard.

Writing and reading texts

Postmodern descriptions of texts, with echoes of the vocabulary of computing processes. A writerly text is constructed so that it can be rewritten, that is to say, re-interpreted by readers. Writerly texts are of a postmodern kind. Readerly texts are like a read-only computer program with an intended and unchangeable message. Readerly texts are by definition more modern rather than postmodern.

The Franco-European Postmodernists

In the twentieth century, a prominent Franco-European influence became identified with emerging postmodern ideas.[14] From the platform of understanding I have selected a few pieces of jigsaw that recur in subsequent writings. As such, they represent contributions that postmodernism offers to those readers who, like myself, approach the subject very much 'from the outside'.

Foucault on power and authority

Michel Foucault (1926–84) gained enormous academic reputation in his years as professor in the history of thought, at the Collège de France, Paris. His various books included studies of insanity and sexuality. A recurrent theme was the manner in which prevailing powerful élites were able to define the conditions of madness, or morality, for the whole of society. Where Foucault differed from earlier generations of revolutionary-minded artists and philosophers was in his explanation of the workings of power. He makes us conscious of the implications of authority in prescribing what is true, as well as what is morally correct. The author of a text exemplifies authorization, authority, authenticity. Yet, Foucault argued, the author has come to exist only in a historical time frame. 'An author's prestige was required for authenticity, and the authority of scientific statements rested upon it. Only later, in the seventeenth and eighteenth centuries, did scientific texts come to be backed up, guaranteed by the scientific community, rather than by specific individuals.'[15] Other texts retained the concept of authorship, but according to Foucault the ownership of the work, even its creativity, cannot be attributed to a unique author.

Foucault indicated that the Enlightenment had offered a promise of emancipation through reason. A double-bind had developed in the manner whereby power and dogma had cornered the market in the establishment of reason. Like Marx, Foucault saw that sweet reason, or even the discovery of the opposing ideas of unreason, would not bring about power shifts and significant social change. Power-brokered reason can be no more than a kind of blackmail inhibiting change.

Foucault's views have been taken up enthusiastically as offering conceptual weight to criticisms of dominant views of rationality. One of the targets for attack is the manner in which prevailing theories have ways of imposing their special truth. Foucault gives encouragement to the unorthodox, to those theories in waiting that are dismissed as unscientific or atheoretical.[16]

Derrida's deconstructionism

'Deconstruction' is a term that slipped into general 'cocktail party' use as a signal that the user is able to converse in postmodern terminology. Jacques Derrida (b. 1930) is regarded as a major pioneer of deconstructionism, 'a form of textual analysis applicable to all modes of writing which seeks to demonstrate the inherent indeterminacy of meaning'.[17]

Derrida places great emphasis on textuality. His notion of a text is a broad one, covering any kind of phenomenon that can be experienced, including cultures and ideologies.[18] The author has, in modernist practice, been assumed to have an intended meaning, expressed in the text. According to Derrida, the author has no claim on a unique interpretation of a text. Such claim survives by suppressing other possible interpretations.

The authority of the text preserves the reality of its power. Cummings and Tsoukas read Derrida as proposing that concepts exist as opposites, one of which gets privileged over the other – good/bad; included/excluded, and so on, and through the functioning of language the text imposes its loaded context on the reader. Postmodernists describe this as the text which is writing the reader – and steering his or her behaviour.[19] 'Privileged terms not only differ from the terms they marginalize, they also defer them . . . Far from being an accessory, the marginalized term is thus a central feature of the privileged.'[20]

Derrida's argument was to lead to the popularization of 'liberating' or 'delimiting' interpretations through critical deconstruction. He contends that under established conventions interpretation is regarded as revealing a hidden truth. The other view, which he considers an escape from established canons of modern thought, regards interpretations as always incomplete, unsuited to such absolute terms as truth. As expressed, the newer kind of interpretation has no claim to replace the earlier kind. Derrida sees such an approach as escape from the inadequacies implied in the methods of earlier searches for enlightenment. His ideas have been accepted as capturing the spirit of postmodernism.[21] However, the natural sciences have also been coming to terms with indeterminacy, and with the impossibility of absolute scientific proof statements. It does not seem too great a distance from Derrida's case for indeterminacy of interpretations.[22]

Baudrillard's ironic timebombs

Jean Baudrillard (b. 1929) has applied a characteristic and personal approach to contemporary life, with particular regard to the consequences of mass media, technology and popular culture. His sociological ideas have been described as taking to the limit the idea of a nightmare world in which reality can be sought but never found. At its bleakest this is the world of Kafka and Orwell; at its most ironic that of Marshall McLuhan.

Baudrillard is nothing if not ironic. Although his early work had Marxist tendencies[23] he later considered that to seek revolutionary goals under any movement claiming a special privileged truth would risk manipulation. His recipe for dealing with the modern condition is to find ways of surviving through detached enjoyment of the hyperreal provided through the multiplicity of images from television and consumerism. His hope is that the system will eventually self-destruct. His writing offers disorienting thoughts on time, space and reality. His commentary on his American experiences includes the thought that Disneyworld is, through its intentional fantasy, a truer reality than other purported realities. He gained a wider notoriety for a while with his observation in a similar vein that the

Gulf War was 'really' a television show. The wider audience reacted to this as to a modernist statement of fact or belief.

Lyotard's notions of narrative

Jean-François Lyotard (b. 1924) reshaped his own earlier Marxist thinking as he grew disenchanted with all forms of totalitarianism. In *The Postmodern Condition*,[24] one of the most-cited books on postmodernism, he develops his opposition to all-embracing belief systems which he terms metanarratives. He lends support to ways in which everyday individual acts can exhibit creativity. These acts have benefits of themselves and have no need for theoretical justification. He called them *petits récits* which in translation become little narratives or micronarratives. 'Even marginalized individuals have the power to subvert repressive social systems simply by acting in contrary and unpredictable ways [leading to] a guerrilla-like attitude of flexible and creative response to pressures emanating from one's particular grand narrative – the ability to "go to a ball in the evening and fight a war at dawn".'[25]

Not surprisingly, such a view offers little hope of direct revolutionary triumph over totalitarian grand narratives. Lyotard holds that grand narrative and *petits récits* coexist. He analyses the impact of the information age as potentially favouring a repressive state, the Orwellian future again; or it could lead to liberation, as information is made freely available to public access.

The End of Modernism or the Beginning of Late Modernism?

One recurring theme in postmodern writings is that earlier modes of thought have been eliminated. This turns out to be a conceptually difficult issue. It is serious enough for us to look at some of the most important 'the end of' claims. We will then look at the consequences of these claims. A particularly coherent alternative has been developed by the English sociologist Anthony Giddens, in which he suggests we are not experiencing the end of modernism but a transition into what he has termed late-modernity.

Why modernism is hard to kill off

The era we have identified as modern had its fill of critics who vigorously attacked various aspects of the general modernist set of beliefs. The end of modernism has been accompanied with arguments for the end of history.[26] We can learn nothing from past experiences in this new era. It has been accompanied with claims that rationality can no longer 'work' under conditions of chaotic uncertainty. In the next chapter, we find that even contemporary economics is threatened as hopelessly outmoded.

Nietzsche is regarded as a precursor to postmodern thinking.[27] In one sense, his invective on 'The Death of God' might seem like the quintessential modernist raging against residual premodern superstitions. However, he was also deeply convinced that science had replaced cultural values, and called for rejection of those who were weakened by social conventions. These themes have a postmodern tone to them.

Yet these 'death of' claims bring with them a difficulty. At the core of postmodernism is opposition to any dominant 'voice' that seeks to eliminate other 'voices'. It is not easy to argue the case that modernism is dead from a position that is uncomfortable with such totalizing assertions. Various attempts have been made to get round this difficulty. For example, ambiguity and paradox may be accepted as useful components within a postmodern view. Another strand of postmodern thinking[28] is to accept the co-existence ('differance') of modernism and postmodernism, each always being read in part in association with the differences associated with the other, in a process that persists as long as both terms 'have work to do' in their use.

Rather than kill off modernity, some writers have proposed the need for rethinking the conditions of modernity in contemporary organizational life. We will now look briefly at one such proposal that offers considerable promise.

Reflexive ('High') Modernity

In the 1990s the status of postmodernism was being debated energetically among sociologically-minded organizational theorists.[29] The thrust of the debate is whether contemporary controversies on the nature of organizational life require a radical new way of thinking, or adaptation of older ways of thinking. One of the most influential figures in the debate is the English sociologist Anthony Giddens, who was appointed to lead the London School of Economics in 1997. His scholarly work established him as a revolutionary thinker. A whole industry has sprung up exploring Giddens and his ideas. One team of writers concluded: 'The world of sociology does not quite know what to make of Anthony Giddens and his theory of structuration.'[30]

Giddens, a prolific, and contextually complex, writer has indicated that his development of a theory of structuration was directed towards 'a conceptual investigation of the nature of human action, social institutions and the interrelations between actions and institutions'.[31] At the core of structuration theory might be placed the 'heretical' notion that structures of interest to social scientists are not 'things' that exist independently of people, but rather help shape and are shaped by actions of those involved with the structures. From such a perspective there is little need for postmodernism as an alternative to modernism. Giddens argues that we are living in a time which he calls high modernity. This is located in a time frame and in an empirical world where there are globalizing influences accelerating with technological changes. Modernity may have been transformed, but it can hardly be said to have died.

Giddens has chosen to rework the sociological world to account for these changes. He suggests that the new modernity is characterized by a far greater and reflexive kind of self-awareness of what is going on. This has been taken to mean that there is no real-world case for a new way of thinking based on the demise of modernism. Rather, modernism has taken a reflexive 'turn' and can be understood in these terms.[32]

Management researchers have approached the work of Giddens much as they did that of Foucault and the postmodernists. He has a secure reputation as a major thinker in the social sciences. In the bits of jigsaw puzzling out postmodernism he appears as a different kind of heretic. Giddens has made a major contribution to a late twentieth-century debate about the nature of social life. Whatever the verdict of history may be, he has suggested in rich conceptual terms ways in which the form of modernism so dominant in business studies might be challenged.

Postmodernism and the Gender Issue

Postmodernist reasoning acknowledges the hidden voices which it seeks to liberate. In one sense, that provides some common ground for interest groups claiming unfair and unequal treatment. In the workplace, the struggles for equality have been fought on various grounds. In orthodox management texts, these struggles have been ignored. This was the case within all the handfuls of books examined in the chapters on mainstream management thought.

Some aspects of postmodern approaches are attractive to supporters of libertarian groups. The work concerning gender makes a good illustration of the opportunities and challenges in deploying postmodern methods to these ends. It is relatively easy through postmodern deconstruction for a feminist researcher to reveal mechanisms of self-protection against minority views within the mainstream management texts.[33] Less easy is to find means of moving from understanding to influencing.

Political correctness

The battles of political correctness have emerged out of recognition of the postmodern textual influences of language. Language that is taken for granted is challenged so as to reveal the subtext of dominance and oppression.[34] As sensitivities change, so do reactions towards vocabulary. Battles still rage, which might be taken as evidence of the capacity of vocabulary to become part of a struggle of conflicting ideas.[35] Further evidence of the potency of the approach is the anger and ridicule with which the approach is received by those who regard the advocates as members of dangerous and revolutionary political groupings.

In the nineteenth century, social correctness was instilled through knowledge of etiquette. This served to preserve the niceties that distinguished the genteel from the common people, thus perpetrating the social differences. In the twentieth century, political correctness seeks to disrupt those conventions that reinforce the social dominance of one group over others. At the surface level, the debate is over what I should say about different people, different races, genders, differently privileged classes. At another level it is about how what I say reflects how I treat other people.

The feminist movement has effectively drawn attention to the vocabulary in Western literature, and its continued evidence of the dominance of what has been called the white, middle-class, male voice. Awareness has been rising for several decades. Not surprisingly, it is a matter of debate whether consciousness raising is an effective primary strategy for social change.

Rewriting gender into organizational theorizing

Marta Calás and Linda Smircich are faculty members at the School of Management of the University of Massachusetts. At a recent conference on rethinking organizational theory, they brought together their interests in feminist theorizing and postmodernism. They make it clear that there is no one feminist theory or position. As with so many other bodies of knowledge derived from particular perspectives, the term captures a diversity of views within a more general belief that there are widespread cultural forces of male dominance denying equality to women. The inequality can be found in the organizational places of work, although these represent only one specific aspect of the wider cultural conditions.

Feminine scholarship examines such gaps, and here the deconstructionist methods are shared with postmodern approaches. The missing and biased values are examined and a case made for their right to a voice. Rewriting gender leads to a recognition that gender is an issue that cannot be loaded as a problem on to women. Men and women alike have gender, and gender responsibilities.

Postmodernism opposes totalizing views. It acts as a defence against replacement of one totalitarianism with another. Here is where Calás and Smircich see the productive tension between feminist studies and postmodernism. There can be no last word on the matter, only a struggle sometimes in concert, sometimes independently, towards a less unjust set of social conditions.

More complex postmodern examinations are beginning to emerge. For example, the writings on workplace equality have been studied to suggest that the claims for change are being severely diminished through the prevailing assumptions of the superiority and special qualities of the types of people who get to the top of the corporate ladders, and the inadequacies of those who do not. Classic management texts have been taken apart so as to release other interpretations and voices.[36]

Postmodern methods serve as weapons deployed in the service of those seeking a voice. In this sense the approach is not essentially left or right wing, nor of itself supportive of causes. Gender issues may well find some starting point for change through postmodern critique, although, as some feminists argue, substantial progress will require more action-oriented methods.[37]

Taking Stock: Postmodernism and its Relevance to Management Studies

Any educational endeavour attempts to equip its recipients for the most difficult intellectual challenges they are likely to encounter. Business education has to find some way to introduce its recipients to the challenges to the very core of business thinking. For that reason alone accommodation must be sought with the challenges posed by the postmodern movement.

There are reasons more directly connected with the contents of this book. The attention to suppressed voices is very much an approach suggested by postmodern thinking. Our methods demonstrate one way in which postmodernism provides a vehicle for new ways of thinking. Postmodern awareness sensitizes us to assertions that a particular belief is the only way of seeing things. In particular we may be sensitized to the beliefs about the irrationality or unscientific nature of beliefs that challenge the orthodox views on business and rationality.

Such considerations open the way to the acceptance as legitimate aspects of knowledge that are not currently on the business curriculum. These include the social sciences in their new developing forms. They also include creativity and other expressions of human development. For example, a reported series of classroom projects at Loyola University draws attention to ways of disrupting the taken-for-granted in thinking.[38] The methods include searching for dualities and dichotomies. Another approach involves reversal of perspective, again an invitation that would not be difficult to incorporate into a creativity training programme. Creativity training encourages search for the unusual, the impossible, the distorted.[39] In some respects, then, deconstruction might be regarded as a more sophisticated version of creative problem-solving, with processes seeking to create new thought products.

Some postmodern reflections

Don't trust experts or the assertions within expertly constructed grand narratives.

Don't trust history to report what really happened or what is definitely going to happen.

Treat texts as the material from which the reader creates meaning.

Truth claims are not in this part of the universe – they only belong in the modernist world, in which they are not recognized as being manifestations of power, and of suppression of alternative possibilities.

Beware of claims that someone 'speaks for' an entire group in democratic politics, or within organizational processes.

Progress is one possible way of understanding events over time. There are explanations that do not necessarily require a belief in technological, economic or ethical advances. Nor need such possibilities be absolutely discounted.

Postmodernism helps put an ironic front on things, so lighten up. Don't take anything totally seriously, including these ideas . . . With practice you can get to appreciate the irony in day-to-day experiences, which at least beats scientific determinism or religious fatalism.

The postmodern movement will perhaps compromise to survive within the world retaining modernist beliefs. Or it will adhere to its beliefs without compromise – in which case it is likely to remain excluded from that world.

Postmodernism, for all its infuriating self-indulgence, has been struggling with the issues of paradigm change. The exploration of paradox, for example, may help those who wish it to travel back and forth across paradigmatic customs posts. There is a sense that creative opportunities may be lurking within the various postmodern themes, challenging authority and the taken-for-granted assumptions of organizational realities of the late twentieth century.

Notes

1 Rosenau (1992: 8).
2 Hollinger (1994: xi).
3 Zohar & Marshall (1993: 263).
4 Burrell (1996: 652). He recommends Dreyfuss & Rabinow (1982) as a good introduction to Foucault's writings.
5 Did you wonder what sort of footnote this might be? Has this been a helpful footnote? Is there something paradoxical about this footnote?
6 Constructions such as this, with their indications of paradox and layers of meaning, are a postmodern convention.
7 Questioning the need for a reason in this way is a rather rationalistic and modern preoccupation.
8 My early guide was Rosenau (1992), who had come highly recommended from colleagues already interested in postmodernism. I later came to rely on Hollinger (1994) as a thoughtful thematic review of the field, and Giddens (1990) as a critic of developing themes in postmodernism. Reed & Hughes (1992); Boje et al., (1996) and Linstead et al. (1996) were more concerned with organizational themes. Discussions with Professor Hari Tsoukas (and Tsoukas, 1994) and Dr Christian de Cock were also of immense value during my efforts to find shortcuts into this area of organizational silences.
9 After Tsoukas (1994).
10 See, for example, Hollinger (1994), who warns of the complexities of defining modernism and postmodernism, asking whether they reflect *periods or styles.*
11 Hollinger (1994: 7).
12 Baudrillard, for example, teaches us that our views of reality are challenged by Disneyworld. Inasmuch as Disneyworld sets out to create its own fantasy it has a reality that is not shared with much else in a modernist world. Such postmodern insights suggest that 'Bluffer's Guides' might create their own innocent type of deception, and might even be called a real Mickey-Mouse description of postmodernism.
13 'Bluffer's Guides' tend not to quote sources. My 'Bluffer's Guide' has been constructed from my handfuls of books. I am not really sure about footnotes, and this service has been suspended for the duration of the bluffer's guide.
14 Because of its reluctance to give one interpretation a privileged position over another, postmodernism can be explored with modern and/or postmodern methods. In searching for the views of pioneering figures I am rather uneasily sticking to my modernist knitting.
15 Rosenau (1992) quoting Foucault (1979).
16 Burrell (1996) warns of the subtleties in Foucault's writings. These are likely to be even harder to appreciate across cultural borders.
17 Sim (1995: 102).
18 'Text is all' (Derrida, 1976: 158).
19 Cummings & Tsoukas (1995).
20 Cummings & Tsoukas (ibid: 31–2).
21 'Deconstruction – a post-modern method of analysis. Its goal is to undo all constructions. Deconstruction tears a text apart, reveals its contradictions and assumptions.

Its intent, however, is not to improve, revise, or offer a better version of the text.' (Rosenau, 1992: xi).

[22] Science can make absolute claims within systems that are closed off from inputs that might alter those claims. Social systems are always open to possibilities of self-reinvention, the so-called double hermeneutic of changing through self-awareness.

[23] Sim (ibid.).

[24] Sim (ibid.), who cites Lyotard (1984), a translation of *The Postmodern Condition*, by Bennington & Massaumi.

[25] Sim (ibid.: 271) where Lyotard's references to the scientific theories of chaos and catastrophe are also noted.

[26] Fukuyama, F. (1992).

[27] Hollinger (1994); Rosenau (1992); Sim (1995), among others.

[28] After Derrida's proposals of the significance of difference and deferring.

[29] See for example the debate in Organization Studies between Parker (1992) and Tsoukas (1992).

[30] Bryant & Jary (1991: 1).

[31] Giddens (1991: 201).

[32] This is roughly the argument and the terms used in Turner (1994).

[33] Calás & Smircich (1992) give a clear account of the postmodern and feminist theoretical overlaps. Other examples, by Bradshaw and Calton & Kurland, can be found in Boje et al. (1996).

[34] See Dunant (1994) for perspectives within the political correctness debate.

[35] 'We have gone overboard with all this political correctness crap. There's nothing wrong with calling a spade a spade.' Politically disingenuous?

[36] Boje et al. (1996) includes several examples. I particularly liked Patricia Bradshaw's examination of women as constituent directors, and her noting of Mumby & Putnam (1992), who examined Simon's bounded rationality and explored the hidden possibility of bounded emotionality.

[37] Rosenau (1992) cites Harding (1990).

[38] Rosile & Boje (1996).

[39] 'An effective program to nurture creative behavior attempts to establish *habits against habits (a set against set)*.' Parnes (1992: 138).

chapter 10 Economics and Beyond

The difficulty lies, not in the new ideas, but in escaping from the old ones.

***John Maynard Keynes*[1]**

Marshall's world of competitive entrepreneurs, maximizing consumers, and a suitably reticent state continues to serve the ends of comfortable orthodoxy today. It does not describe the world as it is. . . . But to have mastered Marshall was a good thing. To know what is right, one must grasp what is wrong.

***J. K. Galbraith*[2]**

Simple as they are, the basic concepts of conventional international trade theory turn out to be as inaccessible to the anti-mathematical intellectual as those of quantum mechanics. And so the same ideas that seem clear, beautiful and compelling to most economists seem like obscure mumbo-jumbo to many highly intelligent people.

***Paul Krugman*[3]**

The emerging infrastructure will so fundamentally change the rules of supply and demand that a new economic order will result.

***Blake Ives and Sirkka Jarenpaa*[4]**

Introduction

By the late 1990s, technological advances had permitted the globalization of financial markets. The interdependence of regional markets might be assumed to have had a stabilizing effect. Yet the most obvious consequence of turbulence in one region was a cascading effect around the world. In 1998, the financial shock waves from Asia's economies were felt from Tokyo to New York. Among the uncertainties there was one incontestable fact: conventional economic analysis had failed to identify the extent of the vulnerabilities of the Asian economies, just as it had failed to anticipate in advance their growth potential.

Economists were all too painfully aware that non-economists were no more able to follow their explanations than were non-scientists able to understand explanations of the changing worlds of nuclear physics, genetic engineering and information technology.

Yet the methods outlined in previous chapters can still offer an approach – even for non-economists – that helps in the understanding of the critical assumptions underpinning economic thinking about the global economy. The methods will also indicate possible challenges to the economic orthodoxy.

In this last chapter we will once again look for the platform of understanding of the dominant paradigm, which has become known as neoclassical economics. We will then consider ways in which the orthodoxy might have silenced other 'voices', before considering possibilities that address today's real world challenges to the dominant belief system.

The economic jigsaw puzzle

Pieces of the economic jigsaw were not difficult to find. The difficulty was more the question of selection so that the jigsaw did not become intolerably complicated. The handfuls of books took a great deal longer to collect than had been the case in previous expeditions.[5] A fascinating story emerged from the earliest days of economic thought, through to the newest challenges posed by contemporary economic conditions. The main bits of the economics jigsaw eventually selected are shown in figure 10.1.

At some risk of mixing metaphors, the bits of a jigsaw could also be seen in terms of a family tree as shown in figure 10.2. In the following sections we will see how the family tree developed from its historical roots.

Early Economic Ideas

Although economic thought can be traced to ancient writings on household management, economic histories tend to begin with two political movements in France, the mercantilists and the physiocrats.

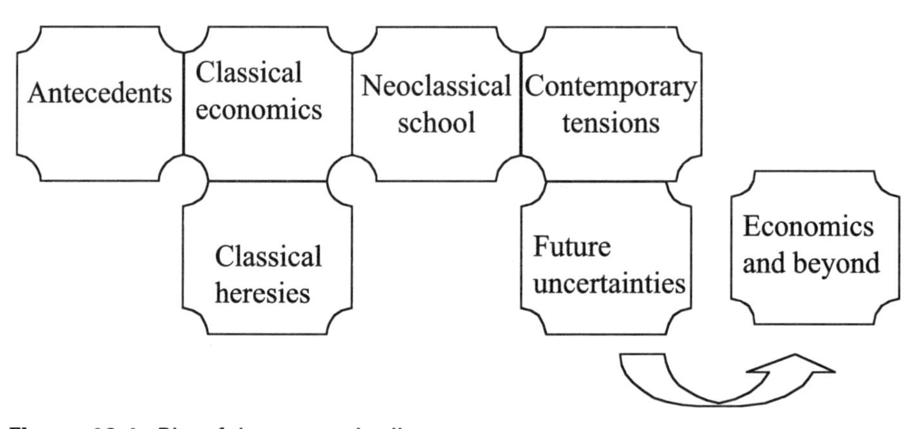

Figure 10.1: Bits of the economics jigsaw

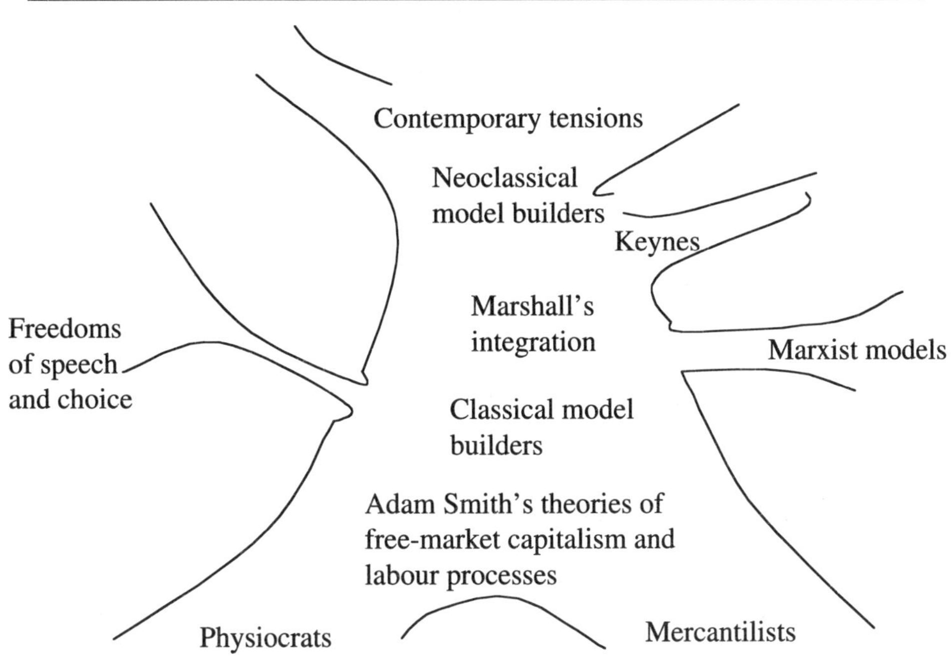

Figure 10.2: Antecedents of economic orthodoxy

The French mercantilists

The mercantilists of early seventeenth-century Europe saw trade and the accumulation of trade surpluses as means of supporting professional soldiers, and thereby a means to retaining power. The convenient universal medium of exchange was gold. The accumulation of reserves of gold was taken as an indicator of a nation's progress and strength. Mercantilist pamphleteers argued vehemently that it was vital to retain a trade surplus as gold reserves. If necessary, imports should be restricted as a means of retaining an international surplus. The mercantilist policies eventually disappeared, as France declined in economic power relative to England where the ideas had never held sway.

The physiocrats

The failure of mercantilism led France to turn to the ideas of the physiocrats, whose central premise was that land was the ultimate generator of economic wealth. These economic thinkers pioneered what today would be called an early form of microeconomics, and began to explore the nature of individual creation of value.

Adam Smith and *The Wealth of Nations*

Adam Smith's most influential work, on the nature of the wealth of nations, is often compared, in impact and intellectual power, to Darwin's *Origin of Species*. Smith was active during a time of both political and intellectual revolution. Political movements in France and America were building to their respective revolutionary outcomes. The intellectual revolution known as the Enlightenment was enthusiastically extending the scope of scientific thought to replace old, 'unenlightened' beliefs, in the two spheres of rational reasoning and empirical investigation or experimentation.

Adam Smith laid the foundations for today's economics, the study of wealth creation and its differential distribution across nations. This gives him his status as a pioneer of classical economics. He also made influential contributions to the theory of business organization. He anticipated the economic gains in efficiency that could derive from new methods of production, and particularly through the division and specialization of labour (illustrated with his still famous pin-making 'manufactury') and competition. We can trace from his observations the production line and the workings of the great manufacturing systems of the twentieth century.

Smith and enlightened self-interest

Smith built his theories from meticulously assembled arrays of observations and examination of the available documentary evidence. At the individual level, Smith argued, the economic mechanism is that of self-interest. However, self-interest goes beyond that attributed to all other animals that do not have the capacity to reason. Among humans there can be found a rational or enlightened self-interest whereby exchange or trade occurs. The consequence of enlightened exchange is the possibility of gaining increasing levels of economic benefits from one's efforts. Trade or exchange permits personal wellbeing. Since Smith, enlightened self-interest has become a shorthand way of dealing with economically rational behaviour.

Smith's insight was that self-interest at the level of the individual also works at the level of the community. Wealth of individuals means wealth of nations. Smith rather briefly attributes this to the workings of an invisible hand of natural processes. The terminology of the invisible hand of the market makes Smith's concept more appealing to those who place their political faith in the workings of a free market. This suggests how Smith has become regarded as supporting a right-wing political philosophy.[6]

The Development of Classical Economics

Classical economics is a term assumed to capture the ideas pioneered by Adam Smith. The concepts were developed in the late eighteenth century and early nineteenth century by thinkers among whom Thomas Malthus and David Ricardo were particularly influential.[7]

Malthus

The Reverend Thomas Malthus was the first economics professor appointed in the English-speaking world.[8] Malthus showed how scientific analytical methods could be applied to a body of empirical data. These were increasingly to become the methods associated with economics. The substance of his theory of population growth and subsequent apocalyptic famine did not survive. It is perhaps ironic that the fame brought by a theory that was to be discredited also served to attract attention to his analytic methods.

Ricardo

Ricardo developed his ideas in the eye of the storm of the industrial revolution in Britain. One of his important contributions was a theoretical analysis that demonstrated the continued benefits of a free trading policy regardless of absolute level of economic efficiency across sectors. Specifically, Britain at the time was more efficient in manufacturing agriculture. Ricardo showed that under such conditions there is still economic benefit in trading for goods of lower economic value (agriculture) while concentrating on the sector of greater economic gains (manufacturing).

Ricardo and Malthus made a particular contribution in pioneering the use of mathematical modelling of economic theory. As we will see, this became the orthodoxy of the neoclassical mainstream.

Labour theory of value

One of the challenges to classical economics was to develop a theory of the nature of economic value. Efforts to develop a more scientific analysis of human needs had presented the classical economists with considerable difficulties. To get round these difficulties required an ingenious shift towards valuing human needs in terms of perceived worth or utility. The vocabulary of the shift has been retained into today's economics. The enthusiasm for scientific rationality prompted this shift towards a measurable 'objective' base for economic theory.

The Transition to the Neoclassical School

Throughout the handfuls of books I came across frequent references to neo-classical economics, expressed in the clearest possible terms as the received wisdom of modern economics, against which all new ideas are to be judged. The Chicago School, in the United States, and The London School of Economics, in England, were particularly frequently mentioned as the most respected English-speaking representatives of the canon.

When a distinguished group of economists got together in the early 1980s to discuss the crisis in economic theory, deliberations centred around challenges to neoclassical ideas.[9] In essence they were all neoclassicists, albeit with divergent views on how the most basic tenets impacted on empirical measures of economic variables.

Today, the neoclassical school is regarded as originating in the 1870s. The platform of understanding of economics texts tells a story that begins with two scientifically trained academics, Stanley Jevons at the University of Manchester and Leon Walras at Lausanne. Although working independently, Jevons and Walras developed similar mathematical formulations that became regarded as the bedrock of modern neoclassical economic theory.[10] The work was popularized by the influential teaching of Alfred Marshall at Cambridge University, England, and by his influential text *The Principles of Economics*, published in 1890.[11] The most famous of Marshall's students was John Maynard Keynes, who will figure later in our story.

The defining characteristics of neoclassical orthodoxy

Jevons and Walras wanted to get back to basics and create a sound mathematical basis for economics. The much-admired methods of the empirical sciences had been enormously successful in taking a simple or ideal case and working out the mathematical relations of that case. Jevons and Walras would have been well acquainted with the emerging mathematical ideas of James Clerk Maxwell (1831–79) that were to lead to the kinetic theory of gases and theory of electromagnetic radiation.

In the spirit of such scientific discoveries, the neoclassical school begins by postulating a simple model, and seeing what explanatory power it possesses. Producers and consumers in the system have all the information needed to make informed ('rational') decisions. The so-called principles of diminishing marginal returns apply, and there is perfect competition for supply and demand.

Within the assumptions made for the models, neoclassical methods show that economic systems operate according to the price principle. The system can be shown mathematically to reach an equilibrium position. That is important. Even more important, the position is one that is considered economically efficient. That is to say, no alternative equilibrium position can be attained that does not disadvantage one or more of those participants within the economic system.

This is the bedrock of neoclassical economics. It forms the basis of the so-called marginal revolution – that is to say of the revolution in economic thinking brought about by models of the kind described, based on equilibria resulting from the principle of diminishing marginal returns. The emphasis of the paradigm is primarily micro-economic.[12] Through it, the economic agent, *Homo economicus*, is given life.[13]

The Development of the Keynesian Consensus

Keynes and inflation

Keynes is regarded today as an important revolutionary figure who challenged the economic orthodoxy developing around the theories of competitive equilibria of economic systems. To understand how this might be we have to look at his most important contributions in the context of his time. The great social and economic problems of Keynes' time were connected with economic slump and mass unemployment. Keynes was concerned with unemployment, and tended to be less concerned with inflation. In later decades attention was to switch to inflation, when emerging monetarist ideas were to establish a new consensus. He regarded the 1930s slump as a distortion of 'normal' economic conditions, and set about developing theory to support policies that could help restore the 'normal' employment and market conditions.

Keynes' case for intervention

In his *General Theory*, we find a remarkable accumulation of ingenious concepts combining old and new ideas. Keynes proposed that aggregate supply and demand did not smoothly equilibrate under the realistic conditions in which workers had options of saving some portion of their wages. The intervening factor was the nature of money and investment. In a lengthy, but not conceptually difficult, argument, Keynes reasoned that economic orthodoxy had assumed that saving levels did not influence growth.[14] His point was that savings took money away from investment leading to growth. Then he reached, among other conclusions, the practically important point that there were ways of re-injecting investment that would produce a gain in growth through employment gains. Keynes' ***multiplier*** relates investment to increases in income. He shows that his multiplier is related to, but not identified with, an employment multiplier.

The rise of a new orthodoxy

For a while in America and England, Keynesian ideas acquired the status of a dominant orthodoxy, and were seized upon as having practical policy implications. At first, investment through great public works programmes led to growth.[15] Keynes was hailed as an economic miracle worker. However, his policy prescriptions were always vulnerable to criticisms of being too liberal (or socialistic) in America and Britain. As long as they appeared to work in practice, theoretical criticisms could be managed. The theories were increasingly open to challenge as the 1950s and 1960s witnessed the failure of orthodox economic policies to deal with economics of stagflation, especially in the United Kingdom and the USA, the two countries which had been the most enthusiastic about Keynesian ideas. A new orthodoxy arose, popularly described as monetarism, and associated with the work of Milton Friedman.

The Nature of Monetarism

Monetarist ideas had been developed among a group of economists over a period of some years, partly as a response to what they saw as the ill-conceived ideas of Keynes. Strictly speaking, economists tend to use the term monetarist to refer to someone who believes that inflation is a monetary phenomenon. Their opposition to Keynes arises from this belief. However, as often happens, terminologies change. Popularly, monetarists have become identified with the belief that free markets are supreme. An economist colleague put it this way: 'An economist would use the term monetarist as someone who believes that inflation is a monetary phenomenon, regardless of what he believed about free markets. Someone who believes in the supremacy of free markets is a free market economist, or in the vernacular a "Chicago economist". This opens up the possibility that some monetarists are not free market economists. Indeed, in the days of Laidler and Parkin in Manchester in the early 1970s, one of their disciples was a monetarist Marxist. This might seem like an advanced form of schizophrenia, but to the economist it is a logical (if unusual) perspective.'[16]

The monetarists find a powerful case against Keynesian policies

A particularly damaging blow to Keynesianism came through empirical evidence that supported the monetarists and their assumptions of non-intervention from their micro-economic models.

Milton Friedman with co-worker Anna Schwartz developed comprehensive empirical evidence that showed Keynesian policies were failing to achieve their intended increase in economic outputs. This led Friedman to predict that interventionist policies could be demonstrated as making things worse, and were contributing to inflation through inattention to the significance of money supply growth. When inflation soared and output growth slowed in the 1970s, his position was accepted as fully vindicated.

Thatcherism, Reaganomics and the decline of Keynesian influence

The economic debates set a climate for an alternative to Keynesianism that found expression in the West in the 1980s under the American President Ronald Reagan and the British Prime Minister Margaret Thatcher. A common simplification of the position of these politicians is to label them as monetarists. As we have seen, a professional economist would be more inclined to see this as showing political instincts towards unregulated free markets, financial discipline and traditional (family) values.[17]

The Neoclassical Positions on a Political Spectrum[18]

The economic left flank

Neo-Keynesians such as J. K. Galbraith, Joan Robinson and Lord Kaldor would be numbered among those who would regard money as an indicator of economic distortions of social privilege. As such they tend to be regarded as on the political left flank. The British journalist Will Hutton has recently argued eloquently along these lines and can claim influence in developing a coherent political philosophy within Tony Blair's New Labour movement.[19]

The Keynesian successors

Keynes had rather less concern for income distribution or social ('normative') grounds than the left flankers, and would be located towards the right of the Neo-Keynesians. The economists regarded as the most consistent heirs to Keynesian principles would currently include the British economist G. L. S. Shackle and the American Paul Davidson.

The Neo-Austrians

These have been discussed in chapter 3 as concerned with what other neoclassicists would call externalities leading to innovation and growth. The early ideas of the school came from Karl Menger. His ideas were subsequently developed by von Mises and Hayek. Kirzner, a more recent Austrian school economist, sums up the contributions of the school as recognizing the individualistic and subjective nature of choice.

The neoclassical Keynesians

Efforts to integrate Keynes into a neoclassical format[20] align with what in the UK would be called right of centre policies. Inflation is now treated as a monetary phenomenon, especially 'in the long run'. Their modelling assumes full employment, with unemployment regarded as a temporary disequilibrium position.

The monetarists

We have already indicated the popular extension of the economic view of a monetarist. If Friedman is taken as the leading figure, monetarists have become aligned with more right wing economic policies.[21] Friedmanite interventions are assumed to achieve full employment in the (economic) long run. Inflation is primarily a monetary policy.

The New Classical economists

In the United States the New Classical school was developed by Professors Robert Lucas and Thomas Sergent. In England, Professor Patrick Minford became a highly visible representative of their views in the 1980s and 1990s, as well as a member of a governmental advisory group of influential economists. The New Classical view considers that markets have the classically attributed property of rapid equilibrating. Government intervention tends to make things worse. Wage rates must be allowed to rise or fall in the interests of the free market's healthy functioning. Distortions in practice are due to such factors as negotiated wage settlements which unexpected 'jolts' shift out of equilibrium. However, tight monetary policy is considered a means of not interfering (with market mechanisms), and is therefore a good thing.

The Themes of the Neoclassical Jigsaw

Can all these views be reconciled in some way? After all, they have sufficient cohesion to debate one with the other so it should be possible for a 'voice' to be heard indicating the agreements and differences. The repeated concerns found in the literature are shown in figure 10.3.

The voice that might be heard dealing with the concerns of the orthodoxy 'as a whole' might be expected to have a shared, paradigmatic view on the importance of the themes in figure 10.3. It may be difficult for non-economists to understand the significance of the themes, or to follow the mathematical treatments of them in neoclassical texts. Their nature is, however, revealing of the nature of the orthodoxy, and its preoccupations. For instance, the themes imply a shared methodology, a shared belief in what kinds of knowledge are valid, and what types of economic phenomena are 'real' and worthy of study. In some contrast, the most central issues seem rather remote from the day-to-day concerns of people engaged in economic activities.

Why prediction is difficult yet important

Economists are under pressure to predict economic figures over very short time-periods from powerful political, administrative and commercial forces. Cautionary warnings of 'all other things being equal' tend to be ignored by non-economists. However, economists can point to predictive successes over substantial time-periods when models are used within their declared limits.

On equilibrium of economic systems

Neoclassical economics has been built around the belief that markets come into balance between supply and demand. That is the most important type of economic

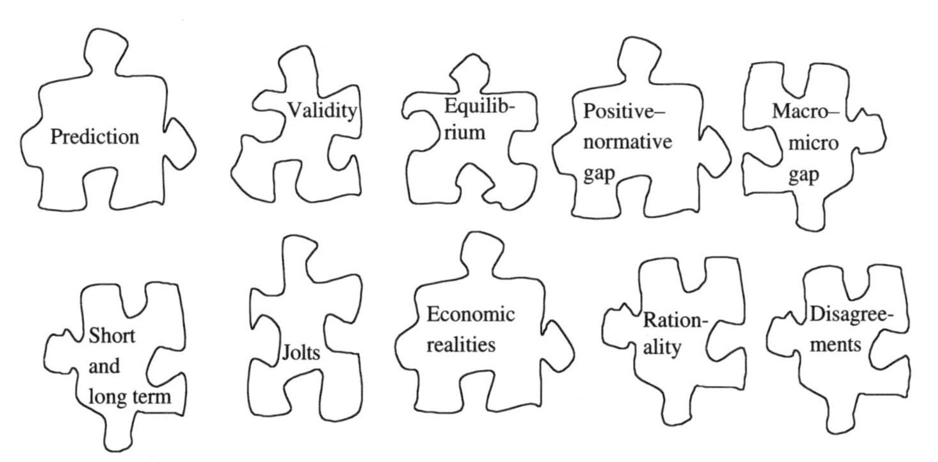

Figure 10.3: Puzzling out *homo economicus*

equilibrium. The main debates centre around the speed at which this happens. The Keynesians question whether the market regains its old equilibrium position after some jolt or shock.

On positive and normative economics

Positive economics deals with economic variables that can be scientifically characterized and measured so as to provide predictions of outcomes. Normative economics deals with the sort of economic policies needed to achieve social ends or norms. Normative issues deal with value judgements, for example to do with the wellbeing of different groups.

On the macro-micro economics gap

Micro-economics deals with sub-components that are derivable from macro-economic principles. The subject is concerned with how individuals make choices of one commodity over another. Essentially, micro-economics makes a partial analysis, like any other science, to get into a subject in great depth. Macro-economics is concerned with the great global economic issues of trade and business cycles, and wealth formation. There is still a lot of interesting work to be done at the micro-economics and macro-economics interface.

Long and short term

In the short term economists examine what happens under the assumption there are no substantial changes to the production/market system. In the long run costs taken as fixed in the short run have to be discounted somehow. The longer-term analyses have to study and account for major economic shifts, for example when an organization invests in a totally new technology.

On reality

Economics has had to arrive at positive (scientifically characterized) values for various items such as money. Although a dollar or a pound note has a nominal figure on it, the purchasing power varies. The real value has to be estimated and distinguished from the nominal value. Real wages are quite different from the nominal value of the wage, which is very important, for example, under inflationary conditions.

On rationality

Individuals behave with economic rationality if they act to get the best economic outcome for themselves that they can. Instances of irrational behaviour are generally dismissed as non-economic. The rational expectations school suggested that if a labour force appeared to behave irrationally, it was due to lack of information. So provision of information permits the rational expectations of workers to appear, and work through, even in the short term.

On jolts and expectations

Economic theory now takes into account people's future expectations. Theories of rational and adaptive expectations are complicated when the economy experiences a shock such as the famous oil-price rises of OPEC in the 1970s. This shifts the equilibrium relationship. Current theorizing is unclear on how to shock the global economy deliberately, to achieve desired economic stability.

Neoclassical disagreements[22]

The disagreements, as we have seen, arise from differences of opinion over assumptions and interpretations. To some degree (but not completely), the paradigm can argue that the problems come from efforts to deal with 'normative' issues – in terms of value judgements of an ethical or political kind, and do not impact on the validity of positivist economic theory.

Neoclassical Framing of Other Economic Positions and Places

Our jigsaw puzzling has been useful in getting to the core of neoclassical orthodox concerns. There still remain a great variety of writings to be studied in and around that orthodoxy. Our experiences of earlier chapters suggest that less central economic ideas will be isolated outside the orthodoxy. Or, when commented upon from within the dominant position, will be done so according to the beliefs of the orthodoxy. We can make a first simplification locating groups of 'heresies' according to our distinctions of radical versus regulatory, and subjective versus objective dimensions. In this process we find some integration of the material covered in chapter 3 on innovation.

Marxism as economic heresy

Economic orthodoxy has long assumed a natural and healthy state of competition among all individuals; Marx argued for unbridgeable divisions between those who own resources, and who are able to maintain and increase their economic wealth; and those who are exploited and deprived, thereby existing in a condition of alienation. For Marx, there is no benign and invisible hand of the market. Rather, under the prevailing political conditions, the distribution of power is a structural condition sustained by the unequal ownership of resources, and specifically of property. He postulated that the prevailing economic system was oppressing the vast majority, the workers, and benefiting only a few 'capitalists', supported and sustained by a political superstructure. He further predicted that revolution would sweep aside the capitalist superstructure, eliminate the competitive forces of the market system, and produce a convergence of individual and societal needs.

Marx retained the Enlightenment respect for the liberating power of objective scientific thought. However, he reached an intellectual position in which radical change was a pre-determined and logical outcome of his analysis. Revolution was presented as a historical necessity, scientifically established, to achieve the objectively determined outcome of society. For over a century the intellectual efforts directed to exploring, sustaining or refuting Marxist thought have been immense. All our earlier chapters indicate the forces that have kept Marxism off the business studies agenda as a theoretically unsound notion. Since the fragmentation of the regimes of the former Soviet Union, it has become easier to reject all of Marx's theoretical work by reference to the general economic failures of the regimes claiming to apply Marxist principles. Yet it should be remembered that the Marxist position was firmly off the Western business curriculum throughout the era when Marxism was a dominant philosophical and political ideology. In some contrast, Marx has been more accepted as a powerful influence in the social sciences, particularly as a pioneer of sociology.[23] Its simplest location is as a radical and objective economic model although its richness permits multiple interpretations.

The Austrian school and Schumpeter's creative gales

The Austrian school was considered briefly, together with Schumpeter's work, in chapter 3, for their contributions to innovation theory. Overall, the Austrian school might be seen as more concerned with macro-economic mechanisms and have been more willing to explore the psychological and sometimes philosophical aspects of individual behaviours. For them, individual creativity and organizational innovations are important factors in economic growth.

Schumpeter, while sharing the interest in entrepreneurial activities of his fellow Austrians, does not fit within the Austrian school. According to Schumpeter, the role of the entrepreneur is a far more revolutionary one. The economic gales generated by entrepreneurs were exactly those violent disruptions to markets that are not easily explained through neoclassical models that exclude messy subjectivities associated with entrepreneurs and technological innovation. These factors are sometimes referred to as externalities, that is to say beyond the scope of the economic models. This point was also considered important by evolutionary economists (see below). Schumpeter can be seen as a highly revolutionary and somewhat subjectivist theorist.

Hayek

Friedrich August von Hayek was an Austrian by birth, British by adaption, and a member of the Austrian school of economists by repute. He held professorial positions at London, Chicago and Freiburg. His writings have far transcended the rather technical controversies that are regarded as the main contributions of the Austrian school. One of the few things that united Margaret Thatcher and her turbulent chancellor Nigel Lawson was a recognition of the importance of Hayek's ideas on free choice and free markets.[24]

A historian as well as an economist, Hayek had considerable appeal to those of a right-wing political persuasion. His view of the development of markets is striking. In it he outlines the origins of trade emerging under conditions of such complexity that they prohibit planning and design as mechanisms for what he called the 'extended order'. The mechanisms, emergent and unplannable, support a traditionalist ('conservative') political philosophy. His penetrating insights were rewarded with a Nobel prize in 1974. Among recent advocates can be found Tom Peters, who celebrates Hayek's ideas in one of his books.[25]

Yet Hayek remains a silenced voice in economics textbooks. An explanation is not difficult to find. While his appeal to policy makers has been great, his work can not easily be incorporated into the neoclassical models that occupy so many pages of economic textbooks. These are based on very well-behaved markets. Hayek sees markets as essentially unpredictable. He has made his unpopular position clear in opposition to what he has described as 'scientism' in economics, noting that 'We have at the moment little cause for pride; as a profession we have made a mess of things.'[26] Hayek shares Schumpeter's respect for radical theory incorporating the subjective side of economic life.

Industrial economics and related micro-economic voices

Industrial economics has a strong claim to have developed a powerful body of knowledge of clear relevance to managers and organizational theorists. Its theories offer ideas of relevance to strategy, innovation, industrial regeneration and growth, mergers and acquisitions, and more recent concepts such as supply chain management. The subject has found an interesting niche position, attracting economic and managerial theorists. It shares with neoclassical theory some assumptions regarding rationality of economic actors, while exploring methods to understand the observed structures and functioning of organizations.

One leading theorist identified five related views.[27] The first is the population ecology model. This is a natural selection approach that perhaps appeals to the free market economic beliefs,[28] and offers one way in which an 'invisible hand' may be in play. The second view is the resource-dependent one. Here the decisions within organizations are studied in the context of resource constraints.[29] The model provides a role for managerial choice so that it offers a more active role for managers as strategy-making agents. Both population ecology and resource dependence models have tended to avoid the issue of managerial goals. These are introduced in the third approach known as rational-contingency theory.[30]

The fourth approach is known as the transaction cost economics model. It is associated with a well-respected body of work developed by Oliver Williamson.[31] The model constructs an explanation for the diversity and functioning of firms that eludes the orthodox economic approach. Williamson departs from the orthodox focus on production and replaces it with transactions. This analysis admits the uncertainties within 'real' transactions and leads to emergence of structures, and in particular to hierarchies, which serve to reduce transaction costs. Williamson has tended to regard the approach as one that complements other organizational theories.[32] One important feature of transaction cost theory is the recognition that agents undertaking transactions may cheat, introducing monitoring costs. This also raises the issue of trust within trading relationships.

The final approach is that of institutional economics.[33] Its emphasis has been to explain convergence of organizational structures. The notion of 'institutional isomorphism' combines sociological observations and theorizing. It has various applications, such as a contribution to theories of diffusion of innovation.

Evolutionary economics

This piece of the jigsaw probably would not have come to light if I had begun my handfuls of books search at the economics shelves of the library. Because the starting points had been theories of creativity and innovation, and subsequently the management of change I had been sensitized to valuable insights into evolutionary economics. The work of Richard Nelson and Sidney Winter has been particularly influential in the innovation field. It now receives recognition as stimulus in areas such as organizational ecology and the economics of networks.[34] They consider economic orthodoxy to have failed to deal with technology as a force for driving change. In a major treatise they indicate the special features of creativity within technological discovery that contribute to the problem. 'Creative intelligence, in the realm of technology as elsewhere, is autonomous and erratic, compulsive and whimsical. It does not lie plausibly within the prescriptive and descriptive constraints imposed by outsiders to the creative process, be they theorists, planners, teachers or critics.'[35]

They identified one assumption of contemporary economics that was holding back the development of effective growth theory. This was the principle of profit maximization. Citing Milton Friedman as an exemplar of the view, they suggest that a more dynamic view would be needed to indicate the mechanisms of economic growth. In particular, they have devoted a great deal of effort to illustrating how the impact of technology has been discounted as a major contributor to economic change.

More recent advocates of evolutionary economics have offered means of examining the evolution of market structure, and the connections between corporate vision and technological change.[36] The approaches have favoured mathematical modelling, and may be moving towards a radical structural alternative to neoclassical orthodoxy.

Puzzling Out *Homo economicus*

The points made in the last section reveal the voice through which neoclassical economists are heard. The next step is to look carefully at the voice and listen for the hidden voices that the orthodoxy tends to ignore.[37]

The modernist trajectory of economics

Today's economic orthodoxy has developed in a way that parallels the development of modern scientific knowledge. Adam Smith was part of the ferment of a transition period from the premodern to modern eras. Nevertheless, we must remember that Smith was inevitably writing as one who had a 'premodern' education. It has been argued that Smith was steeped in a premodern tradition that chose a rhetorical style of logic. It was a style that persisted well into the era of classical economics.[38] He wrote as a humanist with humanist concerns.[39] It would be dangerous to attribute one 'reading' to such a rich (and chronologically distant) work. That he is seen as a founder of today's right-wing economic views is an example of the economic orthodoxy 'selecting out' humanist and 'subjective' ideas that are inconvenient to their core beliefs.

The contributors to the classical school of economic thought were still working away at complex social issues of growth, trade, and even destitution and social implosion. Nevertheless, the application of newer analytical methods further tamed such 'subjective' elements as human needs, and substituted measures easier to build into abstract models.[40]

As the methods became more sophisticated, 'growth was simply taken for granted, and the problems of economic fluctuations and unemployment, which featured strongly in the classical writings, simply disappeared'.[41] The key issue became that of efficient distribution of resources illustrated by the preoccupations of the neoclassical school indicated above. This trajectory towards 'purer' scientific methods explains the divergence of interest between neoclassical economists, and the theorists within the 'heresies' still seeking real-world answers to social and economic problems. The orthodoxy increasingly treated real-world messiness as on the margins of their theories. The behaviours of exceptional and successful firms were not easily studied, and were left to others.

The historical path led to a splitting of management schools from the departments of economics. Economics textbooks put some emphasis on positive and normative economic perspectives. Based on the 'readings' we have discovered and outlined above we might conclude that the orthodoxy of contemporary economics is theoretically more self-confident with a positivist approach whereas the managerial preoccupation calls for a normative perspective.[42]

Peter Drucker, as in so many other issues, writes instructively about this. He has suggested that the micro-economics taught in college courses needs to attend less to the question of profit maximization and should concentrate on developing a theory that offers more for explaining and influencing growth, innovation and change.

> The next economics will not, it is reasonably certain, have the luxury to choose between microeconomics and macroeconomics. It will have to do what Marshall tried and failed to do: integrate both. Macroeconomics has proven itself – for the second time – to be unable to handle supply, that is, productivity and capital formation. Yet microeconomics alone is not adequate for economic theory or for economic policy in a world of mixed economies, multinational corporations, non-convertible

> currencies, and governments that redistribute half their nations' incomes. But what the term 'macroeconomy' will actually mean in the next economics is anything but clear and will be highly controversial.[43]

In considering the components of a post-industrial society, Daniel Bell draws on the words of the distinguished economist Robert M. Solow to the effect that economic man in future has to be regarded as a social category. He is not too sanguine about the possibility. In the same passage, reflecting on the possibility of economics forming some liaison with sociology, Bell commented 'For the hard-nosed economist, this is a fate feared worse than the pox.'[44]

Towards a New Economic Paradigm

We can conclude that the economic orthodoxy can be understood from the perspective of the neoclassical voice. Its influence pervades the economic world. We hear the voice explaining the workings of international trade, and the economic policy of governments. We also hear commentaries on inflation, exchange rates, regional development, job creation and unemployment. The voices come from policy-makers, political journalists and financial gurus.

It is therefore easy to confirm on a regular basis that the voices share the platform of understanding of the neoclassical orthodoxy we have but glimpsed in this chapter. They also indicate a deep belief in a few particularly salient features of the orthodoxy. In these pronouncements we detect the belief in the 'near perfect' functioning of today's unremitting capital markets networked through the great nodes at New York, London and Tokyo. We also detect the economic orthodoxy that regional or government interference with markets is on principle unsound and likely to be unproductive. Deregulation is in contrast 'a good thing' for over-regulated central banking systems. When regional government policies threaten to distort the system, the World Bank has the economic power to force appropriate changes, usually toward prudence. Financial stability is generally a good thing.[45]

Listening to the silenced voices

Let us now apply the mapping of heresies and orthodoxy on to the economic picture we have been examining. The familiar form of our map is shown in figure 10.4.

The map shows that the same kind of suppression and taming processes by an orthodoxy that we found in our visits to other territories. Once the trajectory to a neoclassical orthodoxy was underway, the subjective and the radical were under pressure. How is sense made of Keynes' animal spirits? Or Smith's invisible hand? Or Schumpeter's creative gales of destruction? As we might expect, these topics are almost all off limits, in economics courses, all conveniently ignored.

What does all this mean to the student of business? Above all the student has to be prepared to accept that the knowledge on offer of economics is an expression

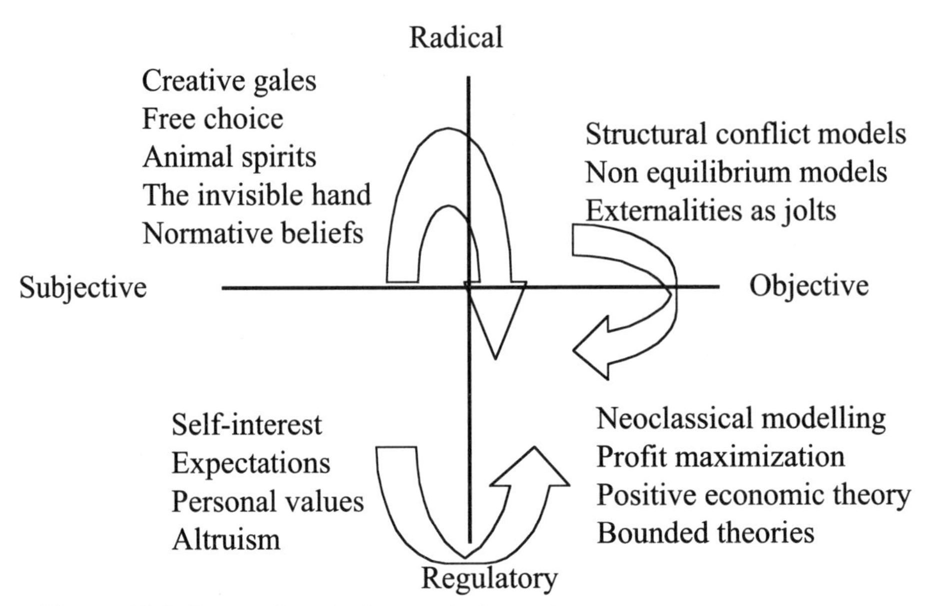

Figure 10.4: Economic orthodoxy and other voices

of one particular way of looking at the world. It is a way that rightly can claim to have made great advances in our understanding of a multitude of issues covered in economics textbooks. For those who approach the subject not as professional economists, there will always be the need to puzzle out explanations and explore alternative theoretical positions in the interests of intelligent business practices.

From creativity to economics and back

In our earlier journeys we found evidence for practitioner enthusiasm for creativity and innovation as topics of some practical importance. The enthusiasm extends to topics such as leadership, strategy and marketing. Cultures and climates that support creativity and innovation are considered desirable. The efforts to achieve creative and innovative results lead to theories of change management, which are again regarded as having considerable practical importance to managers and professionals. The enthusiasm of practitioners is shared by management consultants, who have been active in offering technologies for change, such as quality, and business process reengineering.

Yet, despite practical interest in the subjects they remain theoretically out in the cold, having no satisfactory home at present, either in economics or orthodox management science. In the case of creativity, the vocabulary of management orthodoxy brands it as something associated with danger, unpredictability, or even madness. At best it is regarded as a necessary evil, to be controlled and confined to the safety of creative professionals, brought in from the outside on a temporary basis. Innovation has less negative connotations among practitioners and some policy makers. However, we have seen the evidence of innovation being treated as a heresy within economic orthodoxy.

This book is an attempt to escape from the cover-up that denies legitimacy to a range of topics in orthodox management theory. In essence, the escape route for those who wish to take it can be found through applying those methods of discovery with which we have familiarized ourselves.

It has demonstrated an approach for identifying those assumptions within any orthodoxy that can be tested against heresies, some of which will be hinted at, usually dismissively, within that orthodoxy. The new assessment of realities opens up ways of discovering and dealing with new institutional forms.[46]

We may be able to start processes that create our way out of such iron cages. Chapters 8 and 9 touched on the forces that are disturbing the old orthodoxy. The world in which this new approach has to find application is in transition away from the stable organizational structures, and the old theories of organization. Technological progress has been granted a role of high significance as a driver of change throughout the modernist era. One aspect of technology, namely information technology, seems more central to the concerns of the contemporary period. How might our beliefs about reality change through interaction with information technology?

Just as work becomes blurred with leisure, so does learning become merged with experience. Learning is no longer split off from other activities, but connected in and through actions. The evidence suggests that organizational experiences in the contemporary world are increasingly revealing gaps in the core topics of business orthodoxy. Throughout this book the gaps have been brought more sharply into focus in a variety of ways. Readers will have every chance to take the new ideas and apply them in action. One of our messages has been that actions under conditions of environmental uncertainties can never be completely planned for in advance. That is the paradox of action. Conversely, the orthodoxy described as managerialism has been too readily accepted as a kind of economic predestination within which there is no scope for individual creativity. Yet to accept that and do nothing cuts across the essential idea of managerial action. That is the paradox of inaction.

A start has been made in this book to address these issues. Creativity and the management of change are just two among the range of currently suppressed voices which may help in the resolution of these critical organizational issues. A wider question is whether economic theory and business theories might benefit from a closer encounter with contemporary 'heresies'. I believe that the answer is an emphatic and unambiguous yes. I hope others will reach a similar conclusion. More importantly, I hope that I have indicated approaches for puzzling out the answers that will be of some interest and value to those who wish to search beyond the current platform of understanding of business studies.

Notes

1 Keynes (1936: viii).
2 Galbraith (1981: 39).
3 Krugman (1996: 16).

[4] Ives & Jarenpaa (1996: 33).

[5] I drew heavily on Begg et al. (1994); and Parkin (1993). Somewhat against the advice of colleagues I read a recent annotated edition of Smith's *Wealth of Nations* (1776); and Keynes' *General Theory* (1936), gaining great pleasure and enlightenment in each case. I had read Marx's *Capital* some years ago, and resisted the temptation to repeat the experience. My other handfuls of books were Copley & Sutherland (1995), and Ross (1995) for the historical Adam Smith; Arestis et al. (1997); Bell & Kristol (1981); Chrystal & Price (1994) and Galbraith (1981) for contemporary controversies. Bootle (1996), Ormerod (1994) and Hutton (1995) were excellent challenges to conventional economic thinking. Lawson (1992) spoke as a policy maker at the heart of the Thatcherite economic revolution of the 1980s.

[6] A rejoinder to this might be that in *Capital* Marx was far more scathing of Ricardo than he was of Adam Smith.

[7] It was Marx who bundled together the political economists since Smith as the classical school.

[8] Heinzelman (1995).

[9] Bell & Kristol (1981).

[10] Ormerod (1994) and FitzRoy et al. (1998) give good introductory accounts of the neo-classical school.

[11] This view is somewhat at odds with those held by Keynes, who tended to see Marshall as a follower of the classical traditions. Keynes saw himself as originating a more significant shift in economic thinking.

[12] In contrast to the macro-economic aggregates of Keynes.

[13] A term coined by one of the early neoclassicists, Pareto, according to Bell (1981).

[14] We must recall that Keynes was modelling the macro-economic world, and concerned himself with aggregate variables such as total savings, employment, growth and so on.

[15] Further theoretical support came from empirical studies by Kuznets in which consumption patterns over various periods were shown to be determined (as predicted) by disposable income levels.

[16] I am grateful to Professor Peter Swann who pointed out this distinction.

[17] Lawson (1992). For a more scholarly analysis of the dissolution of the Keynesian consensus see Dean (1981).

[18] I have extended the grouping suggested in Begg et al. (1994) to include the Neo-Austrians towards its right flank.

[19] Hutton (1995).

[20] Solow, Samuelson and Hicks would be generally listed among the leaders of this tendency.

[21] Karl Brunner coined the term in 1968, according to Meltzer in Bell & Kristol (1981).

[22] See Chrystal & Price, 1994, for a concise account of contemporary controversies in macro-economics.

[23] Fukuyama (1992, 1995) claims the end of Marxism as another historical necessity because of the economic supremacy of global capitalism. Samuelson suggests that Marx has been dismissed without serious critique by the economics paradigm, although his own reading suggests that 'In sum, at its heart Marx's paradigm was hopelessly flawed' (Samuelson 1997: 190).

[24] Lawson (1992) especially pp. 13–14.

[25] Peters (1992) who quotes from Hayek (1988 *trans).*

[26] Quoted in Coats (1997: 343).

[27] Hall (1991) drawing on Pfeffer (1982).

[28] Amburgey & Rao (1996) gives an overview for a special edition of *Academy of Management Journal.*
[29] Aldrich & Pfeffer (1976).
[30] Hall (1991).
[31] Williamson (1975).
[32] Williamson (1985).
[33] Scott (1987).
[34] See the *Academy of Management Journal* forum on innovation, vol 39, no. 5; see also Cohendet et al. (1998).
[35] Nelson & Winter (1982: vii).
[36] Swann & Gill (1993); Swann (1993).
[37] This is the approach we followed throughout the book. After chapter 9 it might be seen as a form of deconstruction of the text of orthodox neoclassical economics.
[38] See Heinzelman (1995).
[39] Tribe.
[40] Ormerod (1994).
[41] Ormerod (1994: 42).
[42] According to Giddens (1971), Durkheim worked at producing a positivist social science but found issue with Smith's view of enlightened self-interest which he saw as leading to the cult of individualism. Contemporary social scientists continue to dispute the cult of the individual, and even of the possibility of the economic 'rational being' (Barnes, 1995).
[43] Drucker (ibid.: 15).
[44] Bell (1981: 78).
[45] There is ambivalence towards the financial stability associated with more repressive regimes.
[46] Charles Handy, for example, invites us to consider new organizational forms using metaphors of a shamrock or an inverted doughnut. He also suggests that: 'the doughnut image is a conceptual way of relating duty to a fuller responsibility in every institution and group in society . . . It is a visual tool for balancing what often seem contradictions' (Handy, 1994: 66).

References

Aacer, D. A. (1991) *Managing brand equity: capitalizing on the value of a brand name*, New York: The Free Press.

Aacer, D. A. (1996) *Building strong brands*, New York: The Free Press.

Abrahamson, E. (1991) 'Managerial fads and fashions: the diffusion and rejection of innovations', *Academy of Management Review*, vol. 16, no. 3, pp. 586–612.

Ackoff, R. L. (1978) *The art of problem-solving*, New York: Wiley.

Ackoff, R. L. (1979) 'The future of operational research is past', *Journal of the Operational Research Society*, vol. 30, no. 2.

Ackoff, R. L. & Vergara, E. (1981) 'Creativity in problem-solving and planning: a review', *European Journal of Operational Research*, vol. 7, pp. 1–13.

Ackroyd, S. (1992). 'Paradigms lost: paradise regained?', in M. Reed & M. Hughes (eds.), *Rethinking organization: New directions in organization theory and analysis*, London: Sage, pp. 102–19.

Adair, J. (1989) *Great leaders*, Guildford, UK: Talbot Adair Press.

Adler, N. J. (1983) 'Cross-cultural management research: the ostrich and the trend', *Academy of Management Review*, vol. 8, no. 2, pp. 226–32.

Adler, N. J. (1991) *International dimensions of organizational behavior* (2nd edn), Boston, Mass.: PWS Kent.

Aldrich, H. E. (1992) 'Incommensurable paradigms? Vital signs from three perspectives', in M. Reed & M. Hughes (eds.), *Rethinking organization: new directions in organization theory and analysis*, London: Sage, pp. 17–45.

Aldrich, H. E. & Pfeffer, J. (1976) 'Environments and organizations', *Annual Review of Sociology*, vol. 2, Palo Alto, Ca.: Annual Review.

Almaraz, C. (1994) 'Quality management and the process of change', *Journal of Organizational Change Management*, vol. 7, no. 2, pp. 6–14.

Amabile, T. M. (1982) 'Social psychology of creativity: a consensual assessment technique', *Journal of Personality and Social Psychology*, vol. 43, pp. 997–1013.

Amabile, T. M. (1990) 'Within you, without you: the social psychology of creativity and beyond', in M. A. Runco & R. S. Albert (eds.), *Theories of creativity*, Newbury Park, Ca.: Sage.

Amabile, T. M. (1996) *Creativity in context*, Boulder, Co.: Westview.

Amabile, T. M., Conti, R., Coon, H., Lazenby, J. & Herron, M. (1996) 'Assessing the work environment for creativity', *Academy of Management Journal*, vol. 39, no. 5, pp. 1154–84.

Ambler, T. (1997) 'Building brand relationships' in S. Bickerstaffe (ed.), *Mastering management*, London: Pitman Publishing, pp. 175–82.

Amburgey, T. L. & Rao, H. (1996) 'Organizational ecology: past, present and future directions', *Academy of Management Review*, vol. 39, no. 5, pp. 1265–85.

Ansoff, H. I. (1965) *Corporate strategy*, New York: McGraw Hill.

Arestis, C., Palma, G. & Sawyer, M. (eds.) (1997) *Capital controversy, post-Keynesian economics and the history of economic thought: essays in honour of Geoffrey Harcourt*, vol. 1, London: Routledge.

Argyris, C. (1990) *Overcoming organizational defenses: facilitating organizational learning*, Boston, Mass.: Allyn & Bacon.

Astrachan, B. M. (1975) 'The Tavistock model of laboratory training', in K. D. Benne, L. P. Bradford, J. R. Gibb & R. O. Lippitt (eds.), *The laboratory method of changing and learning: theory and application,* Palo Alto, Ca.: Science and Behavior Books, Inc.

Atkinson, R. C. & Shiffrin, R. M. (1971) 'The control of short-term memory', *Scientific American*, vol. 225.

Barnes, B. (1995) *The elements of social theory*, London: UCL Press.

Bass, B. M. & Avolio, B. J. (1990) 'The implications of transactional and transformational leadership for individual, team, and organizational development', *Research in Organizational Change and Development*, vol. 4, pp. 231–72.

Bass, B. M. & Avolio, B. J. (1994) *Improving organisational effectiveness through transformational leadership*, Thousand Oaks, Ca.: Sage.

Bateson, G. (1979) *Mind and nature: a necessary unity*, London: Fontana.

Baumol, W. J. (1959) *Business behavior, value and growth*, New York: Macmillan.

Bazerman, M. H. (1994) *Judgment in managerial decision making* (3rd edn), New York: Wiley.

Bédard, J. (ed.) (1994) *Proceedings, 1994 International Creativity and Innovation Networking Conference*, Quebec City, Quebec: Transphere Publishers.

de la Bedoyere, Q. (1988) *Managing people and problems*, Aldershot: Gower Press.

Beer, S. (1966) *Decision and control*, Chichester: Wiley.

Beer, S. (1979) *The heart of enterprise*, Chichester: Wiley.

Beer, S. (1981) *The brain of the firm*, Chichester: Wiley.

Beer, S. (1994) *Beyond dispute: the invention of team syntegrity*, Chichester: Wiley.

Begg, D., Fischer, S. & Dombusch, R. (1994) *Economics* (4th edn), London: McGraw-Hill.

Bell, D. (1981) 'Models and reality in economic discourse', in D. Bell & I. Kristol (eds.), *The crisis in economic theory*, New York: Basic Books, pp. 46–80.

Bell, D. & Kristol, I. (eds.) (1981) *The crisis in economic theory*, New York: Basic Books.

Benbasat, I. & Lim, L. H. (1993) 'The effects of group, task, context and technology variables on the usefulness of group support systems: a meta-analysis of experimental studies', *Small Group Research*, vol. 24, no. 4, pp. 430–62.

Benne, K. D., Bradford, L. P., Gibb, J. R. & Lippitt, R. O. (1975) *The laboratory method of changing and learning: theory and application*, Palo Alto, Ca.: Science and Behavior Books, Inc.

Bennett, P. D. (1988) *Dictionary of marketing terms*, Chicago: American Marketing Association.

Bennis, W. G. (1959) 'Leadership theory and administrative behavior: the problem of authority', *Administrative Science Quarterly*, 4, pp. 259–60.

Bennis, W. & Nanus, B. (1985) *Leaders*, New York: Harper & Row.

Bennis, W., Parikh, J. & Lessem, R. (1994) *Beyond leadership: balancing economics, ethics, and ecology*, Oxford: Basil Blackwell.

Benson, B. S. (1957) 'Let's toss this idea up . . .' *Fortune*, October, pp. 145–6.

Benson, J. K. (ed.) (1977) *Organisational analysis: critique and innovation*, London: Sage.

Bertalanffy, L. von (1968) *General systems theory*, New York: Braziller.

Bessant, J. (1991) *Manufacturing advanced manufacturing technology: the challenge of the fifth wave*, Manchester: NCC Blackwell.

Bessant, J., Caffyn, S. & Gilbert, J. (1996) 'Learning to manage innovation', *Technology Analysis and Strategic Management*, vol. 8, no. 1, pp. 59–69.

Biggerdike, E. R. (1981) 'The contributions of marketing to strategic management', *Academy of Management Review*, vol. 6, no. 4, pp. 621–32.

Blake, R. B. & Mouton, J. S. (1964) *The managerial grid*, Houston, Tex: Gulf Publishing Company.

Blake, R. R., Mouton, J. S. & McCanse, A. A. (1989) *Change by design*, Reading, Mass.: Addison-Wesley OD Series.

Blakesee, T. R. (1980) *The right brain*, Garden City, NY: Anchor Press.

Blanchard, E. & Johnson, S. (1982) *The one-minute manager*, New York: William Morrow.

Boden, M. A. (1994a) 'What is creativity', in Boden, M. A. (ed.), *Dimensions of creativity*, Cambridge, Mass.: The MIT Press, pp. 75–118.

Boden, M. A. (ed.) (1994b) *Dimensions of creativity*, Cambridge, Mass.: The MIT Press.

Bogan, J. E. (1969) 'The other side of the brain II: an appositional mind', *Bulletin of the Los Angeles Neurologial Sciences*, vol. 34, no. 3, pp. 135–62.

Boje, D. M., Gephart, R. P. Jr. & Thatchenkery, T. J. (eds.) (1996), *Postmodern management and organization theory*, Thousand Oaks, Ca.: Sage.

Boje, D. M. & Winsor, R. D. (1993) 'The resurrection of Taylorism: Total Quality Management's hidden agenda', *Journal of Organizational Change Management*, vol. 6, no. 4, pp. 57–70.

Bootle, R. (1996) *The death of inflation: surviving and thriving in the zero era*, London: Nicholas Brealey.

Bowers, D. G. & Seashore, S. E. (1966) 'Predicting organizational effectiveness with a four-factor theory of leadership', *Administrative Science Quarterly*, vol. 11, pp. 238–63.

Bryant, C. & Jary, D. (eds.) (1991) *Giddens' theory of structuration: a critical appraisal*, Routledge: London.

Bryant, J. (1989) *Problem management: a guide for producers and players*, Chichester: Wiley.

Bryman, A. (1992) *Charisma and leadership in organizations*, Newbury Park, Ca.; London, UK: Sage.

Buchanan, D. & Huczynski, A. (1997) *Organizational behaviour: an introductory text* (3rd edn), Prentice Hall Europe: Hemel Hempstead.

Burgoyne, J. G. (1979) 'A behavioural science perspective of operational research practice', in M. C. Jackson, P. Keys & S. A. Cropper (eds.), *Operational research and the social sciences*, New York: Plenum Press, pp. 3–12.

Burnes, B. (1992) *Managing change*, London: Pitman.

Burns, J. M. (1978) *Leadership*, New York: Harper and Row.

Burrell, G. (1996) 'Paradigms, metaphors, discourses, genealogies', in S. R. Clegg, C. Hardy, & W. R. Nord (eds.), *Handbook of organization studies*, London: Sage, pp. 642–708.

Burrell, G. & Morgan, G. (1979) *Sociological paradigms and organisational analysis: elements of the sociology of corporate life*, London: Heinemann.

Buttle, F. (ed.) (1996) *Relationship marketing*, London: Paul Chapman.

Calás, M. B. & Smircich, L. (1992) 'Re-writing gender into organizational theorizing: directions from feminist perspectives', in M. Reed & M. Hughes (eds.), *Rethinking organization: new directions in organization theory and analysis*, London: Sage, pp. 227–53.

Carroll, D. T. (1983) 'A disappointing search for excellence', *Harvard Business Review*, November–December, pp. 78–88.

Carson, J. W. (1989) *Innovation: a battle plan for the 1990s*, Farnborough, Hants: Gower.

Carson, J. W. & Rickards, T. (1979) *Industrial new-product development*, Farnborough, Hants: Gower.

Cartwright, D. & Zander, A. (eds.) (1968) *Group dynamics: research and theory* (3rd edn), London: Tavistock.

Chambers Biographical Dictionary (1990) (5th edn), Edinburgh: Chambers (ed. M. Magnusson.).

Champy, J. (1995) *Reengineering management: managing the change to the reengineering corporation*, London: Harper Collins.

Chandler, A. D. (1962/1966) *Strategy and structure*, Cambridge, Mass.: The MIT Press.

Cheah, Hock Beng (1993) 'Dual modes of entrepreneurship: revolution and evolution in the entrepreneurial process', *Creativity and Innovation Management*, vol. 2, no. 4, pp. 243–51.

Checkland, P. B. & Scholes, S. (1990) *Soft systems methodology in action*, Chichester: Wiley.

Child, J. (1972/1977) *Organization: a guide to problems and practice*, London: Harper and Row.

Chrystal, K. A. & Price, S. (1994) *Controversies in macroeconomics* (3rd edn), Hemel Hempstead, Herts: Harvester Wheatsheaf.

Churchman, C. W., Ackoff, R. L. & Arnoff, E. L. (1957) *Introduction to operations research*, New York: Wiley.

Clegg, S. R., Hardy, C. & Nord, W. R. (eds.) (1996) *Handbook of organization studies*, London: Sage.

Coats, A. W. (1997) 'The nobel prize in economics', in C. Arestis, G. Palma & M. Sawyer, (eds.), (1997) *Capital controversy, post-Keynesian economics and the history of economic thought: essays in honour of Geoffrey Harcourt*, vol. 1, London: Routledge, pp. 337–51.

Cohendet, P., Llerena, P., Stahn, H. & Umbhauer, G. (eds.) (1998) *The economics of networks: interactions and behaviours*, Berlin, Germany: Springer-Verlag.

Colemont, P., Groholt, P., Rickards, T. & Smeekes, H. (eds.) (1988) *Creativity & innovation: towards a European network*, Amsterdam: Kluwer.

Collins, J. C. & Porras, J. I. (1994) *Built to last: successful habits of visionary companies*, New York: Random House.

Conger, J. A. (1989) *The charismatic leader: beyond the mystique of exceptional leadership*, San Francisco: Jossey-Bass.

Conti, R. F. & Warner, M. (1994) 'Taylorism, teams and technology in "Reengineering" work organization', *New Technology, Work and Employment*, vol. 9, pp. 93–102.

Cooper, R. G. (1992) 'The NewProd system: the industry experience', *Journal of Product Innovation Management*, vol. 9, no. 2, pp. 113–27.

Cooper, R. G. & Kleinschmidt, E. J. (1987) 'New products: what separates winners from losers?', *Journal of Product Innovation Management*, vol. 4, no. 3, pp. 169–84.

Copley, S. & Sutherland, K. (eds.) (1995) *Adam Smith's Wealth of Nations: new interdisciplinary essays*, Manchester: Manchester University Press.

Couger, J. D. (1995) *Creative problem solving and opportunity finding*, Danvers, Mass.: Boyd & Fraser.

Crawford, C. M. (1984) 'Protocol: new tool for product innovation', *Journal of Product Innovation*, vol. 2, pp. 85–91.

Cummings, S. & Tsoukas, H. (1995) 'Awakenings: the rediscovery of ancient Greek wisdom in management theory', Warwick working paper, presented at Manchester Business School.

Cyert, R. M. & March, J. G. (1963) *A behavioral theory of the firm*, Englewood Cliffs, NJ: Prentice Hall.

Daft, R. L. & Lengel, R. H. (1986) 'Organizational information requirements, media richness and structural design', *Management Science*, vol. 32, no. 5, pp. 554–71.

Damian-Knight, G. (1986) *The I Ching on business and decision-making*, London: Rider.

Dando, M. R. & Sharp, R. G. (1978) 'Operational research in the UK in 1977: the causes and consequences of a myth', *Journal of the Operational Research Society*, vol. 29, p. 939.

Davis, M. S. (1971) 'That's interesting! Towards a phenomenology of sociology and a sociology of phenomenology', *Philosophy of Social Science*, vol. 1, pp. 309–44.

Dawson, P. (1994) *Organizational change: a processual approach*, London: Paul Chapman.

Day, D. V. & Lord, R. G. (1988) 'Executive leadership and organizational performance: suggestions for a new theory and methodology', *Journal of Management*, vol. 14, pp. 453–64.

Day, G. S. (1994) 'The capabilities of market-driven organizations', *Journal of Marketing*, vol. 58, pp. 37–52.

de Bono, E. (1971) *Lateral thinking for management*, London: McGraw-Hill.

de Bono, E. (1990) *I am right you are wrong*, London: Viking.

de Bono, E. (1992) *Serious creativity: using the power of lateral thinking to create new ideas*, London: Harper Collins.

De Cock, C. (1993) 'A creativity model for the analysis of continuous improvement programmes: a suggestion to make continuous improvement continuous', *Creativity and Innovation Management*, vol. 2, no. 3, pp. 156–65.

De Cock, C. (1996) An investigation into the introduction of planned organizational change: theoretical and empirical considerations. Unpublished doctoral dissertation, University of Manchester.

De Cock, C. & Rickards, T. (1996) 'Thinking about organizational change: towards two kinds of process intervention', *International Journal of Organizational Analysis*, vol. 4, no. 3, pp. 233–51.

Deal, T. & Kennedy, A. (1982) *Corporate cultures*, Reading, Mass.: Addison-Wesley.

Dean, J. W. (1981) 'The dissolution of the Keynesian consensus', in D. Bell & I. Kristol (eds.), *The crisis in economic theory*, New York: Basic Books, pp. 19–34.

Deci, E. L. & Ryan, R. M. (1985) *Intrinsic motivation and self-determination in human behavior*, New York: Plenum.

Denison, D. R. (1996) 'What *is* the difference between organizational culture and organizational climate? A native's point of view on a decade of paradigm wars', *Academy of Management Review*, vol. 21, no. 3, pp. 619–54.

Derrida, J. (1976) *Of grammatology*, trans. G. Spivak, Baltimore, Md: Johns Hopkins University Press.

DeSanctis, G. & Gallope, R. B. (1987) 'A foundation for the study of group decision support systems', *Management Science*, vol. 33, no. 5, pp. 589–609.

Dickson, T. & Bickerstaffe, G. (eds.) (1997) *Mastering management*, London: Pitman Publishing.

Dingli, S. (ed.) (1994) *Creative thinking: a multifaceted approach*, Valetta, Malta: Malta University Press.

Donaldson, L. (1988) 'In successful defense of contingency theory: a routing of the critics', *Organization Studies*, vol. 9, no. 1, pp. 28–32.

Donaldson, L. (1996) *For positivist organization theory*, London: Sage.

Downs, G. W. R. Jr. & Mohr, L. B. (1976) 'Conceptual issues in the study of innovation', *Administrative Science Quarterly*, vol. 21, pp. 700–14.

Doyle, P. (1994) *Marketing management & strategy*, Hemel Hempstead: Prentice Hall International (UK) Ltd.

Dreyfus, H. & Rabinow, P. (1982) *Michel Foucault: beyond structuralism and hermeneutics*, Brighton, UK: Harvester.

Drucker, P. F. (1961/1964) *Managing for results*, London: Heinemann.

Drucker, P. F. (1968 [1955]) *The practice of management*, London: Pan.

Drucker, P. F. (1981) 'Towards the next economics', in D. Bell & I. Kristol (eds.), *The crisis in economic theory*, New York: Basic Books, pp. 4–18.

Drucker, P. F. (1985) *Innovation and entrepreneurship*, London: Heinemann.
Dunant, S. (ed.) (1994) *The war of the words: the political correctness debate*, Virago: London.
Dung, P. (1994) 'Introducing creativity methodologies into Vietnam', *Creativity and Innovation Management*, vol. 3, no. 4, pp. 240–2.
Dung, P. (1995) 'Inventive creativity based on the laws of systems development', *Creativity and Innovation Management*, vol. 4, no. 1, pp. 19–30.
Easingwood, C. (1986) 'New product development for service companies', *Journal of Product Innovation Management*, vol. 4, no. 2, pp. 269–75.
Eden, C. & Huxham, C. (1996) 'Action research for the study of organizations', in S. R. Clegg, C. Hardy & W. R. Nord (eds.), *Handbook of organization studies*, London: Sage, pp. 526–42.
Ekvall, G. (1987) 'The climate metaphor in organization theory', in B. M. Bass & P. J. D. Drenth (eds.), with P. Weissenberg, *Advances in organizational psychology: an international review*, Beverly Hills Ca.: Sage, pp. 177–90.
Ekvall, G. (1991) 'The organizational culture of idea management: a creative climate for the management of ideas', in J. Henry & D. Walker, *Managing innovation*, London: Sage, pp. 73–9.
Ellinor, L. & Gerard, G. (1998) *Dialogue: rediscover the transforming power of conversation*, New York: Wiley.
Enthoven, G. (1997) 'Ideology, 200 years young: the actual impact of the science of ideas', in T. Rickards, S. Moger, M. Tassoul, I. van de Kimmenade & J. van den Beuken (eds.), *Creativity and innovation: Impact*, Maastricht: EACI.
Evans, R. & Russell, P. (1989) *The creative manager*, London: Unwin Hyman.
Eysenck, H. J. (1994) 'The measurement of creativity', in M. A. Boden, ed. *Dimensions of creativity*, Cambridge, Mass.: The MIT Press, pp. 199–243.
Festinger, L. (1957) *A theory of cognitive dissonance*, Evanston, Ill.: Row, Peterson.
Fiedler, F. E. (1967) *A theory of leadership effectiveness*, New York: McGraw Hill.
Fisher, L. (1994) 'Total quality: Hit or miss?', *Accountancy*, April, pp. 50–1.
FitzRoy, F. R., Acs, Z. J. & Gerlowski, D. A. (1998) *Management and economics of organization*, London: Prentice Hall Europe.
Flood, R. L. & Jackson, M. C. (1991) *Creative problem solving: total systems intervention*, Chichester: Wiley.
Ford, C. M. & Gioia, D. A. (1995) *Creative actions in organizations: ivory tower visions and real world voices*, Thousand Oaks, Ca.: Sage.
Forrester, J. (1961) *Industrial dynamics*, Cambridge, Mass.: The MIT Press.
Foster, R. N. (1986) *Innovation: the attacker's advantage*, London: Pan.
Foucault, M. (1979) 'What is an author', in J. Hariri (ed.), *Textual strategies: perspectives in post-structuralist criticism*, Ithaca, NY: Cornell University Press.
Freeman, C. (1982) *The economics of industrial innovation* (2nd edn), London: Pinter.
French, W. L. & Bell, W. H. (1978) *Organization development* (2nd edn), Englewood Cliffs, NJ: Prentice-Hall.
Frost, P. J. (1989) 'Creating scholarship and journeying through academia: Reflections and interpretations from the field', *Journal of Applied Behavioural Science*, vol. 25, no. 4, pp. 399–418.
Frost, P. J., Moore, L. F., Louis, M. R., Lundberg, C. C. & Martin, J. (1985) *Organizational culture*, Beverly Hills, Ca.: Sage.
Frost, P. J., Moore, L. F., Louis, M. R., Lundberg, C. C. & Martin, J. (1991) *Reframing organizational culture*, Beverly Hills, Ca.: Sage.
Fukuyama, F. (1992) *The end of history and the last man*, London: Penguin.

Fukuyama, F. (1995) *Trust: the social virtues and the creation of prosperity*, Hamish Hamilton, London.
Galbraith, J. K. (1981) *A life in our times: memoirs*, London: Corgi Books.
Gallupe, R. B. & Cooper, W. H. (1993) 'Brainstorming electronically', *Sloane Management Review*, Fall, pp. 22–36.
Gause, D. C. & Weinberg, M. (1982) *Are your lights on? How to figure out what the problem really is*, Cambridge, Mass.: Winthrop Publishers, Inc.
Geschka, H., Moger, S. T. & Rickards, T. (eds.) (1995) *Creativity and innovation: the power of synergy*, Darmstadt, Germany: Geschka Associates.
Giddens, A. (1971) *Capitalism and modern social theory: an analysis of the writings of Marx Durkheim and Max Weber*, Cambridge, UK: Cambridge University Press.
Giddens, A. (1990) *The consequences of modernity*, Cambridge, UK: Polity Press.
Giddens, A. (1991) 'Structuration theory: past, present, and future', in C. Bryant and D. Jary (eds.), *Giddens' theory of structuration: a critical appraisal*, Routledge: London, pp. 201–21.
Gilbreth, F. B. (1911) *Motion study*, New York: Van Nostrand.
Glover, J. A., Ronning, R. R. & Reynolds, C. R. (eds.) (1989) *Handbook of creativity: perspectives on individual differences*, New York: Plenum.
Goldratt, E. & Cox, J. (rev. edn, 1989) *The goal*, Aldershot: Gower.
Gough, J. & Hill, S. (1979) *Fundamentals of managerial economics*, London: Macmillan.
Graves, D. (1986) *Corporate culture: diagnosis and change*, London: Frances Pinter.
Gray, I. (1984) *Fayol's general and industrial management*, New York: IEEE Press.
Grint, K. (1994) 'Reengineering history: social resonances and business process reengineering', *Organization*, vol. 1, pp. 179–201.
Grönhaug, K. & Kaufmann, G. (1988) *Innovation: a cross-disciplinary perspective*, Oslo: Norwegian University Press.
Gruber, H. E. (1995) 'Insight and affect in the history of science', in R. J. Sternberg & J. E. Davidson, *The nature of insight*, Cambridge, Mass.: The MIT Press, pp. 397–461.
Gryskiewicz, S. S. (ed.) (1993) *Discovering creativity: proceedings of the 1992 international creativity & innovation conference*, Greensboro, NC: Center for Creative Leadership.
Guilford, J. P. (1959) 'Traits of creativity', in H. H. Anderson (ed.), *Creativity and its cultivation*, New York: Harper, pp. 142–61.
Guilford, J. P. (1970) 'Traits of creativity', in P. E. Vernon (ed.), *Creativity*, Harmondsworth: Penguin, pp. 167–88.
Haensly, P. A. & Reynolds, C. R. (1989) 'Creativity and intelligence', in J. A. Glover, R. R. Ronning & C. R. Reynolds (eds.), *Handbook of creativity: perspectives on individual differences*, New York: Plenum, pp. 111–32.
Hall, R. H. (1991, 5th edn) *Organizations: structures, processes, and outcomes*, London: Prentice Hall.
Hamel, G. & Prahalad, C. K. (1989) 'Strategic intent', *Harvard Business Review*, May–June, pp. 63–76.
Hammer, M. (1990) 'Reengineering work: Don't automate. Obliterate', *Harvard Business Review*, July–August, pp. 104–12.
Hammer, M. & Champy, J. (1993) *Reengineering the corporation: a manifesto for business revolution*, London: Nicholas Brealey.
Hampden-Turner, C. (1990) *Corporate culture: from vicious to virtual circles*, London: Economist Books.
Handy, C. (1976) *Understanding organisations*, Harmondsworth: Penguin.
Handy, C. (1988) *The age of unreason*, London: Hutchinson.

Handy, C. (1994) *The empty raincoat*, London: Hutchinson.

Harding, S. (1990) 'Feminism, science, and the anti-enlightenment critique', in L. J. Nicholson (ed.), *Feminism/Postmodernism*, New York: Routledge.

Hayek, F. A. (1988) ed. W. W. Bartley III *The fatal conceit: the errors of socialism*, Chicago: University of Chicago Press.

Heinzelman, K. (1995) 'The last georgic: *Wealth of Nations* and the scene of writing', in S. Copley & K. Sutherland (eds.), *Adam Smith's Wealth of Nations: new interdisciplinary essays*, Manchester: Manchester University Press, pp. 171–96.

Hennessy, B. A. & Amabile, T. M. (1988) 'The conditions of creativity', in R. J. Sternberg (ed.), *The nature of creativity*, Cambridge, Mass.: Cambridge University Press, pp. 11–38.

Henry, J. (1991) *Creative management*, London: Sage.

Henry, J. & Walker, D. (eds.) (1991) *Managing innovation*, London: Sage.

Hersey, P. & Blanchard, K. (1988 [1977]) *Management of organizational behavior* (4th edn), Englewood Cliffs, NY: Prentice Hall.

Hicks, M. J. (1991) *Problem solving in business and management: hard, soft and creative approaches*, London: Chapman & Hall.

Hocevar, D. & Bachelor, P. (1989) 'A taxonomy and critique of measurements used in the study of creativity', in J. A. Glover, R. R. Ronning & C. R. Reynolds (eds.), *Handbook of creativity: perspectives on individual differences*, New York: Plenum, pp. 53–75.

Hofstede, G. (1980) *Culture's consequences: international differences in work related values*, Beverly Hills, Ca.: Sage.

Hofstede, G. (1991) *Cultures and organizations: software of the mind*, Maidenhead, UK: McGraw-Hill.

Hogarth, R. (1987) *Judgement and choice* (2nd edn), New York: Wiley.

Hollinger, R. (1994) 'Postmodernism and the social sciences: a thematic approach', *Contemporary social theory*, vol. 4, London: Sage.

House, R. J. & Mitchell, T. R. (1974) 'Path-goal theory of leadership', *Journal of Contemporary Business*, vol. 3, pp. 81–97.

Huber, G. P. (1998) 'Synergies between organizational learning and creativity and innovation', *Creativity and Innovation Management*, vol. 7, no. 1, pp. 3–8.

Huczynski, A. & Buchanan, D. (1997) *Organizational behaviour: an introductory text* (3rd edn), London: Prentice Hall.

Hunt, J. G. (1991) *Leadership: a new synthesis*, Newbury Park, Ca.: Sage.

Hutton, W. (1995) *The state we're in*, Jonathan Cape: London.

Independent on Sunday (1995) 'Profile on Gerry Robinson: portrait of a predator as an artist', 3 December, Business Section, p. 5.

Inkeles, A. & Levinson, D. J. (1969) 'National character: the study of modal personality and sociocultural systems', in G. Lindsey & E. Aronson (eds.), *The handbook of social psychology* (2nd ed.), vol. 4, Reading, Mass.: Addison-Wesley.

Isaksen, S. G. (ed.) (1987) *Frontiers of creativity research: beyond the basics*, Buffalo, NY: Bearly.

Isaksen, S. G., Murdock, M. C., Firestien, R. L. & Treffinger, D. J. (eds.) (1993a) *Nurturing and developing creativity: the emergence of a discipline*, Norwood, NJ: Ablex.

Isaksen, S. G., Murdoch, M. C., Firestien, R. L. & Treffinger, D. J. (eds.) (1993b) *Understanding and recognising creativity: the emergence of a discipline*, Norwood, NJ: Ablex.

Ise, M. (1995) 'Entrepreneurial innovation: beyond Schumpeter', *Creativity and Innovation Management*, vol. 4, no. 1, pp. 40–4.

Ives, B. & Jarenpaa, S. L. (1996) 'Will the internet revolutionize business education and research?', *Sloane Management Review*, Spring, pp. 33–41.
Janis, I. L. (1972) *Victims of groupthink*, Boston: Houghton Mifflin.
Johnson-Laird, P. N. (1993) *Human and machine thinking*, Hillsdale, NJ: Lawrence Erlbaum Associates.
Kahn, R. L. & Katz, D. (1953) 'Leadership practices in relation to productivity and morale', in D. Cartwright and A. Zander (eds.), *Group dynamics*, New York: Harper and Row.
Kanter, R. M. (1985) *The change masters: corporate entrepreneurs at work*, London: Counterpoint (Unwin) paperbacks.
Kapferer, J.-N. (1997) *Strategic brand management: creating and sustaining brand equity long term*, London: Kogan Page.
Kerr, S., Schriescheim, C. A., Murphy, C. J. & Stodgill, R. M. (1974) 'Towards a contingency theory of leadership based on the consideration and initiating structure literature', *Organizational Behavior and Human Performance*, 12, pp. 62–82.
Ketchum, L. D. & Trist, E. (1992) *All teams are not created equal: how employee empowerment really works*, Newbury Park, Ca.: Sage.
Kets de Vries, F. R. (1989) *Prisoners of leadership*, London: Wiley.
Keynes, J. M. (1936) *The general theory of employment interest and money*, London: Macmillan.
Kim, S. H. (1990) *Essence of creativity: a guide to tackling difficult problems*, New York; Oxford, England: Oxford University Press.
Kindler, J. & Kiss, I. (1984) 'Future methodology based on past performance', in R. Tomlinson & I. Kiss (eds.), *Rethinking the process of operational research and systems analysis*, Oxford: Pergamon, pp. 1–17.
King, N. (1990) 'Innovation at work: the research literature', in M. A. West & J. L. Farr (eds.), *Innovation and creativity at work: psychological and organizational strategies*, Chichester: Wiley.
Kingston, W. (1984) *The political economy of innovation: studies in industrial organization*, vol. 4, The Hague: Martinus Nijhoff.
Kirton, M. J. (1994) *Adaptors and innovators: styles of creativity and innovation* (2nd edn), London: Routledge.
Kirzner, I. M. (1973) *Competition and entrepreneurship*, Chicago: University of Chicago Press.
Kleiner, A. (1996) *The age of heretics: heroes, outlaws, and the forerunners of corporate change*, New York: Nicholas Brealey.
Koestler, A. (1964) *The act of creation*, London: Hutchinson.
Kolb, D. A., Rubin, I. M. & Osland, J. S. (1991) *The organizational behavior reader* (5th edn), Englewood Cliffs, NJ: Prentice-Hall International.
Kotler, P. (1976) *Marketing Management*, Englewood Cliffs NJ: Prentice Hall.
Kotler, P. & Armstrong, G. (1994) *Principles of marketing* (6th edn), Englewood Cliffs, NJ: Prentice Hall.
Kotler, P., Armstrong, G., Saunders, J. & Wong, V. (1996) *Principles of marketing: the European Edition*, London: Prentice Hall.
Kristol, I. (1981) 'Rationalism in economics', in D. Bell & I. Kristol (eds.), *The crisis in economic theory*, New York: Basic Books, pp. 201–19.
Kroeber, A. L. & Kluckhohn, F. (1952) *Culture: a critical review of concepts and definitions*, Peabody Museum papers, vol. 47, no. 1, Cambridge, Mass.: Harvard University Press.
Krugman, P. (1996) 'The implausible pundits', *Times Higher Educational Supplement*, 10 May, pp. 18–19.

Kuhn, T. (1967) *The structure of scientific revolutions*, Chicago: University of Chicago Press.
Lakatos, I. (1970) 'Falsification and the methodology of scientific research', in A. Musgrave and I. Lakatos (eds.), *Criticism and the growth of knowledge*, Cambridge, UK: Cambridge University Press.
Lawler, E. E. (1973) *Motivation in the work organization*, New York: Brooks-Cole.
Lawrence, P. R. & Lorsch, J. W. (1968) *Organizations and environment*, Boston, Mass.: Harvard Business Press.
Lawrence, R. J. & Thomas, M. J. (eds.) (1971) *Modern marketing management*, Harmondsworth: Penguin.
Lawson, N. (1992) *The view from No. 11: memoirs of a tory radical*, London: Bantam Books (Corgi edn, 1993).
Leonard, A. (1994) 'The very model of a modern system-general: how the viable system actually works', in S. Beer, *Beyond dispute: the invention of team syntegrity*, Chichester: Wiley, pp. 346–56.
Leonard-Barton, D. (1995) *Wellsprings of knowledge*, Cambridge Mass.: Harvard University Press.
Lessem, R. (1990) *Managing corporate culture*, Aldershot: Gower.
Levitt, T. (1960) 'Marketing myopia', *Harvard Business Review*, July–August, pp. 26–37.
Lewin, K. (1947) 'Group decision and social change', in T. M. Newcombe & E. L. Hartley (eds.), *Readings in social psychology*, New York: Holt, Reinhart and Winston.
Ley, R. (1990) *A whisper of espionage: Wolfgang Kohler and the apes of Tenerife*, New York: Avery Publishing Group.
Lim, L-H. & Benbasat, I. (1996) 'IT support for reducing group judgment bias', in J. F. Nunamaker Jr. & R. H. Sprague Jr. (1996) *Information systems – decision support and knowledge-based systems*, Washington, DC: IEEE Computer Society Press, vol. IV, pp. 98–108.
Linstead, S., Small, R. G. & Jeffcutt, P. (eds.) (1996) *Understanding management*, London: Sage.
Lord, R. G. & Maher, K. J. (1993) *Leadership and information processing: linking perceptions and performance*, London: Routledge.
Lyotard, J.-F. (1984) *The postmodern condition: a report on knowledge*, trans. G. Bennington & B. Massaumi, Minneapolis: University of Minnesota Press.
MacKinnon, D. W. (1978) *In search of human effectiveness: identifying and developing creativity*, Buffalo, NY: Creative Education Foundation.
McCormack, M. H. (1984) *What they don't teach you at Harvard Business School*, London: Collins.
McDonald, M. H. B. (1995) *Marketing plans: how to prepare them, how to use them*, Oxford: Butterworth Heinemann.
McGrath, R. G., MacMillan, I. C., Yang, E. A. Tsai, W. (1991) 'Does culture endure, or is it malleable? Issues for entrepreneurial economic development', *Journal of Business Venturing*, vol. 7, pp. 441–58.
McGregor, D. (1960) *The human side of enterprise*, New York: McGraw-Hill.
McReynolds, P. (1990) 'Motives and metaphors: a study in scientific creativity', in D. E. Leary (ed.), *Metaphors in the history of psychology*. Cambridge, UK: Cambridge University Press.
Magyari-Beck, I. (1993) 'Creatology: a potential paradigm for an emerging discipline', in S. G. Isaksen, M. C. Murdoch, R. L. Firestien & D. J. Treffinger (eds.), *Understanding and recognising creativity: the emergence of a discipline*, Norwood, NJ: Ablex, pp. 48–82.
Majaro, S. (1988) *The creative gap: managing ideas for profit*, London: Longman.
Mandela, N. (1994) *A long walk to freedom*, London: Little, Brown and Company.

Manimala, M. J. (1992) 'Entrepreneurial innovation: beyond Schumpeter', *Creativity and Innovation Management*, vol. 1, no. 1, pp. 46–55.
March, J. G. & Simon, H. A. (1958) *Organizations*, NY: Wiley.
Marris, R. L. (1963) 'A model of the managerial enterprise', *Quarterly Journal of Economics*, vol. 77, pp. 185–209.
Marshall, A. (1890), *Principles of economics*, London: Macmillan.
Maslow, A. (1943) 'A theory of human motivation', *Psychological Review*, vol. 50, no. 4, pp. 370–96.
Mayer, R. E. (1995) 'The search for insight: grappling with gestalt psychology's unanswered questions', in R. J. Sternberg & J. E. Davidson, *The nature of insight*, Cambridge, Mass.: The MIT Press, pp. 3–32.
Mervis, P. H. & Berg, D. N. (eds.) (1977) *Failures in organizational development and change: cases and essays for learning*, New York: Wiley Interscience.
Meyerson, D. (1991) 'Acknowledging and uncovering ambiguities', in P. Frost, L. F. Moore, M. R. Louis, C. C. Lundberg, C. C. & J. Martin (eds.), *Reframing organizational culture*, Beverly Hills, Ca.: Sage, pp. 254–70.
Miles, R. E. & Snow, C. C. (1984) 'Designing strategic human resource systems', *Organizational Dynamics*, Summer, pp. 36–52.
Miller, E. & Rice, A. K. (1967) *Systems of organization: the control of task and sentient boundaries*, London: Tavistock Publications.
Mintzberg, H. (1976) 'Planning on the left and managing on the right', *Harvard Business Review*, vol. 54, no. 4, pp. 49–58.
Mintzberg, H. (1979) *The structuring of organizations*, Englewood Cliffs, NJ: Prentice Hall International Editions.
Mintzberg, H. (1987) 'The manager's job: folklore and myth', *Harvard Business Review*, vol. 53, no. 4, pp. 49–61.
Mintzberg, H. (1994) *The rise and fall of strategic planning*, Englewood Cliffs, NJ: Prentice Hall International Editions.
Moger, S. T. (1994) 'Creativity and entrepreneurs', in S. Dingli (ed.), *Creative thinking: a multifaceted approach*, Valetta, Malta: Malta University Press, pp. 111–21.
Mohamed, M. Z. & Rickards, T. (1996) 'Assessing and comparing the innovativeness and creative climate of firms', *Scandinavian Journal of Management*, vol. 12, no. 2, pp. 109–21.
Montuori, A. & Purser, R. E. (1996) *Social creativity*, Creskill, NY: Hampton Press, vol. 1.
Morgan, G. (1985, 1998) *Images of organization*, Newbury Park, Ca.: Sage.
Mumby, D. & Putnam, L. (1992) 'The politics of emotion: a feminist reading of bounded rationality', *Academy of Management Review*, vol. 14, no. 3, pp. 465–86.
Mumford, E. (1981) *Values, technology and work*, The Hague, Netherlands: Martinus Nijhoff.
Mumford, M. D. & Gustafson, S. B. (1988) 'Creativity syndrome: integration, application and innovation', *Psychological Bulletin*, vol. 103, pp. 27–43.
Nadler, D. A. & Tushman, M. L. (1989) 'What makes for magic leadership?', in W. E. Rosenbach and R. L. Taylor (eds.), *Contemporary issues in leadership*, Boulder, Co.: Westview.
Nelson, R. & Winter, S. (1977) 'In search of a useful theory of innovation', *Research Policy*, vol. 5, pp. 36–76.
Nelson, R. & Winter, S. (1982) *An evolutionary theory of economic change*, Cambridge, Mass.: Harvard University Press.
Newell, A. & Simon H. A. (1972) *Human problem-solving*, Englewood Cliffs, NJ: Prentice Hall.

Nonaka, I. & Kenney, M. (1991) 'Towards a new theory of innovation management', *Journal of Engineering and Technology Management*, vol. 8, pp. 67–83.

Nonaka, I. & Takeuchi, H. (1995) *The knowledge creating company: how Japanese companies create the dynamics of innovation*, Oxford: Oxford University Press.

Nunamaker, J. F. Jr., Briggs, R. O. & Mittleman, D. D. (1996) 'Lessons from a decade of group support systems research', in J. F. Nunamaker Jr. & R. H. Sprague, Jr. *Information systems – decision support and knowledge-based systems*, Washington, DC: IEEE Computer Society Press, vol. III, pp. 418–27.

Nunamaker, J. F. Jr. & Sprague, R. H. Jr. (1996) *Information systems – decision support and knowledge-based systems*, Washington, DC: IEEE Computer Society Press.

Nyström, H. (1990a) 'Organizational innovation', in M. A. West & J. L. Farr (eds.), *Innovation and creativity at work: psychological and organizational strategies*, Chichester: Wiley, pp. 143–61.

Nyström, H. (1990b) *Technological and market innovation: strategies for product and company development*, Chichester: Wiley.

Ohmae, K. (1982) *The mind of the strategist: the art of Japanese management*, New York: McGraw-Hill.

Ormerod, P. (1994) *The death of economics*, London: Faber and Faber.

Ornstein, R. (1972/5) *The psychology of consciousness*, New York, W. H. Freeman Co/London: Jonathan Cape.

Ornstein, R. (1975, 1986) *The psychology of consciousness* (2nd rev. edn), Harmondsworth: Penguin.

Osborn, A. F. (1953) *Applied imagination, principles and procedures of creative problem-solving* (3rd edn), New York: Charles Scribner's Sons.

Osborn, A. F. (1992) 'How to think up', in S. J. Parnes (ed.), *Sourcebook for creative problem-solving*, Buffalo, NY: Creative Education Foundation Press, pp. 4–14.

Ouchi, W. G. (1981) *Theory Z: how American business can meet the Japanese challenge*, Reading, Mass.: Addison-Wesley.

Parker, M. (1990) *Creating shared vision*, Clarendon Hills, IL: Dialog International.

Parker, M. (1992) 'Post-modern organizations or post-modern organization theory?', *Organization Studies*, vol. 13, pp. 1–17.

Parkin, M. (1993) *Macroeconomics* (2nd edn), Reading, Mass.: Addison-Wesley.

Parnes, S. J. (1988) *Visionizing*, East Aurora, NY: D.O.K. Publishers.

Parnes, S. J. (ed.) (1992) *Sourcebook for creative problem-solving*, Buffalo, NY: Creative Education Foundation Press.

Parnes, S. F., Noller, R. B. & Biondi, A. M. (1977) *A guide to creative action* (revised workbook), New York: Charles Scribner's Sons.

Pascale, R. T. & Athos, A. G. (1981) *The art of Japanese management: applications for American executives*, New York: Simon and Schuster.

Payne, R. L. & Pugh, D. S. (1976) 'Organisational structure and climate' in M. D. Dunnette (ed.), *Handbook of industrial and organizational psychology*, Chicago, Rand-McNally, pp. 1125–73.

Perkins, D. N. (1994) 'Creativity: beyond the Darwinian paradigm', in M. A. Boden, (ed.), *Dimensions of creativity*, Cambridge, Mass.: The MIT Press, pp. 119–42.

Perrow, C. (1984) *Normal accidents*, NY: Basic Books.

Perry, N. (1992) 'Putting theory in its place: the social organization of organizational theorising', in M. Reed & M. Hughes (eds.), *Rethinking organization: new directions on organization theory and analysis*, London: Sage, pp. 85–101.

Peters, T. (1988) *Thriving on chaos: handbook for a management revolution*, London: Macmillan.

Peters, T. (1992) *Liberation management: necessary disorganization for the nonsecond nineties*, New York: Alfred Knopf; London: Macmillan.
Peters, T. & Waterman, R. (1982) *In search of excellence*, New York: Harper & Row.
Pettigrew, A. (1979) 'On studying organisational culture', *Administrative Science Quarterly*, vol. 24, pp. 570–81.
Pettigrew, A. & Whipp, R. (1991) *Managing change for competitive success*, Oxford: Blackwell.
Pfeffer, J. (1982) *Organizations and organization theory*, Boston: Pitman.
Polya, G. (1957) *How to solve it: a new aspect of mathematical method* (2nd edn), Princeton: Princeton University Press.
Porter, M. E. (1980) *Competitive strategy: techniques for analysing industries and competitors*, New York: The Free Press.
Porter, M. E. (1985) *Competitive advantage: creating and sustaining superior performance*, New York: The Free Press.
Porter, M. E. (1990) *The competitive advantage of nations*, New York: The Free Press.
Prahalad, C. K. & Hamel, G. (1990) 'The core competence of the corporation', *Harvard Business Review*, May–June.
Pugh, D. S. (ed.) (1971) *Organization theory*, Harmondsworth: Penguin.
Pugh, D. S., Hickson, D. J. & Hinings, C. R. (1969) 'An empirical taxonomy of structures of work organisation', *Administrative Science Quarterly*, vol. 14, pp. 115–26.
Pugh, D. S., Hickson, D. J. & Hinings, C. R. (1971) (2nd edn) *Writers on organizations*, Harmondsworth: Penguin.
Putnam, L. L., Phillips, N. & Chapman, P. (1996) 'Metaphors of communication and organization', in S. R. Clegg, C. Hardy & W. R. Nord (eds.), (1996) *Handbook of organization studies*, London: Sage, pp. 375–408.
Pylyshyn, Z. W. (1979) 'Metaphoric imprecision and the "top down" research strategy', in A. Ortony (ed.), *Metaphor and thought*, Cambridge, UK: Cambridge University Press.
Raiffa, H. (1982) *The art and science of negotiation*, Cambridge, Mass.: Harvard University Press.
Raina, M. K. (1996) 'The Torrance phenomenon: extended creative search for Lord Vishvakarma', *Creativity and Innovation Management*, vol. 5, no. 3, pp. 151–68.
Ramqvist, L. (1994) 'The UK innovation lecture', London: Department of Enterprise, DTI/Pub 1231/10K/2.94/NJ.
Reed, M. & Hughes, M. (1992) *Rethinking organization: new dimensions in organization theory and analysis*, Newbury Park, Ca.; London: Sage.
Reichers, A. E. & Schneider, B. (1990) 'Climate and culture: an evolution of constructs', in B. Sneider (ed.), *Organizational climate and culture*, San Francisco: Jossey-Bass, pp. 5–39.
Rhodes, J. M. (1957) 'The dynamics of creativity; an interpretation of the literature on creativity with a proposed procedure for objective research', *Dissertation Abstracts*, vol. 17, p. 96.
Rhodes, J. M. (1961) 'An analysis of creativity', *Phi Delta Kappa*, April, pp. 305–11.
Rhodes, J. M. (1987) 'An analysis of creativity', in S. G. Isaksen (ed.), *Frontiers of creativity research: beyond the basics*, Buffalo, NY: Bearly, pp. 216–22.
Rickards, T. (1973) *Problem-solving through creative analysis*, Epping, Essex: Gower.
Rickards, T. (1985) *Stimulating innovation*, London: Frances Pinter.
Rickards, T. (1990) *Creativity and problem-solving at work*, Farnborough, UK: Gower.
Rickards, T. (1991) 'Creativity and innovation: woods, trees, and pathways', *R & D Management*, vol. 21, pp. 97–108.

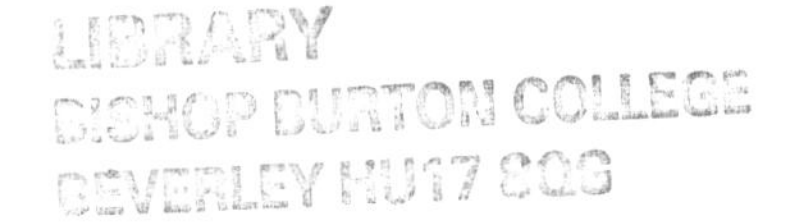

Rickards, T. (1994) 'Brainstorming electronically', *Creativity and Innovation Management*, vol. 3, no. 1, p. 76.
Rickards, T. & Freedman, B. L. (1979) 'A reappraisal of creativity techniques', *Journal of European and Industrial Training*, vol. 3, no. 1, pp. 3–8.
Rickards, T. & Jones, L. J. (1991) 'Towards the identification of situational barriers to creative behaviors: the development of a self-report inventory', *Creativity Research Journal*, vol. 4, no. 4, pp. 303–15.
Rickards, T. & Moger, S. T. (1999) *Handbook for creative team leaders*, Aldershot, Hants: Gower.
Rickards, T., Moger, S., Colemont, P. & Tassoul, M. (eds.) (1992) *Creativity and innovation: quality breakthroughs*, Delft, The Netherlands: TNO.
Robinson, P. (1994) *Snapshots from hell: the making of an MBA*, New York: Warner Books.
Rogers, E. M. (1995) *Diffusion of innovation* (4th edn), New York: The Free Press.
Rosenau, P. M. (1992) *Post-modernism and the social sciences: insights, inroads, and intrusions*, Princeton: Princeton University Press.
Rosile, G. A. & Boje, D. M. (1996) 'Pedagogy for the postmodern classroom: Greenback company', in D. M. Boje, R. P. Gephart, Jr. & T. J. Thatchenkery (eds.), *Postmodern management and organization theory*, Thousand Oaks, Ca.: Sage, pp. 225–50.
Ross, I. S. (1995) *The life of Adam Smith*, Oxford: Clarendon Press.
Runco, M. A. & Albert, R. S. (eds.) (1990) *Theories of creativity*, Newbury Park, Ca.: Sage.
Samuelson, P. A. (1997) 'Isolating sources of sterility in Marx's theoretical paradigm', in C. Arestis, G. Palma & M. Sawyer (eds.), *Capital controversy, post-Keynesian economics and the history of economic thought: essays in honour of Geoffrey Harcourt*, vol. 1, London: Routledge, pp. 187–98.
Sayer, A. (1992) *Method in social science* (2nd edn), London: Routledge.
Schaffer, S. (1994) 'Making up discovery', in M. A. Boden, (ed.), *Dimensions of creativity*, Cambridge, Mass.: The MIT Press.
Scheerer, M. (1963) 'Problem-solving', *Scientific American*, vol. 208, pp. 118–218.
Schein, E. H. (1969) *Process consultation*, Reading, Mass.: Addison-Wesley.
Schein, E. H. (1979) 'Organizational socialization and the profession of management', in D. A. Kolb, I. M. Rubin, & J. M. McIntyre (eds.), *Organizational psychology: a book of readings* (3rd edn), Englewood Cliffs, NJ: Prentice Hall, pp. 9–23.
Schein, E. H. (1985) *Organizational culture and leadership: a dynamic view*, San Francisco: Jossey-Bass.
Schein, E. H. (1991) 'What is culture', in P. J. Frost, L. F. Moore, M. R. Louis, C. C. Lundberg & J. Martin (eds.), *Reframing organizational culture*, Newbury Park, Ca.: Sage, pp. 243–53.
Schein, E. H. & Beckhard, R. (1989) 'Foreword', in R. B. Blake, J. S. Mouton & A. A. McCanse, *Change by design*, Reading, Mass.: Addison-Wesley OD Series, pp. vii–viii.
Schneider, B. (ed.) (1990) *Organizational climate and culture*, San Francisco: Jossey Bass.
Schooler, J. W., Fallshore, M. & Fiore, S. M. (1995) 'Epilogue: putting insight into perspective', in R. J. Sternberg & J. E. Davidson (eds.), *The nature of insight*, Cambridge, Mass.: The MIT Press, pp. 559–88.
Schumpeter, J. A. (1934) *The theory of economic development*, Cambridge, Mass.: Harvard University Press (English trans.).
Schumpeter, J. A. (1947) *Capitalism, socialism and democracy* (2nd edn), New York: Harper and Brothers.
Schwartz, P. (1991) *The art of the long view: planning for the future in an uncertain world*, New York: Doubleday. [Also (1996), Chichester, UK: Wiley.]

Scott, W. R. (1987) 'The adolescence of institutional theory', *Administrative Science Quarterly*, 32. no. 4. (December), pp. 493–511.
Senge, P. M. (1990) *The fifth discipline: the art and practice of the learning organization*, New York: Doubleday.
Shewhart, W. A. (1931) *The economic control of quality of manufactured product*, New York: McGraw Hill.
Shils, E. (1968) 'Charisma', in D. Shils (ed.), *International encyclopedia of the social sciences*, vol. 2, London: Macmillan.
Sim, S. (1995) *The A–Z guide to modern literary and cultural theorists*, London: Prentice Hall/Harvester Wheatsheaf.
Simmons, K. (1986) 'Marketing as innovation: the eighth paradigm', *Journal of Management Studies*, vol. 23, no. 5, pp. 479–99.
Simon, H. A. (1960) *The new science of management decision*, New York: Harper and Row.
Simon, H. A. (1986) 'What we know about the creative process', in R. L. Kuhn (ed.), *Creative and innovative management*, Cambridge, Mass.: Ballinger, pp. 3–22.
Simon, H. A. (1997) *Models of bounded rationality: empirically grounded economic reason*, vol. 3, Cambridge, Mass.: The MIT Press.
Smith, A. (1776) *An enquiry into the nature and causes of the wealth of nations*, vols 1–5, London: printed for W. Strathan and T. Cadell. (Modern editions: Books 1–111, 1970, etc.; Selected edn, 1993; London: Penguin.)
Smith, S. M. (1995) 'Getting into and out of mental ruts: a theory of fixation, incubation and insight', in R. J. Sternberg & J. E. Davidson (eds.), *The nature of insight*, Cambridge, Mass.: The MIT Press, pp. 229–51.
Sperry, R. W. (1964) 'The great cerebral commissure', *Scientific American*, pp. 44–52.
Starratt, R. J. (1993) *The drama of leadership*, Washington, DC: The Falmer Press.
Stein, M. I. (1974–5) *Stimulating creativity*, vols 1–2, New York: Academic Press.
Sternberg, R. J. (1988) *The nature of creativity*, Cambridge, UK: Cambridge University Press.
Sternberg, R. J. (1985) *Beyond IQ: a triarchic theory of human intelligence*, Cambridge, UK: Cambridge University Press.
Sternberg, R. J. & Davidson, J. E. (eds.) (1995) *The nature of insight*, Cambridge, Mass.: The MIT. Press; Bradford Books.
Stodgill, R. M. (1974) *Handbook of leadership: a survey of theory and research*, New York: The Free Press.
Sundbo, J. (1998) *The organisation of innovation in services*, Frederiksberg, Denmark: Roskilde Press.
Sunderland, K. (1993) 'Introduction and commentary', in K. Sunderland (ed.), *Adam Smith: Wealth of Nations*, Oxford: Oxford University Press, pp. ix–lii.
Susman, G. I. & Evered, R. D. (1978) 'An assessment of the scientific merits of action research', *Administrative Science Quarterly*, vol. 23, pp. 582–603.
Sutton, R. I. & Hargadon, A. (1996) 'Brainstorming groups in context: effectiveness in a product design firm', *Administrative Science Quarterly*, vol. 41, pp. 685–718.
Swann, P. (1993) *New technologies and the firm: innovation and competition*, London: Routledge.
Swann, P. & Gill, J. (1993) *Corporate vision and rapid technological change*, London: Routledge.
Tannenbaum, R. & Schmidt, W. H. (1973) 'How to choose a leadership pattern', *Harvard Business Review*, May–June, pp. 162–75, 178–80.
Tarr, G. (1973) *The management of problem-solving: positive results from productive thinking*, London: Macmillan.

Taylor, C. W. & Barron, F. (eds.) (1963) *Scientific creativity: its recognition and development*, pp. 153–60, New York: Wiley.
Thomas, A. B. (1993) *Controversies in management*, London: Routledge.
Thomas, H. & Gardner, D. (eds.) (1985) *Strategic marketing and management*, New York, Wiley.
Tidd, J., Bessant, J. & Pavitt, K. (1997) *Managing innovation: integrating technological, market and organizational change*, London: Wiley.
Toffler, A. (1972) *Future shock*, London: Bodley Head.
Tomlinson, R. & Kiss, R. (eds.) (1984) *Rethinking the processes of operational research and systems analysis*, Oxford: Pergamon Press.
Torrance, E. P. (1962) *Guiding creative talent*, Englewood Cliffs, NJ: Prentice Hall.
Torrance, E. P. (1993) 'Experiences in developing technology for creative education', in S. G. Isaksen, M. C. Murdock, R. L. Firestien & D. J. Treffinger (eds.), *Understanding and recognising creativity: the emergence of a discipline*, Norwood, NJ: Ablex, pp. 158–201.
Trompenaars, F. (1993) *Riding the waves of culture: understanding cultural diversity in business*, London: Economist Books.
Tsoukas, H. (1992) 'Postmodernism, reflective rationalism and organizational studies: a reply to Martin Parker', *Organization Studies*, vol. 13, no. 4, pp. 643–49.
Tsoukas, H. (1994) *New thinking in organizational behaviour*, Oxford: Butterworth Heinemann.
Tuckman A. (1994) 'The yellow brick road: total quality management and the restructuring of organizational culture', *Organizational Studies*, vol. 15, no. 5, pp. 727–51.
Turner, B. (1994) *Orientalism, postmodernism, and globalism*, London: Routledge.
Tushman, M. L. & Romanelli, E. (1985) 'Organizational evolution: a metamorphosis model of convergence and reorientation', in L. L. Cummings & B. B. Staw (eds.), *Research in organizational behavior*, vol. 7, Greenwich, CT: JAI Press, pp. 171–222.
Tversky, A. & Kahneman, D. (1974) 'Judgement under uncertainty: heuristics and biases', *Science*, vol. 185, pp. 1124–31.
Twiss, B. (1992), *Managing technological innovation* (4th edn), London: Pitman.
Van de Ven, A. H. & Poole, M. S. (1995) 'Explaining development and change in organizations', *Academy of Management Review*, vol. 20, no. 3, pp. 510–40.
VanGundy, A. B. (1988) *Techniques of structured problem-solving* (2nd edn), New York: Van Nostrand Reinhold.
Van Oech (1983) *A whack on the side of the head*, New York: Warner Books.
Vroom, V. H. (1964) *Work and motivation*, New York: Wiley.
Wallas, G. (1970) 'The art of thought', in P. E. Vernon (ed.), *Creativity*, Harmondsworth: Penguin, pp. 91–7.
Walton, M. (1989) *The Deming management method*, London: W. H. Allen; Mercury.
Weber, M. (1947) *The theory of social and economic organization* (A. M. Henderson & T. Parsons (ed.), trans. T. Parsons), New York: Free Press (original work, 1924).
Weick, K. E. (1995) *Sense making in organizations*, Thousand Oaks, Ca.: Sage.
Weisberg, R. W. (1986) *Creativity, genius and other myths*, New York: Freeman.
West, M. A. & Farr, J. L. (eds.) (1990) *Innovation and creativity at work: psychological and organizational strategies*, Chichester: Wiley.
Wiener, N. (1948) *Cybernetics*, New York: Wiley.
Williamson, O. E. (1963) 'A model of rational managerial behavior', in R. M. Cyert & J. G. March, *A behavioral theory of the firm*, Englewood Cliffs, New York: Prentice Hall.
Williamson, O. E. (1975) *Markets and hierarchies: analysis and antitrust implications*, New York: The Free Press.
Williamson, O. E. (1985) *The economic institutions of capitalism*, New York: The Free Press.

Willmott, H. (1989) 'OR as a problem-situation', in M. C. Jackson, P. Keys & S. A. Cropper (eds.), *Operational research and the social sciences*, New York: Plenum Press, pp. 65–78.
Winch, P. (1958, 1980) *The idea of a social science and its relation to philosophy*, London: Routledge & Kegan Paul.
Wood, D. & Gaston, K. (1996) 'The search for and selection of a new product', *Creativity and Innovation Management*, vol. 5, no. 1, pp. 3–12.
Yukl, G. A. (1981) *Leadership in organizations*, Englewood Cliffs, NJ: Prentice Hall.
Yukl, G. A. (1989) *Leadership in organizations* (2nd edn), Englewood Cliffs, NJ: Prentice Hall.
Zaleznik, A. (1977) 'Managers and leaders: are they different?', *Harvard Business Review*, vol. 55, pp. 67–78.
Zartman, I. W. (ed.) (1976) *The fifty-percent solution*, New York: Anchor-Doubleday.
Zaltman, G., Duncan, R. & Holbeck, J. (1973) *Innovations and organizations*, Chichester: Wiley.
Zohar, D. & Marshall, I. (1993) *The quantum society: mind, physics, and a new social vision*, London: Harper Collins.

Index